SEVEN CONTEMPORARY PLAYS
FROM THE KOREAN DIASPORA
IN THE AMERICAS

SEVEN CONTEMPORARY PLAYS FROM THE KOREAN DIASPORA IN THE AMERICAS

EDITED AND WITH AN INTRODUCTION BY **ESTHER KIM LEE**

Duke University Press
Durham and London
2012

© 2012 Duke University Press
History K by Edward Bok Lee © 1998
99 Histories by Julia Cho © 2004
American Hwangap by Lloyd Suh © 2007
Hongbu and Nolbu: The Tale of the Magic Pumpkins
by Jean Yoon © 2005
Yi Sang Counts to Thirteen by Sung Rno © 2000
Satellites by Diana Son © 2006
Mina by Kyoung H. Park © 2004
All rights reserved.

Designed by Amy Ruth Buchanan
Typeset in Minion and Lato by Tseng Information Systems, Inc.
Library of Congress Cataloging-in-Publication Data appear on
the last printed page of this book.

Frontispiece: Photo of the 2009 production of Sung Rno's
Yi Sang Counts to Thirteen in Seoul, Korea. Photo by
Jong Hyun Seo.

For My Daughters

CONTENTS

ix   Acknowledgments

xi   Introduction

1   Edward Bok Lee, *History K*

21   Julia Cho, *99 Histories*

85   Lloyd Suh, *American Hwangap*

151   Jean Yoon, *Hongbu and Nolbu: The Tale of the Magic Pumpkins*

195   Sung Rno, *Yi Sang Counts to Thirteen*

247   Diana Son, *Satellites*

321   Kyoung H. Park, *Mina*

ACKNOWLEDGMENTS

Editing a collection is truly a collaborative enterprise. This anthology could not have been possible without the playwrights, their agents, and colleagues who provided generous support. I would also like to thank my persistent research assistants, Sandra Lee, Mina Sohaj, and Youngji Jeon, who assisted me at every stage of the project. Many thanks go to Mina for her thorough reading of scripts and for her organized method in obtaining information. Special thanks are due the Asian American Studies Program at the University of Illinois at Urbana-Champaign (UIUC) for the Amy Ling Research Grant that supported this project. The Department of Theatre and the College of Fine and Applied Arts at UIUC also provided financial and intellectual support. I owe much gratitude to Kathy Perkins, who guided me from the start and generously answered all my questions on editing a play anthology. At Duke University Press, Courtney Berger's encouragement and advice gave me the motivation and stamina to complete the collection. She and her colleague Christine Choi have been my partners in making this collection come to life. Three reviewers provided invaluable comments as the anthology evolved through several drafts, and I thank them for helping me ground the introduction theoretically and historically. Many thanks go out to all Korean diasporic playwrights who generously sent their scripts to me. Even their plays that are not included here informed me greatly, and I hope they see echoes of their work in this collection. Finally, my greatest thanks go to the seven featured playwrights who have worked with me patiently through this long process. Their words continue to move me, and I hope the magic of their plays will touch many other souls throughout the diaspora and beyond.

INTRODUCTION

In 2000 the East West Players (EWP) in Los Angeles produced the Korean American playwright Euijoon Kim's new play *My Tired Broke Ass Pontificating Slapstick Funk*, which represented a new direction for the EWP. As the premier Asian American theater company, EWP was known for its long association with Little Tokyo, a Japanese American community in Los Angeles, and its loyal subscribers consisted mostly of older Japanese Americans. With Kim's provocative play, the company aimed to reach out to new audiences, especially those of the younger generation in Koreatown across the city. The theater critic Julio Martinez described the play as representative of "a vibrant but embryonic culture struggling to establish its own identity out of the myriad influences that are constantly bombarding it."[1]

At the time, I was in Los Angeles to attend a panel discussion on the future of Asian American drama and to interview Asian American theater artists. I also had a personal investment in Kim's play. As a Korean American of the generation Kim writes about, I wanted to see what he had to say about the direction of the emerging culture cultivated in Koreatown. I grew up in Southern California and recognized his characters and their issues. Kim was also a panelist, and I wanted to hear what he had to say.

Led by Alice Tuan, the panel included more established writers such as Sandra Tsing Loh and Chay Yew. As the youngest member of the panel, Kim was expected to speak for the new generation of Asian Americans in the twenty-first century and to articulate the significance of his play. Instead, Kim took a nap onstage, or at least made it look as if he was. While the other writers on the panel spoke, he closed his eyes, crossed his arms, and tilted his head while sitting in his chair. The audience initially laughed at this, but we soon realized he was not going to speak at all. Recalling the event, Kim says that he was annoyed with the questions he received and did not care for the "flowery, poetic Asian American" topic.[2] Bored, angry, and annoyed, Kim remained onstage as a nonparticipant. His performance was in stark contrast to the polite audience and his fellow panelists who remained throughout the discussion. In one sense, at least, the EWP had gotten its wish: the company wanted to rebel against its own tradition, and the rebel was literally onstage. As I sat in the audience, I watched Kim and thought about what the moment signified. Many compared Euijoon Kim to Frank Chin, the iconic Chinese American playwright who debuted in American theater in 1972 with the play *Chickencoop Chinaman*. The hypermasculine anger toward society and a sense of youthful angst were the obvious points of comparison, but Kim, unlike the loquacious Chin, had not figured out a way to verbally express his frustrations. Kim, a young Korean American from Koreatown, was out of place in Little Tokyo, and the majority of the conference attendees did not understand his world. In 2000, a Korean American playwright had much explanation to do before he could tell his story, and Kim was still struggling to find his voice as a playwright.

Euijoon Kim is one of what I call the Korean diasporic playwrights, some of whose plays are represented in this collection. At the dawn of the new millennium, only a handful of plays about the Korean diaspora in the Americas had been written, and playwriting was not a common choice of profession. But within ten years, theater had attracted a growing number of talented writers who used the stage to dramatize and crystallize the world they know. They are no longer silent and displaced as playwrights. Rather, they command attention, and the purpose of this collection is to capture the quality and dynamism of the writers and their plays. The collection features seven contemporary plays about the Korean diaspora, written by Korean diasporic playwrights in the Americas. Included are five full-length plays and two one-acts; the writers include one from Canada, one from Chile, and five from the United States. The dates of the plays span about ten years since the late 1990s, and all have received professional productions or workshops. The plays were selected carefully to demonstrate the vast diversity of themes and styles of playwriting, but they were also chosen to represent common motifs in plays about the Korean diaspora in the Americas.

KOREAN DIASPORA IN THE AMERICAS

The phrase "Korean diaspora in the Americas" is used broadly to include Korean immigrants and their descendants in the United States, Canada, and Latin America. It is not meant to replace ethnic or cultural groupings such as "Korean American"; rather it functions as an inclusive term to provide a hemispheric perspective of Korean immigration and diasporic histories in the Americas. I use "Korea" to signify the entire peninsula before the Korean War (1950–53), but I also use it interchangeably with "South Korea" to refer to its history after the war. After World War II, the country was divided into North and South, and immigration to the Americas came mostly from South Korea. But immigration began decades earlier. From the first decade of the twentieth century, Korean laborers arrived in Hawaii to work on sugar plantations. And starting in the 1960s, immigration laws in both the Americas and Korea were significantly eased.[3] After 1965, the number of immigrants grew exponentially, and it is estimated that by 1980, over a half million had immigrated to the Americas from Korea. Many immigrants who left Korea for the Americas after 1965 were professionals, students, wives of American military personnel, adoptees, and relatives of those already residing in the host country. Some were also illegal immigrants who had to travel through a third country in order to arrive at their final destination. Whatever the backgrounds and reasons for immigration, the majority of immigrants settled in urban enclaves. According to the 2005 data reported by the Overseas Koreans Foundation, it is estimated that 6.6 million Koreans live in 160 different countries worldwide. The United States is home to the second largest Korean immigrant population with 2.08 million (China being the largest, with 2.43 million). Canada has almost 200,000, and about 107,000 live in Central and South America.[4]

Korea was occupied by Japan from 1910 to 1945 during the latter's imperialist expansion into Asia. After Japan's defeat in World War II, Korea depended on the United States for its postwar recovery, with a constant U.S. military presence at home and a growing number of Koreans immigrating to the United States. Accordingly, studies on the Korean diaspora in the Americas have been dominated by U.S.-based scholars, and Korean American studies have grown steadily as an important area study. Among U.S. cities, Los Angeles has received much scrutiny because the city has the largest concentration of Koreans outside of Korea and because of the Los Angeles riots in 1992 that garnered international attention. Victims of the riots quickly became the public face of the Korean diaspora, as the news media disseminated images of frustrated business owners left on their own to protect their properties and families. Speaking broken English and looking painfully displaced, these Korean immigrants embodied the failure to achieve the American Dream.

Attempts to explain the causes and consequences of the riots have led to a popular yet reductive narrative of survival and perseverance. Koreans in the United States and elsewhere have been described as a strong diasporic people who would sacrifice themselves for the betterment of their children's future. A father with a college education from a top university in Korea would own a swap-meet store downtown while his wife would toil away at a garment factory receiving minimum wage. Their children would be accepted to Ivy League schools to become lawyers, doctors, and engineers. Such iterations of the American Dream would inspire more Koreans to leave their homeland. Images of the broken merchant from the L.A. riots were quickly replaced with those of successful Korean immigrants throughout the Americas. From politics to popular culture, descendants of Korean immigrants have been visible front and center and often in unexpected professions. For instance, in the United States, the law professor John Yoo became known for having authored the most controversial part of the Patriot Act during the Bush administration. Jun Choi was elected in 2005 as mayor of Edison, New Jersey. In Canada, Yonah Kim-Martin became the first Korean Canadian to hold federal office. In popular culture, the Canadian-born actress Sandra Oh won a Golden Globe Award in 2006, and in 2008 Yul Kwon became the winner of the popular American television show *Survivor*. Korean American and Korean Canadian actors such as Yunjin Kim, John Cho, Grace Park, and Daniel Dae Kim have played major roles in television shows and films that have been seen worldwide. Yunjin Kim in particular has had transnational success by appearing in both American and Korean productions. Margaret Cho, with her biting humor, has been recognized as one of the funniest comedians in the United States. In literature, mainstream critics have taken notice of writers such as Chang-Rae Lee and Min Jin Lee. There is also a growing list of professional athletes with Korean roots: Angela Park (golf, Brazil), Jim Paek (ice hockey, Canada), and Hines Ward (football, United States), to name only a few. The seeming suddenness of such collective achievements has led many to wonder what has happened since the L.A. riots, when the popular image of Koreans was that of desperate, unassimilated immigrants who had lost everything.

For second-generation Koreans in the Americas (including those who were born in Korea and immigrated before adulthood, sometimes called the "1.5 generation"), opportunities for success are abundant compared to those of their parents' generation, and many have taken full advantage of it. But research in the social sciences has also shown that narratives of immigrant success do not reveal the full picture of the Korean diasporic history in the

Americas. For every success story, there is an unsuccessful and even tragic one. Indeed, the popular images tell only the most visible part of the story, but the Korean diasporic communities in the Americas are vastly complex and contradicting. With the increase in population and diversity, definitions of success and identity have varied, and there is no longer a clear pattern to singularly describe the Korean diaspora in the Americas.

Complicating the individual achievements of the second generation has been what is commonly known as *hallyu*, or the Korean Wave, which has made popular South Korean entertainment fashionable in Asia and beyond. For example, the singer Rain performed in Madison Square Garden to sold-out audiences, and South Korean television soap operas have inspired women in Southeast Asia to undergo cosmetic surgery to look "Korean." Second-generation Koreans in the Americas have witnessed the global renaissance of the Korean culture during the past decade. The distinction between "Korean" and "abroad" has all but been erased with the Internet, satellite television, and global film distribution. In theater, musicals such as *The Last Empress* and *Nanta* have toured internationally and received recognition for creating intercultural forms of theatrical expression. The sudden popularity of *hallyu* has been seen as a by-product of the equally sudden rise of the South Korean economy, which has grown from almost nothing to a trillion U.S. dollars in less than half a century. The South Korean economy, described as the "Miracle on the Han River," now ranks fifteenth in the world.[5] In the 1990s, South Korea was one of the "Asian tigers" recognized for extraordinary economic growth. When the vast majority of Korean immigrants left for the Americas in the 1970s and 1980s, there was little doubt that they were in search of better employment and educational opportunities in a foreign land. In succeeding years, however, the Korean economy became far more industrialized globally, with brands such as Samsung and Hyundai projecting home-grown opportunities for the twenty-first century. Korean Americans could listen to Korean popular music (K-Pop) on their Samsung smartphones, but the music would be among thousands of songs created by artists from all around the world and distributed by multinational corporations. Such flexible ethnic identities are no longer based solely on the impossible choice between the "homeland" or the "host country," but the option to define oneself transnationally and globally. Aided by South Korea's economic rise, *hallyu* has given the Korean diasporic communities a dialectical sense of unified ethnonational pride and wide-open freedom from national boundaries.[6]

Accordingly, the term "diaspora" has been used to signify a sense of decentralized cultural identity, one that requires a new set of questions and descriptors. The parameters that guide identity formations are not limited by nationhood or ethnic enclaves. Rather, the Korean diasporic communities have been influenced by new forms of mobility and groupings. Borrowing from the cultural critics Kandice Chuh and Karen Shimakawa, the concept of Korean diaspora "evokes multiple locations and movements and hesitates to fix itself as static epistemological object."[7] While neither static nor fixed, Korean diaspora as both concept and phenomenon can nevertheless be observed, documented, imagined, and represented. The plays in this collection remind us that the Korean diasporic condition—real or imagined—can be made known.

KOREAN DIASPORA PLAYS

For this collection I have selected plays that have been presented to audiences in fully produced forms or in reading workshops. The process of producing a play has its own internal politics and requires the collaboration of many people, including designers, actors, directors, dramaturgs, producers, and managers. Playwrights need a supportive community and what Rick Shiomi, a Japanese Canadian director, describes as a "theatrical infrastructure."[8] The infrastructure provides the foundation for theater artists to find their niche and voice, and, for young dramatists, finding the right community is often the key to making their work visible. In the United States, the main theatrical infrastructure that has supported Korean diasporic writers has been Asian American theater. As I describe in *A History of Asian American Theatre* (2006), a group of Asian American actors, playwrights, and directors started a movement in the 1960s and 1970s by forming theater companies, producing new plays, and advocating equal opportunity in American theater. In 1965, the EWP (Los Angeles), the first Asian American theater company, was founded, and others followed in New York City, San Francisco, and Seattle. There are now over forty active Asian American and Asian diasporic theater companies and groups around the country.

Over the past fifty years, Asian American theater, with its pan-ethnically formed infrastructure, has provided both space and labor for many Korean American playwrights to debut their work. The EWP have had the longest history of producing plays written by Korean or Korean American writers. Soon-Tek Oh, an actor and cofounder of the EWP, had three plays produced during the early years of the company's history: *Martyrs Can't Go Home* (1967), *Camels Were Two-legged in Peking* (1967), and *Tondemonai-Never Happen* (1970).⁹ Oh's plays are considered the first fully produced plays written by a writer of Korean descent in the Americas. After the departure of Soon-Tek Oh from the company, the EWP did not produce another Korean American play until 1995 with the world premier of *Cleveland Raining*. The play was followed in the 1999 season by a production of Chungmi Kim's *Hanako*, a play about Korean "comfort women" during the Japanese occupation in World War II. During the 1980s, the EWP had a subscription base that was predominantly Japanese American under the leadership of the artistic director Mako. It was only in the mid-1990s that the company explicitly made efforts to include plays about other ethnicities. Production histories are similar for other Asian American theater companies, such as Pan Asian Repertory Theatre (New York City) and the Asian American Theater Company (San Francisco). Korean American plays were rarely produced during the 1970s and 1980s, when plays presented under the category of "Asian American theater" were mostly about the Chinese and Japanese American experiences. One notable exception was the Asian American Playwrights Lab at the Public Theater founded in 1992 by Chiori Miyagawa. It was short-lived, but it introduced Sung Rno and Diana Son to the New York audience. Outside of the infrastructure of Asian American theater, Rob Shin received the Kennedy Center's National Student Playwriting Award in 1990 for his play *The Art of Waiting*. The play was produced in 1993 at the Round House Theatre in Maryland. Korean American playwrights, many of whom are included in this collection, began to emerge as a noticeable cohort starting in the second half of the 1990s.

The Korean American theater critic Terry Hong writes in her article "Times Up: The Moment Is Now" that Korean American playwrights are finally getting attention on their own without the connection to the pan-ethnic rubric of "Asian American." Hong quotes Randy Gener, the senior editor of the magazine *American Theatre*: "In a very real and significant way, I suspect, Korean American writers have been discouraged or eclipsed by the larger rubric of 'the Asian American movement,' a political consciousness that grew out of the late 1960s and early 1970s."¹⁰ While the infrastructure of Asian American theater provided important production opportunities for Korean American playwrights, who would otherwise rarely have such chances, it may have also limited the kinds of topics that they could explore. Earlier generations of Asian American playwrights had to address racism, cultural nationalism, Orientalism, and feminism in the most direct and basic ways because they had to educate the audience who knew very little about Asian Americans. Plays by these writers, including Frank Chin, Wakako Yamauchi, David Henry Hwang, Phillip Kan Gotanda, and Velina Hasu Houston, have defined the purpose and expectation of Asian American drama.

The playwrights in this collection have moved beyond the political consciousness of the 1960s and 1970s and the culture war of the 1980s and 1990s. In their plays, race and ethnicity are not central in obvious ways. Instead, they write about characters with multidimensional human problems that can afflict anyone regardless of their cultural identity. With Korean diasporic writers leading the way, Asian American theater as a whole has also changed. The most representative of such change has been Ma-Yi Theater, an Off-Broadway theater company in New York City. The company initially began as a Filipino American theater group but quickly began to incorporate other voices and promote new plays. Sung Rno and Lloyd Suh have been active as leaders of Ma-Yi's Playwrights Laboratory, which has been a critical entryway for new Korean diasporic writers. Indeed, Asian American theater continues to serve as the artistic home and theatrical infrastructure for many Korean diasporic playwrights, but the writers have also expanded their networks. Plays by Korean diasporic writers have been produced Off-Broadway and by companies in Seoul, the American Midwest, Toronto, and other venues that cannot be categorized racially or ethnically. And as the plays in this collection demonstrate, the writers have taken much freedom in exercising their artistic creativity and in exploring new ways of dramatizing the world they know.

As the de facto theater capital of the United States, New York City has attracted ambitious and talented theater artists around the world for decades, and the city is already becoming the gathering place for actors, designers, and writers of Korean descent. Some have already found respect and reputation, as in the case of the costume designer Willa Kim and the actor Randall Duk Kim, and others are arriving with nothing but the will to achieve their dreams. It remains to be seen whether a theatrical infrastructure for Korean diasporic theater will be centered in New York City, but the big city has been the professional starting point for the majority of the writers in this collection and for the actors who performed in their plays.

In Canada, a theatrical infrastructure did not exist for Asian Canadian theater to start as a movement even until the late 1990s. Some individual artists such as Rick Shiomi, who could not find opportunities in Canada, moved to the United States, and those who stayed in Canada defined their work more broadly as multicultural. For instance, Cahoots Theatre Project (Toronto) has played a significant role in promoting diversity in Canadian theater, and many Asian Canadian artists have made it their home. While the number has been small, Korean Canadian playwrights such as Jean Yoon and M. J. Kang have played central roles in the development of contemporary Canadian theater. Both these women have collaborated in multiple projects and acted in each other's plays. Kang's *Noran Bang: Yellow Room* (1993) premiered at Cahoots Theatre Project while Yoon was the co-artistic director of the company. In fact, Kang's play is one of the earliest written in the Americas to address the second generation's experiences of displacement and identity crisis. Of Yoon's plays, *The Yoko Ono Project* has received attention as one of the most discussed projects in contemporary Canadian theater.[11] Canada has a unique history of government-led efforts to promote multiculturalism, and both Yoon and Kang have been at the forefront of creating and defining both Asian Canadian theater and Canadian multicultural theater.

Unlike the United States and Canada, Latin America has not been studied extensively for its Korean diasporic communities. One reason is the smaller immigration population spread over many different countries, which can make generalization difficult. Another reason has to do with language access and the preference of both Korean and North American scholars to use English in their research. In terms of theater, searching for Korean diasporic artists is a challenging task. Partly because of the cultural differences in how theater is defined and produced, playwriting is not the most accurate way to gauge theatrical activity. Script-based theater is, after all, a European tradition best continued in North America. Besides the Chile-born writer Kyoung H. Park, whose one-act play *Mina* is included in this collection, I am not aware of other Latin American playwrights of Korean descent. Of course, this does not mean that they don't exist. For English-speaking scholars like myself, it is simply easier to find those like Park, who writes in English and works in the United States. Although this collection proposes to represent the entire hemisphere of the Americas, it admittedly comes short in providing more examples of plays from Latin America. With this collection, I hope to open the possibility of emerging playwrights in North, Central, and South America to discover each other and to create a theatrical infrastructure that is truly transnational and diasporic.

In choosing the plays for this collection, I had to exclude a number of works that fully deserve publication. While it has not been easy to make the final selection, I am encouraged to see the surge in both number and quality of plays written by writers of the Korean diaspora in the Americas. Some of those writers include Young Jean Lee, Euijoon Kim, Kimber Lee, M. J. Kang, Ins Choi, Philip Chung, Mia Chung, Suzanne Lee, Susan Kim, Ji Hyun Lee, Nic Cha Kim, Paul Juhn, Patty Jang, Katie Hae Leo, and Paul Lee. The majority of these writers are U.S.-based, and some have long been associated with specific theater companies, as in the case of Philip Chung and the Lodestone Theatre Company in Los Angeles. There are also a couple of Korean adoptee writers (Kimber Lee and Katie Hae Leo) who are beginning to receive professional productions of their plays. Young Jean Lee, in particular, has emerged as a major playwright in American theater with award-winning plays and her own company, Young Jean Lee's Theater Company. She has been recognized as one of the most experimental playwrights of American theater, and critics have described her plays as both subversive and funny. Most of her plays do not deal directly with Korean diasporic topics, but the one that does—*Song of the Dragon Flying to Heaven*—is a jarring take on her discomfort and anxiety in writing an "identity play." A collection of her work, *Songs of the Dragon Flying to Heaven and Other Plays* (2009), is the first single-authored drama anthology by a Korean American writer.[12]

Korean diasporic plays, as a group, vary immensely in terms of specific characters, settings, plots, and dialogues. Some characters are assimilated second-generation college students who try to act like their white friends, while others are first-generation dry cleaners living out the stereotypical immigrant life. Some plays are set in Koreatowns while others take place in the middle of Texas or an abstract location. While most plays are written in the realistic style, a story can also take place entirely in a character's head. And every character speaks in different ways—ranging from Southern California Valley-speak to multilingual gibberish. However, there are several recurring themes and critical issues significant enough to merit a study of the plays as a group.

The word "diaspora," which literarily means scattering, evokes a sense of displacement and loss as well as adaption and survival. The recurring themes and issues in the plays derive from such dispersed sense of existence. At the same time, the existence is dynamic and constantly changing. Social scientists Rhacel S. Parreñas and Lok C. D. Siu, in defining Asian diaspora, write, "Being diasporic requires continual reproduction of certain conditions and identifications."[13] The plays are essentially about such continual reproduction, and the diasporic conditions and identifications are dramatized with themes of belonging, assimilation, family, memory, war, success, and ethnic identity.

The majority of the characters seek to know where they belong and how they should define themselves. The children of immigrants often did not have a say in their family leaving Korea for another continent, and they have difficulty resolving the enormous and sometimes embarrassing differences between their first-generation parents and other people in their surroundings. They may try to assimilate and blend in, but they do so as a consequence of losing a part of themselves. Their family tells them they are not Korean enough and that they have assimilated too much. The society at large tells them that they are too Asian, too Korean, or even foreigners, and their friends want them to be more political as Asian Americans, Asian Canadians, or other hyphenated identifiers. But they know in their hearts that race and ethnicity do not dictate their lives. They leave their family, or their family leaves them. Some visit Korea to find a sense of belonging, but they leave disillusioned and lonelier. They may look physically similar to people on the streets of Seoul but lack the language and cultural familiarity to truly fit in. Some realize that they do not belong anywhere, but they nevertheless continue to seek home, however elusive or imaginary it may be.

The sense of belonging is not limited to finding a home that may be represented with family, homeland, authenticity, or assimilation. Many plays deal with the pressure to succeed financially and professionally. Material success is perceived as the fastest and surest way to adapt and belong in a new society, and the plays portray first-generation characters stopping at nothing for their children's socially upward mobility. The first generation left Korea for a better life, and they do not want their children to live the desperate life many in Korea had to live after the Korean War. The history of the Japanese occupation of Korea, the Korean War, and the U.S. involvement in Korea never disappear as a backdrop to the choices the characters make. In the new country, some parents succeed and become wealthy, but their children see them as money-obsessed capitalists who do not know the value of a well-balanced life. But in most cases, the parents do not achieve the immigrant's dream and find comfort in churches, friends, and videos of Korean soap operas. The parents' impossibly high expectation for material success inevitably leads to a sense of failure for everyone. On the other hand, the second generation deals with material success in varying ways. A character may become an investment banker and proudly declare that he is not like his father, but another may continue to work in the small store he inherits from his parents. Either way, all the characters deal with what it means to succeed and how success should be defined.

The playwrights also dramatize the ways in which gender dictates how success is measured and how the expectations for women differ from those for men. A female character's parents teach her the gender values taught by Confucius and tell her to obey them and her husband. She is told to dress modestly and to focus on finding a good Korean husband. But she finds Korean men unattractive because she thinks they can repress and stifle her individuality and freedom. One of the most common stories in the Korean diaspora drama is the mother-daughter relationship in which the daughter finds non-Korean men attractive. Parents, but mothers in particular, universally represent one's biological and cultural roots, and mothers commonly embody the "old country" even in the process of their rejecting it. Terms such as "mother land" emphasize the ways in which mothers are imagined in the minds of immigrants. When the mother is an immigrant herself, she also represents the choice to start afresh in a new country. In Korean diaspora plays, the trope of the mother, therefore, functions as a symbol of both the past and the future. And the mother-daughter relationships reveal one of the most complicated yet most common aspects of the diaspora. They have obvious love for each other and want the best for the other person, but they are entangled in a destructive web of contradictory goals and notions of success and happiness.

Stories of success and failure are complex and never mutually exclusive in the plays. Many characters hear contradictory messages about what is best for them. Some break down psychologically, while others convert their confusion into anger toward their parents or the society. They also turn to their work, to their church, to alcohol, or to a lover in an attempt to escape their reality. But what makes each play powerful and moving is the characters' sincere struggle to find answers and to make connections with others. The characters may never find resolution, but they continue to evolve and contribute to the collective exploration.

But ultimately, plays are literary works and products of the writers' imagination and creativity. How much the plays represent reality depends on the readers' or spectators' interpretation and reception. The majority of the playwrights have never been to Korea, and what they know of Korean history has small consequence to their everyday existence. None of the plays in this collection intends to be an ethnographic documentation of the Korean diaspora.

Rather, the plays are about what the writers have felt emotionally and imagined intuitively in seeing themselves as part of the Korean diaspora. The plays reflect the world that haunts the writers' minds. As a group, the playwrights have given life to stories that sketch the constantly evolving sense of being and becoming in the Korean diaspora. With the full acknowledgment of their talent and potential, I present the selected seven plays not to indicate a limit but to open the possibility of many more productions and publications to follow in the years to come.

THE SEVEN PLAYS IN THIS COLLECTION

The selection process for this collection was based on my wish to showcase a diverse range of topics and styles, but I have also given preference to plays that directly address Korean diasporic issues written by writers of the second generation. Many of the playwrights included here have written plays that have nothing to do with "Korean" as a cultural identifier, and some reject ethnic-specific labels that may hinder their freedom as writers. However, because the collection is about the Korean diaspora, the plays address it as a theme broadly and collectively. The two one-act plays, *History K* by Edward Bok Lee and *Mina* by Kyoung H. Park, bookend the full-length plays as prologue and epilogue.

History K begins the collection with a haunting monologue of an Asian prostitute named K who allegorically embodies the military occupation in Asia. While she could be of any Asian nationality, K's story can be read as a chronicle of the U.S. involvement in Korea's modern history. Written in the style reminiscent of Samuel Beckett's one-woman plays such as *Not I* and *Rockaby*, *History K* shows a woman painfully victimized by the West's military aggression in Asia. Unable to articulate her existence, K can only show fragmented glimpses of westernization forced onto her both physically and emotionally. The sociologist Grace M. Cho writes in her book *Haunting the Korean Diaspora: Shame, Secrecy, and the Forgotten War*, "The Korean diaspora in the United States has been haunted by the traumatic effects of what we are not allowed to know—the terror and devastation inflicted by the Korean War, the failure to resolve it, and the multiple silences surrounding this violent history."[14] K's inarticulate words and silences create the poetry that serve as the prologue and a haunting background for the other plays in the collection.

Julia Cho's *99 Histories* is representative of many Korean diasporic plays that deal with remembrance, forgetting, and fantasy. In the play, memories are faulty and fluid, and they also evolve over time. Cho tells what is in many ways a classic mother-daughter relationship story. When Eunice, the daughter, shows up pregnant long after running away from home, the mother, Sah-Jin, encourages her to look forward and to rebuild her life. But the daughter cannot move on without finding out about the past, especially about her mother's life in Korea and her father, who died abruptly in Los Angeles. By immigrating to the United States, Sah-Jin attempted to forget both her personal past and Korea's history, and Eunice ran away from her mother in order to escape her childhood, but they ultimately accept their realities and draw strength from the bond they have together. Like the old photographs Eunice finds, the play tells a multilayered story about the events that get documented and remembered and the secrets that get hidden and forgotten. "We remembered the wrong memories," says Eunice at the end of the play, but in embracing that fact, she can finally start to find peace.

Like the family in *99 Histories*, the Chun family in Lloyd Suh's *American Hwangap* has difficulty staying together. When the father returns from Korea after fifteen years, he is the physical reincarnation of the past memories the family has repressed and forgotten. The divorced wife and three grown children try to understand how they can—or would want to—function as a family. The oldest son, David, refuses to come home to celebrate his father's *hwangap* (the sixtieth birthday ritual celebrating the completion of the Eastern zodiac). The wife, Mary, is described as "a modern Asian-American woman" comfortably assimilated in Texas. While she is free from any obligation as a wife, she happily prepares the food for her ex-husband's birthday party. The daughter, Esther, disapproves of her parents, but the youngest one, Ralph, excitedly accepts the estranged father. Min Suk Chun, the father who describes himself as a cowboy, finds happiness and redemption with his broken family, but his children no longer have reasons to stay home. The play tells a Korean American version of the Wild West story with fiercely independent characters, lone wanderers, and survivors. Their humorous dialogues and cynical façades hide deep anger and disappointments, but they somehow continue to live on.

All the plays in the collection deal with myths in a broad sense. Whether it is the myth of the Korean family, the American Dream, or the model minority, the plays dismantle expectations placed on Korean immigrants and their children from both internal and external sources. The plays demonstrate the extreme to which a myth can be reified and destroyed. The worlds created in the plays do not resemble everyday realities, but they can function as abstract parables from the Korean diaspora. Jean Yoon's *Hongbu and Nolbu: The Tale of the Magic Pumpkins* is an adaptation of one of the most commonly known Korean folklores. Children in Korea grow up hearing about the two brothers, Hongbu and Nolbu, whose story teaches them to be kind and honest. Yoon's adaptation was written initially for the audience of the Lorraine Kimsa Theatre, a theater for young people, in Toronto. The production brought together many Korean Canadian families, many of whom attended theater for the first time in Canada. Because of the play's use of Korean drumming, mask dance, and language, it was enthusiastically received by the older generation, and the specific references to popular culture (for example, video games) made the play contemporary and accessible for the younger generation. The play's popularity can also be explained by its self-referential humor in the style of both Korean mask drama and slapstick comedy. In an improvisational mode, actors change characters in front of the audience and tell them what happens next. From one perspective, the play tells a simple and innocent mythical story, but from another, it is a meta-theatrical extravaganza full of bizarre fantasies and dark humor.

Things turn even more bizarre with *Yi Sang Counts to Thirteen* by Sung Rno. The play takes place in "Seoul as reflected through a certain Mr. Yi Sang's strange and twisted brain." The Korean surrealist poet Yi Sang died in 1937 at the age of twenty-seven during the height of Japanese colonial rule in Korea. He is considered a poet genius who has received unprecedented posthumous recognition. Indeed, he is a mythic character in the Korean literary society. Sung Rno presents a surrealistic play inspired by translations of Yi Sang's poems that blur literary genres and defy structural rules. Like Yi Sang's poems, Rno's play is more about patterns, juxtapositions, and permutations, and less about conventional storytelling and character development. The three characters, identified as Blue, Red, and Green, commit to actions and words without the goal to communicate or to further the plot; rather, possibilities are limitless in what they could be or become. The play itself could also be many things, including a postmodern pastiche of the world known to Sung Rno. Or it could be, as the theater critic Adam Klasfeld notes, an inverted tale of the Greek myth about Icarus and his wings.[15] But it is ultimately about the poetic world of Yi Sang as interpreted and recreated by Rno. The work is unique as the first Korean American play to receive a professional production in Korea and has since been revived there, seen as an exemplary dramatization of Yi Sang and his work. A major reason for the play's acceptance in Korea has to do with the fact that the director of the original production was the famed American Lee

Breuer. In 1998, Rno worked on the play with Breuer when the former was the resident artist for the director's company Mabou Mines. The play was then included in the Seoul Theater Festival, which had previously included works by Breuer. The production was heralded as a meaningful coming together of three experimental artists of different generations and backgrounds.

In addition to memories and myths, trauma functions as a leitmotif in Korean diaspora plays. Immigration can be traumatic, and the sense of displacement felt in the new country can be permanently damaging. As dramatized in this collection, the uprooted disruption caused by the physical move can break up families, worsen mental instability, and unsettle ontological awareness. But the disruptions can also open doors for changes in unimagined ways. The plays in this collection exemplify the various ways in which Korean diasporic communities have recreated themselves out of trauma and continue to evolve. Diana Son's *Satellites* shows a Korean American character whose ethnic identity is only one of multiple facets of her existence. The protagonist, Nina, is a successful architect in her thirties. She is driven, ambitious, and focused on success. She is also a new mother who moves to Brooklyn to start a family lifestyle with her African American husband, Miles, who was adopted by a white family and had graduated from a prestigious university with a degree in computer engineering. Nina is overwhelmed with motherhood and hires a Korean woman, Mrs. Chae, as a nanny. As her new life unfolds, Nina finds herself pulled in multiple directions and is forced to make heart-wrenching decisions in order to set her own moral standards and to define her responsibilities to herself and others. At the end of the play, Nina tells Miles that "we can make up the words ourselves," referring to a lullaby they were trying to remember. The freedom to make up the words symbolizes a new life they can create for the baby. Nina projects a future in which categories can be rewritten and identities can be chosen; she does not need to be bounded by social expectations that derive from racial, ethnic, and gendered divisions. She only looks forward into the future for the sake of her new family.

The collection ends with an epilogue in the form of the Korean Chilean playwright Kyoung H. Park's one-act play, *Mina*. Like the character K in *History K* that begins the collection, Mina struggles with a life that has spiraled out of control. Mina is utterly lost between four cultures: Peruvian, Korean, Japanese, and American. She speaks three different languages in the short piece, which reads like a long confessional purging. She is a victim of colonialism and globalization, but unlike K, who is hopeless, she is a survivor who imagines finding herself at the end. She may have no roots she can claim, but she can dream of happiness and hope for the future. It is with this optimistic reading of the piece that I present the following seven plays from the Korean diaspora in the Americas.

NOTES

1. Julio Martinez, "My Tired Broke Ass Pontificating Slapstick Funk," *Daily Variety* (March 22, 2000): 16.
2. Euijoon Kim, email to the author, April 12, 2010.
3. For details of the immigration policies, see Won Moo Hurh, *The Korean Americans* (Westport, Conn.: Greenwood Press, 1998); Elspeth Cameron, ed., *Multiculturalism and Immigration in Canada: An Introductory Reader* (Toronto: Canadian Scholar's Press, 2004); and In-Jin Yoon, "Understanding the Korean Diaspora from Comparative Perspective," conference paper for the session "Transformation & Prospect toward Multiethnic, Multiracial and Multicultural Society: Enhancing Intercultural Communication," Asia Culture Forum, Kwangju, South Korea, 2006.
4. In Central and South America, Brazil has the largest Korean population (48,000), followed by Argentina (22,000), Mexico (12,000), Guatemala (almost 10,000), and Paraguay (5,000). Populations with fewer than 4,000 were not specified in the report. The data are available in Korean at the Overseas Koreans Foundation website (http://www.korean.net/morgue/status_1_2005.jsp?tCode=status&dCode=0101; accessed June 23, 2010).
5. For details on the phrase "Miracle on the Han River," see Bruce Cumming, *Korea's Place in the Sun: A Modern History* (New York: W. W. Norton, 2005), and Jürgen Kleiner's *Korea: A Century of Change* (Singapore: World Scientific Publishing, 2001).
6. I am using the term "ethnonationalism" as defined by Nadia Y. Kim in *Imperial Citizens: Koreans and Race from Seoul to LA* (Stanford: Stanford University Press, 2008).
7. Kandice Chu and Karen Shimakawa, eds., "Introduction," in *Orientations: Mapping Studies in the Asian Diaspora* (Durham: Duke University Press, 2001), 6.
8. Rick Shiomi, "Preface," *Love and RelASIANships: A Collection of Contemporary Asian-Canadian Drama*, vol. 1, ed. Nina Lee Aquino (Toronto: Canadian Drama Publisher, 2009), 4.
9. For details on the history of the EWP, see Yuko Kurahashi, *Asian American Culture on Stage: The History of the East West Players* (New York: Garland, 1999). For a biographical study of Soon-Tek Oh, see my article "Transnational Legitimization of an Actor: The Life and Career of Soon-Tek Oh," *Modern Drama* 48, no. 2 (Summer 2005), 372–406.
10. Terry Hong, "Times Up," *KoreAm Journal* (December 2003), 69.

11. For an expanded study on Jean Yoon and Korean Canadian theater, see my article "'Patient Zero': Jean Yoon and Korean Canadian Theatre," in *Asian Canadian Theatre*, ed. Nina Lee Aquino and Ric Knowles (Toronto: Playwrights Canada, 2011).

12. Young Jean Lee, *Songs of the Dragon Flying to Heaven and Other Plays* (New York: Theatre Communications Group, 2009). For a discussion of the play *Song of the Dragon Flying to Heaven*, see Karen Shimakawa, "Young Jean Lee's Ugly Feelings about Race and Gender," *Women & Performance: A Journal of Feminist Theory* 17, no. 1 (March 2007), 89–102.

13. Rhacel S. Parreñas and Lok C. D. Siu, eds., *Asian Diasporas: New Formations, New Conceptions* (Stanford: Stanford University Press, 2007).

14. I would add that the trauma of the Korean War has affected Korean immigrants in other parts of the world, including Japan, China, and all of the Americas. Grace M. Cho, *Haunting the Korean Diaspora: Shame, Secrecy, and the Forgotten War* (Minneapolis: University of Minnesota Press, 2008), 12.

15. Adam Klasfeld, "*Yi Sang Counts to 13* and *Often I Find That I Am Naked*," *Theatre Mania*, August 15, 2001 (http://www.theatermania.com/new-york/reviews/08-2001/yi-sang-counts-to-13-and-often-i-find-that-i-am-na_1590.html; accessed July 15, 2010).

HISTORY K
Edward Bok Lee

Edward Bok Lee is a poet, fiction writer, and playwright. He was born in South Korea in 1971 and grew up in North Dakota and Minnesota. He became actively involved in theater as one of the original members of Theater Mu during his freshman year at the University of Minnesota. He continued to grow as a playwright while pursuing an MFA degree in Creative Writing at Brown University, where he took several playwriting workshops with Paula Vogel, Chuck Mee, and Aishah Rahman. His plays include *Glow*, *Permanence Collection* (co-written with Kira Obolensky), *Passage*, *St. Petersburg*, *Athens County*, and *10,000 Kilometer*. His work has been produced or developed at the Guthrie Theater, the New York Theatre Workshop, the Public Theater, Theater Mu, Taipei Theatre, East West Players, Thirst Theater, Ma-Yi Theater Company, Trinity Repertory Company, and the Walker Art Center. He has won the McKnight Artists Fellowship, two national Jerome Fellowships, and the Weston Fine Arts Prize for Best Graduate Play at Brown University, as well as fellowships from the Minnesota State Arts Board and the New York Theatre Workshop, where he has served as a playwright-in-residence. He is currently a Core Member at the Playwrights' Center in Minneapolis. He has published his plays with Vintage Books, Smith and Kraus, and Playscripts. A collection of his writings, *Real Karaoke People: Poems and Prose* (New River Press), received the PEN Open Book Award in 2006. His second book, *Whorled* (Coffee House Press), was published in 2011. *History K* (1999) started as a poem and was originally titled "Whorled."

Edward Bok Lee. Photo by Dani Werner.

History K was part of the Jerome Fellowship Five Alive Series at the Playwrights' Center in Minneapolis in 1998. A later staged reading of the play was presented at the New York Theatre Workshop and Ma-Yi Theater Company in 2004. The staged reading at the Playwrights' Center was directed by the playwright and featured Jeany Park in the role of K.

CHARACTERS

K: an Asian prostitute, middle-aged, on her final night of work

TIME AND PLACE

In an Asian country, near a U.S. military base

I. DRESSING TABLE

a vanity table covered with old jars and tubes of cosmetics.
K enters in robe, takes seat, staring front into "mirror."
organizes makeup, etc. a ritual.
eventually begins to apply foundation.
sees postcard in top corner of mirror. removes and stares. lips its written words to herself.
eventually removes cassette from drawer, places it in cassette player on dressing table and pushes play.
while applying foundation to face.

TAPE   "Bonjour"

    (she repeats the French in heavy, artfully "Asian" accent.)

TAPE   *Good day.*

    (she repeats the English in heavy, artfully "Asian" accent.)

TAPE   "Je m'appelle Jacques."

    (she repeats the above.)

TAPE   "My name is Jack."

    (she repeats the above.)

TAPE   "*Quelle heure est-il?*"

    (she repeats the above.)

TAPE   "*What time is it?*"

    (she repeats the above.)

TAPE   "*Voulez-vous du thé?*"

    (she repeats the above.)

TAPE   "*Would you care for some tea?*"

    (she repeats the above. she hits stop. fast forwards.)

TAPE   La Bretagne est la premiere province francaise qu'on ait dotee d'un progamme d'—

    (she hits stop, staring front for some moments, looks at postcard again, turns it over and stares at picture, reads.)

K   Arc de Triomphe

Arc de Triomphe

    (finishes applying foundation; powders throughout rambling.)

Arc de Triomphe. Ah. Ah. Ah

Deu. Deu. Deu

Peu. Pheu. Pheu. Peu

    (stops, closes eyes.)

Apport. Apport

Of a share issue bid for investor. Apport

    (resumes powdering face in "mirror.")

Apport. Apport. A – pp – ort

    (pause.)

Arbitrage

Purchase of a . . . security . . .

Nearly. Instantaneously . . .

In one market . . .

Arbitrage

(pleased, begins makeup again, continues for some seconds, examining face.)

Of purchasing additional shares when . . .

Averaging

(frowns for a moment frozen, finally remembers.)

To bring down . . .

Nearly instantaneously . . .

To bring down . . .

To averaging the . . .

. . . cost

(resumes makeup for a time.)

Averaging. Averaging. Is he averaging, Mr. Lee? Is he averaging again? I'd like to average that. Could we average that, Mr. Lee? Arbitrage. Averaging. Avis d'attribution. Avis d'attribution. Avis d'—

(pause. she then begins to search drawer for Dictionary of the Securities Industries, locates it, reads.)

See Allotment letter.

(turns pages.)

Successful applicant for a new share issue . . . see allotment . . . will receive . . .

(turns page.)

an allotment letter

(contemplates vacantly, then slams book shut, staring front for a moment into "mirror," touches face.)

Arc de Triomphe

(blackout.)

(beat. in darkness, K turns on pink lamp at table and begins powdering while speaking.)

(begins in "daughter's" voice.)

Come live with me in Paris, she says. Earned a little money a dancer and all of a sudden a queen. Queen of France. Not twenty years old. What would I do in France, really, what could I do, did you ever think of that, so young, you can't be so naive, not there, do you know how old I've become in the meantime, did you stop and think, have you ever stopped to think, what I would do there, ever, stop to think, at my age, be someone's maid, or nanny, good for nothing else, tongue all shriveled, eyes weary, wash hardwood floors, on my hands and knees, an immigrant, scrub till my blood and bones are so thin I am part air, do you think of me that way, your own mother . . .

(ceases, has over-powdered.)

a ghost already?

(observes, sees postcard, places back in top corner of mirror.)

(applies eyeliner.)

But then when did you ever think ahead from the time a small girl in coasters, so morose, that button nose, not like you to consider me, across the sea, no, me who did the best she could under the circumstances, yes, all she could, alone in those days, oh yes, no, oh yes, what days they were to have to do all you, gods of fire in the fabric mill leaping from such high high windows

(pause. lost in thought. resumes eyeliner.)

Never thinking ahead, nearly run over, twice that summer, in the street, by the pier, almost fell in looking, your first word: go, flat on her face, crying, laughing, who could tell, quiet child, crying outside while laughing inside, who could tell, by the pier, so fucking morose, then suddenly, did you ever hold such a fucking morose child? a sack of rice full of . . . buttons . . . grasshopper legs . . . then, one by one . . . teeth

(different eyeliner.)

Go go go through to rough years, more alone then ever, no comfort, not a soft moment, stinky pillow, and her, you, Magical Orchid, so silent like sickness, short hair, long hair, old enough for what, short hair, long hair, curly hair, long hair, bleached for a week, scurrying around the house, rabbit, rabbit, maybe you don't deserve to eat, disco queen be inside the head with a hot tip, scalding, because your hair looks like shit, comb it, then yes, go set it on fire for all I care

Cry cry cry

Crazy girl, crazy mother? I want to be a singer, she says, a singer on the base, crazy girl, or in New York or Paris, pipe dreams, sniper sniping cheese, want to sing, so sing, I said, only you'll need a visa, and there's only two ways for that

(long pause.)

What would I know in France, what will I ever know, do, where would I go, music like the teeth of some foreign animal swimming through the air

(staring front into "mirror.")

Yes

No

Did all I could to brighten your moods, even bought that pink terry-cloth summer dress, yes, yellow sandals, a red ice-cream cone in her little hand, melting, traffic passing, how she beamed that day, remember, remember, could have passed for anyone's child on the street, not just mine, not just half mine, around the eyes, the nose

everyone's

anyone's

could have even left you there

   (searches for mascara, applies for several seconds in silence.)

Because they go. Leave

Ah, but a son. A man to hold up your tired bones, maybe dance with you, the cologne you've bought him for his first girlfriend like wings that will bring you grandchildren

But a girl, and one with such a country name. What's so magical? What thinking, like a farm-girl, not thinking, not properly at least, orchid. Magical Orchid. Stupid fucking country name

   (closely examines face so far, left to right, front.)

Because, really, how's she going to be a famous picture star with such a country name, I didn't have to, all the girls, suckling, tit metal and bleeding, what were you thinking, not thinking, Katherine, Marilyn, Genevieve, anything, what were you thinking, because how will she ever become anything better with such a country name and big eyes, to big for her button nose

And no father

Like a stalk of cattail torn open in the wind

   (resumes lipstick.)

Dead log floating home

Rice patty groaning with fallen leaves

   (stops. face now almost freakishly white, pressing lips until pleased. rises and exits. returns in sunflower hat on head, adjusts it, returns. adjusts hat, examines self in mirror. adjusts hat.)

You want them all to be

And yet none can see

Yes

No

"Upper class lady!"

And me placing a coin in his sweet sticky little palm, filthy little beggar boy, and he, smiling, and I, and we giving more to one another than a shiny coin

Through the eyes

   (stares at self in "mirror.")

Did I dream him?

Little beggar boy, little small greasy child, and me in my orange dress, such dead black teeth, spaces, where new ones should be coming in, the old falling away

"Upper-class lady!"

Am I a dreamer?

Because I'll suck your eyes out, I swear, she said

Yes

No

Do I dream too much?

Little boy with the face of a dog

Maybe dreaming right now . . .

   (stares at self in "mirror" for a long time. then:)

Flight in the eye already, child, same size, a stick of peppermint in one hand and my crepe yellow church dress underneath my blue school uniform, and what kind of hat? And black lacquer box, lit on the top-side, mother of pearl, inside no jewels, but photographs, tens of them, twenty-nine, who are they, stuffed into my canvas knapsack, one American dollar against hipbone, sewn, RUN!!!

   (beat. calm, in child's voice.)

Father, where are we going?

(opens eyes.)

No reply

Earthen jar of honey, fallen to polished hardwood, crack of a man's skull with rifle butt in the rainy lot, see the trail of ants, sniffles, a little cough hardly louder than itself, in the next room, baby brother's, sick in the crib, jail-faced, head of dark lychee fuzz

(in child's voice.)

Where will we be when we get there?

No reply

(seated, begins brushing hair, marching legs in place.)

Soldiers' legs redoubled in the street puddles

Olive green trucks, well-weathered, tanks, what little boy, where? charred, rusted underbellies and mud-caked hulls, aching, ticking

(stops brushing, stares.)

Father, look at the red stars

(brushing and brushing. eventually, she seeing all her hair in the brush's teeth; stops, gathers it all in her fist, then places it, ceremoniously, in ashtray, and lights it on fire with a match.

it burns fast, then smokes, she sniffs as if remembering something.)

Father?

Don't point don't look don't think don't feel the cold in your toes anymore, the holes in your socks, boiled grass wadded in your bloated stomach, clumped like a stone, cold and plummeting, nights shrinking days the waiting and frozen waking in darkness and snow warm to numb limb, tanks, Russian, numb, scarring the rice fields that autumn, Father, numb, searing wind with black singe, communism in the nostrils

Nonexistence

(pause.)

Things stick to pricks inside you, Mother always said

> *(picks up curling iron, fingers iron part, pulls away quickly, then grasps the metal in her hand, holding it around the metal, drawing it closely to her face as if about to also burn out her eyeballs. reads:)*

Made in . . . Taiwan

> *(hurls inoperative curling iron across the room.)*

Yes

No

Stupid girl. Because what would I know in France, what will I ever know, do, where would I go, music like the teeth of some foreign animal swimming through the wet filthy air

II. RACK OF DRESSES

> *K, in robe and sunflower hat, picking through wardrobe. holds dress after dress up to her, looking front before "mirror," then throwing down again, until she finally holds an old, absurdly small navy blue schoolgirl uniform.*

K   Mencius, Confucius, xingshan, human nature is good, xing'e, human nature is bad, de, viture, jing, revere, ming, fate, ming, decree, just because you have never read, don't push that on me, I love to read, classics, my favorite, Mencius, your grandfather was a teacher, history, I love to read, such dim eyes, your grandfather the teacher, stony old brow, he taught me something, history, every Sunday, in the wine house, through the winter especially, by the fire, he tested me, always an excellent memory, I had, always the best, always winning peanuts, baisse, a declining price trend, baissier, a bear operator in the market, always the best and most peanuts, his favorite of the bunch, allotment letter, a successful applicant for a new—

> *(pause. takes another dress.)*

What to do with a girl like that, so selfish, a dancer, what kind of dancer, I don't know exactly, one who breaks things no doubt, since she was little, always running about, limbs flaying, never a sound from her mouth though, so odd and morose really, what's wrong with you daughter, I don't know, maybe the American in her, freckles on chin and shoulders, what's wrong with her, I don't know, always breaking things, by just looking at them, picture frames falling, metal cups, spilt her first milk, and such vast wild dances

(stops, takes another dress.)

Grandmother's crane vase, passed down from a grand-aunt, from the north, jadestone, fifteen white cranes, flying where? how could you, where were you running past a wind blur, there's nowhere to want to go that fast, such an unmagical orchid sometimes, not clumsy, uncaring, wild, like a soldier, where were you going so fast to not here or there

Not anywhere

(another dress.)

A lesson then, for punishment: giving over something valuable back, yes, in your room, no not a matchbook, no, not nothing, something, give me something back that you took from me, yes, you, one thing, as a lesson not to forget, something as valuable as grandma's vase, now in pieces, each shard a generation, no, not your jump rope, something more, like that transistor yes the one on your nightstand there, go get it, right now, such an unmagical orchid, how unmagical, no indeed, giving it here right now, RIGHT NOW!!!

(another dress.)

Transistor to the floor, smashed, they'll be other birthdays, next to grandmother's vase, in pieces still, big fat tears, how does it feel, to lose something you cherished, how does it feel?, broken to bits inside itself, jagged edges sticky against darkening clouds

(another dress.)

Won't be running around in here again, will we, no reply, I said we won't run around here again now, will we, trembling lids, floating head, ANSWER ME!!!

(rips dress.)

Crazy girl, it's only a transistor, what's got into you, a cheap transistor, look at the vase, in pieces, broken, memories, and grandmother, her smile, and teeth, broken, her eyes, smashed, with cranes on it, what's left, in a heap, shards, go wash your eyes out, with cool water, not cold or hot, crazy girl, all for a cheap transistor, aren't you ashamed, won't be running past here again, limbs flailing, silent sniveling now, all for a cheap transistor, sulking for an hour, crazy girl, all for a cheap

(white dress. beat.)

Voulez-vous du thé?

nothing like ours, no doubt, no doubt nothing like our tea, too sweet, like all Westerners, creamy and sweet instead of clear green, barley, and the cakes, good flour, much less starch, and sugar, no lard, I wonder, having read of tea, a recent hobby, tea, not reading, of course, I've always read, oh yes, in the evenings, what does anyone do, work, read, study, languages, English, French, Investing, what does anyone do, stocks, for the future, part game, for the stomach, toughens it up, the stock market, up and coming, pacific rim, seven tigers, acid test ratio, the current assets of a company, Hanjin up one and a quarter, Kepco down two, and I read, a great deal now, more and more, it comes with age I suppose, buried habits, surfacing, dead bodies in lakes, first loves, to read, and study, before the war, before you were born, before the fabric mill, if you would have known me then, singing in school, a choir of girls, even acted a little, on stage, which helped me, really, a great deal in life, out there, acting, singing too but not as much, more . . . while bathing mainly, by the river

(trying different pair of shoes, a different scarf.)

No going back, not after that, no, no going back to that, caught, in the fields, after that no going back, on his farm, after the festival, autumn, squash porridge, what was his name, a farmer, much older, from the wine house, wife a tubercular, fat sisters, faint mustache and . . . eyes, wide set

Because I love you, he said

Much older, thick fingers, voice unwavering, I love you, and touched me, all fifteen years, unpeeling in the palm of his hand, mouth, bitter wine, in the brittle fields, autumn, windswept from the north, nestled in an excavated landmine, in his arms, cleared away, a cracked mud bed, a hole, really, detonated already, because, you see, men might have died here, he said, before the tracks were laid, he said, that far sounding train, where do you suppose it's going, I said, or did I only think it, think so much, how to trust, such a warm night on the neck for autumn, then why are you shaking, he said, and touched me with his lips, clumsy, teeth never so long and useless, claws really, of a kitten, a little fumbling kitten on its back

There may be some blood

Yes

No

Moth-gnawed at the edges, see where it's stitched, I did that, I stitched that, borrowed stockings

There may be some blood, but it's normal

Normal, when is blood ever normal, I want to go home

This is special blood

Holy blood

   (beat.)

Am I holy?

See there, when else have you seen the sky so red?

> (fully dressed now in evening attire—e.g., fishnet stockings, dress, stiletto-heeled boots, etc.—all inappropriate for her age. she goes to dressing table, removes butterfly knife from drawer, deftly whirls it open and plays with it for a moment, then slips it professionally into the ankle of her boot, perfumes self perhaps, exits.)

III. NIGHT CAFÉ

background music. late-eighties American pop ballads. disco ball/colored lights.

K seated alone at table with half-full bottle of liquor and two glasses, hers and an empty other's across from her. dressed as in last scene. incongruous sunflower hat.

every so often she stares front at "entrance," apparently waiting for someone.

music plays. eventually, she rises, picks up mic, and begins to sing a melancholic karaoke ballad.

mid-song, music cuts out and lights shift jarringly at sound of gunshot. K stares front toward "entrance."

K   Solitary snipers. Not a soul come evening time. Listen

Cold air crackling since dawn. If not for the down stuffed into the gutted lining of uncle's waistcoat. And me inside, clung like a moth to his bare chest. So warm. What did I say, or think? Mother, is that a man asleep in the wet ditch? An American? Or Russian? Chinese? See, there, on his mouth? Curdled shiny pale and myriad. Stupid girl. Too many questions. White rice eating on his lips

(staring front, in child's voice.)

I'd like some rice too, Mother

(goes to pour another glass. downs it. thinks she hears something; approaches and stares front toward "entrance" again for a time.)

Things stick to pricks inside you

Always the same, in varying order, each night, unrelenting, who would have thought, who could have known, every song, to listen and be lulled, by what, if anything, forty-three different songs, of love, always the same, in varying order

(looks around, a bit drunk.)

Though not more than thirty tonight, yes four times each, nine hours, each song at some four and a half minutes, thirty songs, on a weeknight, some breaks, equals . . . nine hours

(returns to table, sits and smokes.)

Terminal organs dipped in wax

(pause. tries to wait as if underwater. music having slowly returned to normal again.)

And you, back, as if the first time, bar over there, and that thing once there, now there, and something there, where he leaned into me, what does Harry mean in English?, I asked him and this man laughing, thin man, bad skin, balding, not old, not young, not tall, not short

(pours again from bottle.)

Did you enjoy it, asking, afterward, the look in his eyes, me trying not to laugh, joking all night, you can be honest, now serious, or is he, did you enjoy it? They call that a film. And that man? Oh, you mean the actor. No, not the actor, but the man. The character. Who was he?

He was the salesman

Who was the salesman?

The salesman was . . . the salesman. The actor playing the salesman.

Who are any of us, really? When you think of it—

I don't think of it.

Don't we all play a part in a movie? In life? Don't we all sell things?

I don't think of it, I try not to think of it.

Maybe you should.

(pause.)

Not tall not fat not anything not young not old not anything.

(drinks.)

Because if you're going to play a part anyway . . .

(drinks. smokes.)

The kind not to have accomplished much in life, eyes, unknowing down deep, did what I could not to laugh, had to hold my breath until he'd had enough

   (smokes.)

Like a wound, just like a wound, cleansing itself

   (drinks.)

Making a movie, he says, on location, do you like movies, he says, what kind of question is that, I said, who doesn't like Hollywood?

   (stands, approaches "entrance" as if someone is walking in and she will greet him.)

You look like an actress

Would you believe I have daughter this tall?

Yes

No

   (pause. smokes coyly, leisurely.)

Harry, how can you not know what your name even means?

Who doesn't know what their name means?

   (pause. stamps out cigarette. now clearly drunk.)

Everyone knows what their name means

Even if they don't tell anyone

Even if they hide it deep inside their tongue

Even if it was never their tongue in the first place

   (beat. she looks over to someone finally approaching through "entrance.")

IV. LOVE MOTEL

K staring front into "mirror," an unmade queen-size bed behind her. pink neon flashes through window.
she is naked, hair unfurled.

K Because youth is a thing of majesty

he said

A boy still, loitering at the fabric mills, after school, what do you weave, he asked, a boy still really, yet such a pallor, under the eyes, and thin face cut by shadows, face of a nobleman, or civil servant, yes, born just beyond the village

I weave bolt of commercial garment, I said, huge bolts of dark cloth

I like fashion, he said, what is a man without style but an animal, he said, book in hand, as always, what are the materials you weave, he asked, such great concern, do you know me from anyone, such old weak eyes already, trapped in the wrong time and place on his youthful face, a strong black widow's peak, like father's

(begins to dress in regular street wear.)

A poet? What good's a poet during wartime? I said. What good's a drunk? he said. A parentless son. Country noble boy. In his found hat. Where did you get that hat? Did you steal that felt hat? Felt, or silk was it? Mind a blur. Of course not. I was given it, he said. In Pagoda Park. At my feet. Pigeons. Hundreds of them ganging the footpath one moment; now skittering away with one lazy kick of his heavy black boot. Did you steal those boots? I was in the army. The army? What do you know about war? Nothing. Is that why it's so scuffed there? What do you do now?

(thinking, scoffs.)

A poet?

(pause, recalls.)

"If I warm your hand, I mean to kiss your soul. But I can't because life is winter and the sound of distant marching . . ."

Is that a poem?

Yes

People don't talk like that

No

Are you even real?

(stops. still contemplating.)

A scab on his left forefinger pad, tracing my jaw

Things stick to pricks inside you, Mother always said

Cut 'em away like scabs

(holds butterfly knife pulled from purse, deftly slings it open and plays with it in rapid motion.)

Like Hyegyung. Found in a tub drown of her own blood.

(pause.)

Because youth is a thing of majesty, he said

Like a spell

(staring front at "mirror" a long time. half dressed now.)

In a shanty-town. Cinder blocks. Orange canvas tents, flapping raggedy in the polluted wind. Near the National Bank. Under acid-drizzle. How odd to see a shriveled child again. Like a little old man. Is that him? Come again? Nothing on but a tight blue sweater. No pants whatsoever. Or shoes. Naked child. Soft-freeing his bowels right there in the vacant lot under such clear gray skies

Flight in the passing cars. Mercedes-Benz splashing past, Hyundais awhirl, bright as plastic bags skirting the sidewalks, clutching a bare branch for dear life, candy girl! you there!

Bending down, to my girl beside me. Small yet. And my knees already creaking. Pink little terry-cloth dress

Listen to Mommy. Go with Mr. Harry. Don't be afraid. Mr. Harry is a very nice man. Mommy is fond of him. He is very nice to Mommy. He wants you to call him . . . Harry. How should I know what it means? Mommy will meet you afterward. You always wanted to visit France, didn't you always sing of Paris? That song, what was that song, sing that song, no, because Mommy has to work, remember that poster of Paris, like a god, I don't know, maybe a god, but how can a city be a god, a god can only be. . . .

a god.

(watches them leave, then turns.)

Candy-girl! You there! Take this and deliver one of those cones to that too small filthy boy there squatting in the lot yes there don't point please. Hurry now

And she eyeing me. Offensively. Simple ruddy cheeks. Small eyes, ugly really. In her candy hat. With her candy shoes. Nearly jumping when he touched such a sweet red piece of red bean ice in her hand

Little bare-bottomed boy

No, I don't have a daughter

What confusion it must have been for him

Yes

No

I never had a daughter

Candy-girl approaching, and he, so sleepy and slow, gazing up this filthy little nameless boy at such . . . offensiveness, through such . . . gratitude

(beat. loud toilet flush from the bathroom.

K looks, finishes dressing, picks up the money left for her on the dresser and places it in her bag.

she is dressed now fully in regular street clothes (pants, tee-shirt, sneakers, perhaps) appropriate for an average middle-aged woman, no makeup, hair casual, and glasses.

staring front, into "mirror.")

No

Yes

Thank you

I am and always have been alone

(slow fade.)

—— END OF PLAY ——

99 HISTORIES
Julia Cho

Julia Cho. Photo by Jennie Warren.

Julia Cho was born in Los Angeles in 1975 and grew up in Los Angeles County and Arizona. She started taking playwriting classes at Amherst College with Constance Congdon and later completed her MFA in dramatic writing at New York University, followed by a playwriting residency at the Juilliard School. Her plays include *The Language Archive*, *The Piano Teacher*, *Durango*, *The Winchester House*, *BFE*, and *The Architecture of Loss*. Her plays have been produced at the Roundabout Theatre Company, the Public Theater, Vineyard Theatre, Long Wharf Theatre, Playwrights Horizons, South Coast Repertory, New York Theatre Workshop, East West Players, The Theatre@Boston Court, Theater Mu, and Silk Road Theatre Project. Honors include the 2010 Susan Smith Blackburn Award, the Barrie Stavis Award, the Claire Tow Award for Emerging Artists, and the L. Arnold Weissberger Award. Cho refers to *99 Histories* (2001) as her "identity play," one that served as a starting point for her career as a playwright. Although the play is not autobiographical, it is about home, immigration, and family, issues she cares about deeply.

99 Histories was developed at the Sundance Institute Theatre Laboratory and received staged readings at New York Theatre Workshop, Mark Taper Forum's Asian Theater Workshop, and South Coast Repertory's Pacific Playwrights Festival. A workshop production of the play was presented at the Cherry Lane Alternative in 2002. A full production of the play was produced by Theater Mu (Rick Shiomi, artistic director) and Intermedia Art (David Gumnit, executive director) in Minneapolis, opening on April 9, 2004. It was directed by Cecilie D. Keenan; set design was by Rick Paul; the costume design was by Malia Burkhart; the lighting design was by Mike Grogan; the sound design was by Dixie Treichel; the prop design was by Roxanne Skarphol; and the stage manager was Melanie Salmon-Peterson. The cast was as follows:

Eunice	Jeany Park
Sah-Jin	Maria Cheng
Girl / Young Sah-Jin	Cindy Koy
Daniel Merritt / Joe	Sean Logan
Young Woman	Sara Ochs
Paul	Tae-Jung Kwan

SETTING

A suburb of L.A.

CHARACTERS

EUNICE: Female, Korean American, late twenties
SAH-JIN: Female, American Korean, Eunice's mother, fifties
GIRL / YOUNG SAH-JIN: Female, Korean American
DANIEL MERRITT: Male, white American, twenties
YOUNG WOMAN: Female, Korean, twenty
JOE: Male, white American; played by the actor who plays Daniel
PAUL: Male, Korean American, early thirties

(*opposite*) Maria Cheng (Sah-Jin) holding Jeany Park (Eunice) in the Theater Mu production of *99 Histories*. Photo by Charissa Uemura.

NOTE

The scenes are fluid and run into each other, with only occasional brief beats. Keep in mind that scenes have different textures: some are memories, some are dreams, some are everyday realities. The shifts in texture should be reflected somehow, whether it's through a change in lighting, pacing, or tone.

PROLOGUE

The sound of a cello. A young girl plays like a master. SAH-JIN *sits with her eyes closed, listening. The* GIRL *stops and looks at her hands.*

SAH-JIN   What is it?

GIRL   *(Touching her fingertips.)* Hurts.

SAH-JIN   Keep playing. It will go away.

GIRL   I sound awful.

SAH-JIN   No. Beautiful.

GIRL   Bach would turn over in his grave.

SAH-JIN   Someday you can be better than Bach.

GIRL   Don't be ridiculous.

SAH-JIN   Better than Casals. Better than Yo-Yo Ma.

GIRL   *(Thinks about it.)* Maybe.

SAH-JIN   I tell you, you can be anything you want. If you don't get what you want . . .

SAH-JIN *and* GIRL   . . . it just means you didn't want it bad enough.

SAH-JIN   Words become reality.

GIRL   I know.

SAH-JIN   Then again.

(The GIRL *plays. The lights dim.)*

—— END OF PROLOGUE ——

ACT I

SCENE 1

EUNICE's bedroom. EUNICE stands still in the middle of the room. SAH-JIN moves quickly around her. SAH-JIN's hair is swept back in a tight bun. She turns down the bed.

EUNICE   I told you I can sleep on the sofa bed, I don't mind.

SAH-JIN   It's *your* room.

EUNICE   I don't want to be a bother.

SAH-JIN   What bother?

(SAH-JIN opens the closet. She takes out a pillow and a shoebox. She throws the pillow on the bed and hands EUNICE the box.)

SAH-JIN   Here.

EUNICE   What's this?

SAH-JIN   I just saw and thought you would like.

(EUNICE opens the box and holds up a very fancy, black, high-heeled shoe.)

SAH-JIN   That's a good brand, very comfortable.

EUNICE   Yeah, they'll go really well with my sleek maternity fashion.

SAH-JIN   Why are you like this?

EUNICE   Like what?

SAH-JIN   Bitter. Just put it on.

EUNICE   *(Putting on a shoe.)* I am *not* bitter. I am *sarcastic*. There's a difference.

SAH-JIN   *(Admiring the shoe.)* I knew they'd fit.

EUNICE   They're too nice for me.

SAH-JIN   How can you say that? Anyway, I got them on sale.

EUNICE   Where are you going?

SAH-JIN   Service.

EUNICE   Now?

SAH-JIN   Saturday evening service. I play the piano and I'm the alto.

EUNICE   *The* alto?

SAH-JIN   Unless you want to join—

EUNICE   Forget it, I'm not going.

SAH-JIN   Okay.

EUNICE   That's it? No fighting? No pleading?

SAH-JIN   You're a grown woman. If you don't want to go, don't go. Anyway, the people at church don't know you're here. It would just be awkward.

EUNICE   Oh, I'd embarrass you.

SAH-JIN   That is *not* what I said—

EUNICE   Just what do you tell your friends about me?

SAH-JIN   The truth. That you travel a lot. For your. Work.

EUNICE   Good one! They probably think I'm a flight attendant.

SAH-JIN   What I don't understand is, if you like travel so much, why *not* just work for an airline and be something, anything, not just a, a—

EUNICE   Bum?

SAH-JIN   Yes, *bum*. I'm just saying, I didn't even know you were in New York. I thought you were still in Boston. How terrible, own mother not knowing where you are.

EUNICE   I got tired of Boston.

SAH-JIN   Your postcard said you liked it.

EUNICE   Of course it did, it was a *postcard*.

SAH-JIN   I hate those.

EUNICE   Would you rather I didn't write at all?

SAH-JIN   You could call.

EUNICE   I meant to.

SAH-JIN   Meant to is one thing, Eunice. Done is another. I am not embarrassed about you but you—you tell me nothing, about where you are, where you been. I just get a phone call, out of the blue, suddenly I have a daughter again. And you know what she's saying? Not "Hello, I miss you," not "How are you." She's saying, "Hi, Ma, it's me, I don't have AIDS."

EUNICE   You were the one who told me when I left home, "Don't get AIDS and don't get pregnant." I was just trying to ease you into the news.

SAH-JIN   Oh, Eunice.

EUNICE   I'm sorry, okay? I didn't know what to say, I didn't know *how* to say.

SAH-JIN   I am not ashamed of you, but there are some things that are private and some things that are public. *This* is private.

EUNICE   And what is private, you hide, right?

SAH-JIN   You're the one come home to hide. I'm not a foolish old woman, Eunice—yah. I know you haven't come home for me.

    (Pause.)

EUNICE   So were you surprised to hear from me?

SAH-JIN   Not surprised. Shocked. But then I see this nature show, on the satellite TV, about salmon and then I think I understand better.

EUNICE   You bought a satellite dish? We never even had cable.

SAH-JIN   I can watch shows from Korea now, but that is not the point. Point is, salmon are born in one pool and then live the whole life somewhere else. But then they come back. They swim against

	the water, upstream, you know how hard that is? Just so they can come back to where they were born. Like you.
EUNICE	Yeah, and then they die.
SAH-JIN	I'm just saying, you may not know why you're home, but you're like those fish. Something happens, you feel the tug and you come home. No choice. You come home—there's rice in the kitchen, don't forget to eat.
EUNICE	I won't.
SAH-JIN	And if you want to help you can finish cleaning up the room. I'll do the laundry when I get home. Or you can do it. Do some work at home for a change.

(SAH-JIN leaves. The lights shift. JOE appears. He doesn't have a shirt on. He is holding an iron.)

JOE	Eunice. Hey.
EUNICE	Is this a bad time? If it's a bad time, I can—
JOE	It's fine. Just talk to me while I get ready.

(They are in his apartment. He starts ironing his shirt.)

EUNICE	How've you been?
JOE	Good, good. Things are good. You?
EUNICE	Good.
JOE	Well that's . . . good. Guess who I ran into? At the post office? Janet.
EUNICE	Which one's Janet?
JOE	I told you about her. She was before. You never met her. Anyway, turns out she's moved to a place on Seventh. So we're going to hang out.
EUNICE	Is it a date? You don't have to answer that.
JOE	We're just friends. She's got a boyfriend, a serious one.

EUNICE   How do you do that?

JOE   Do what?

EUNICE   Stay friends with all of your exes.

JOE   I don't know. Breaking up doesn't change who you are. You still like who that person is, right? And Janet's great. I mean, when you think about it, it hasn't even been that long since she and I broke up. Year and a half. That's not long at all.

EUNICE   For some people it isn't.

(JOE finishes ironing. He shakes the shirt and then puts it on.)

JOE   I read somewhere that it takes a year to shed one entire layer of skin. So when you think about it that way, it's a whole year before you lose the layer of skin that holds the memory of someone, the touch of someone.

(He leaves the room.)

EUNICE   *(Softly.)* Where does your skin hold the memory of me?

(JOE reenters, holding a tie in each hand.)

JOE   A or B? A . . . B. Neither. You hate them both.

EUNICE   No.

JOE   Then why the face?

EUNICE   Look, I had to run some errands in the neighborhood and just thought I'd stop by and return these. Keys. I thought maybe you'd want them back.

(She digs into her pocket and hands him a ring of keys.)

JOE   I thought you lost these.

EUNICE   Yeah, but I was cleaning and I guess they'd fallen back behind—

JOE   What do you mean you were "cleaning"?

EUNICE   I was putting things away . . . ? Dusting?

JOE   You hate cleaning. I've seen you. You get nervous when things get too organized.

EUNICE   Yeah, well, I was packing some stuff up and I—

JOE   Packing? You're moving.

EUNICE   No. Kind of. Just subletting. I'll only be gone a little bit.

JOE   Where?

EUNICE   L.A.

JOE   What? Why?

EUNICE   You sound like a newspaper article, where, what, when . . .

JOE   Eunice.

EUNICE   It's just for a little while, just to see my mother.

JOE   Your mother. You told me your parents were dead.

EUNICE   I told you my *father* was dead. My mother, she's. She's in L.A.

JOE   Did something happen? Is she sick?

EUNICE   No, nothing like that.

JOE   Then what?

EUNICE   I don't know. You always got a reason for what you do?

JOE   Yes.

EUNICE   I don't always know if I do.

JOE   Well, let's start small. Why are you here? (*EUNICE doesn't say anything.*) All right. I'm out. You know what your problem is? You're like Russia.

EUNICE   What's that supposed to mean?

JOE   It's like when Napoleon went to war with Russia. He amasses this huge army and drives into Russian territory, hungry to fight. He can't wait. So he gets his men ready and then the next morning, he goes out to the battlefield and charges the enemy. Except the field is totally empty. There isn't a Russian to be seen. He keeps chasing them farther and farther into the interior, and they just keep withdrawing until finally Napoleon and his men are starving and exhausted and defeated.

EUNICE   So I'm a big land mass?

JOE   Exactly.

EUNICE   Well, why didn't you tell me we were at war.

JOE   I am not your enemy.

EUNICE   You were the one who called me Russia!

JOE   I'm just saying that you have a habit of doing that. Withdrawing. You know I tried. Even when we were together, I always felt alone. And I'd only brought so many supplies with me and they only lasted so long.

EUNICE   I know. You don't have to say. *(A small silence.)* Listen. You want to hear a story?

JOE   Is it scary? It looks scary.

EUNICE   No, funny.

I went to the doctor the other day and you know how they make you pee in those little cups? I'm in the bathroom and you know usually you never see any graffiti in those bathrooms, they're always squeaky clean, right?

But there I am, on the toilet, staring at the door and there's something written on it. Someone had scratched the words right into the metal, like with a key. And it said:

Hit me

hurt me

call me Eileen.

Except there wasn't any punctuation. I couldn't figure out if it was a directive *to* an Eileen: "Hit me, hurt me, call me *(Brief pause.*) Eileen," or a directive in general: "Hit me, hurt me, call me Eileen." It's been driving me crazy. I can't do anything but meditate on the various states of Eileen.

JOE That's funny.

EUNICE Uh huh.

JOE So why were you at the doctor's?

EUNICE It reminds me of a joke, you know, one of those name jokes? What do you call a girl with one leg?

JOE Eunice, why were you at —

EUNICE No, not Eunice. Another name. Come on. Answer. Guess.

JOE I don't know.

EUNICE Eileen. You call her Eileen. Get it?

(She looks at him. He's not laughing.)

JOE Why — were — you —

EUNICE Well, hit me, hurt me, call me Eileen, I'm pregnant, Joe.

(A long, awful pause.)

JOE I thought we were — ?

EUNICE We were.

JOE Then how?

EUNICE I don't know.

JOE How long?

EUNICE Four weeks.

JOE That's not a very long time.

EUNICE For some people it isn't.

(Pause.)

JOE Have you thought about — ? I mean, are you going to — ?

EUNICE   Adoption. I decided on adoption.

JOE   You're sure that's what you want?

EUNICE   Well, I can't . . . so is there any other option? *(Pause.)* Didn't think so.

JOE   Eunice, you can't just spring this on me and then disappear to California. What am I supposed to do with that?

EUNICE   I have no choice. Don't you understand?

JOE   Do you need money, is that it? How much?

EUNICE   No, no. I don't want anything from you.

JOE   But I want to—

EUNICE   No. The agency will pay for the—it's all worked out, you don't have to. That's why I'm going home, just until . . . It's fine. It's like the prodigal son always said, right? There's no place like home.

JOE   That was Dorothy.

EUNICE   Whatever. The thing about home is it always takes you back—rent-free.

JOE   Stop making jokes.

EUNICE   *(Defensively.)* What. I'm sorry. I'm just so bad at this.

JOE   Adoption.

EUNICE   Yeah. It really is for the best. I have thought about it. A lot.

JOE   I just. Need some time to think, okay? Will you call me? From L.A.?

EUNICE   Sure.

(They both know she won't.)

JOE   You call me if you need anything.

EUNICE   Okay, Napoleon.

JOE   What's your number there?

EUNICE	When I call I'll give it to you. *(Pause.)* I should get going.	
JOE	I'll walk you out.	
EUNICE	No, it's okay. You go wherever you need, take your time.	
JOE	I'm glad you told me.	
EUNICE	Well, that was always the thing, right? I could always tell you anything.	
JOE	You could. But you hardly ever did.	

(JOE is gone.)

SCENE 2

EUNICE sits, writing. It's very late.

EUNICE Dear . . . whatsyourname.

To Whom It May Concern, I was your mother, no.

To . . . you.

To you.

I know you're hoping for some kind of epiphany or revelation. Well, I have nothing like that for you. The simple fact is, I was not made for you. That mother smell, that softness. I wasn't made for that. I was just a temp on Wall Street, a sad-faced, pale little office worker like Bartleby the Scrivener, looking out a window that faced only a wall. Speaking of which, optional reading list, books I like: *Bartleby the Scrivener*, Melville.

As for where you come from . . . well, there isn't much to tell. I come from a family that doesn't really talk about the past. For instance, my mother has a scar on her throat but I still don't know exactly how she got it. When I was a kid, I thought she said it was a "star," and so for most of my growing up, I thought she had some magic in her, right there, shaped like a mini-explosion.

I remember once, when I was in eighth grade, I had to make a family tree as a class project.

(Visual of a diagram with very few boxes and a lot of white space.)

Me. Only child. My father with two half-brothers I've never met. My mother: one sister who died when she was just a child. My father's parents, my mother's parents—grandfathers dead on both sides before I was even born. And that's it. Ta-Dah.

I took this chart to school, very proud of what I had done. And who was up first, but my best friend, Liz Grady.

(Visual of a diagram with boxes and lines branching out in wild proliferation.)

Her family tree was the size of a Volvo. She had people like Anne Boleyn, George Washington. Liz Grady oozed history. She once showed me the contents of her Hope Chest: linens from her grandmother, silver from her great-aunt, stuff that had been passed down for generations. I looked at it and thought to myself: I have no hope chest. I have no hope.

I'm just saying, so what if you grew up not knowing where you were from? Maybe more than hair color or eye shape, it's that feeling that proves you are mine.

SCENE 3

Late afternoon the next day. SAH-JIN *and* PAUL *are sitting at the dining table. Above the table is a faded photo of* EUNICE's *father when he was impossibly young and good-looking.*
EUNICE *enters. She is still in her pajamas.*

SAH-JIN   Eunice-ya! There you are. You've been hiding in your room all day. Dinner's ready. And look who's here.

(PAUL *stands up and offers his hand.* EUNICE *is dumbfounded.*)

PAUL   Hey, I'm Paul. Your mom's told me a lot about you.

EUNICE	That's. Great. Mom.	
SAH-JIN	I've been meaning to invite Paul and his sister over to dinner, but the one night we all get around to it, she has to work! But at least Paul could make it.	
PAUL	I don't get home-cooking like this very often.	
EUNICE	She didn't make any of it. It comes in containers from the Korean supermarket.	
SAH-JIN	Eunice.	
PAUL	Well, it's still delicious.	
SAH-JIN	*(To EUNICE.)* Sit. *(To PAUL.)* You'll have to excuse how she's dressed. She hasn't been feeling well lately.	
PAUL	Sorry to hear it. How're you feeling now?	
EUNICE	Nauseous, thanks for asking.	
SAH-JIN	She's really not usually like this.	
EUNICE	It's just the pregnancy—	
SAH-JIN	Eunice!	
EUNICE	—morning sickness and all.	
PAUL	Maybe I can help.	
SAH-JIN	Paul's a doctor.	
EUNICE	Well, of course he is!	
SAH-JIN	That's enough. Was that the phone?	
EUNICE	I didn't hear—	
SAH-JIN	I'll get it! You two talk, get to know each other.	

>(SAH-JIN *leaves.* PAUL *and* EUNICE *sit in awkward silence. Finally,* PAUL *picks up his chopsticks and begins to eat.* EUNICE *watches* PAUL *eat. She can't take it anymore; she picks up her chopsticks and starts eating too. She realizes she's ravenous.)*

PAUL   Good, huh?

(EUNICE *nods.*)

EUNICE Can you hand me that stuff?

PAUL   The kong-na-mul?

(She nods. He hands a dish to her.)

EUNICE Thanks. So how'd my mom rope you into dinner?

PAUL   She didn't. I like her. She's so funny.

EUNICE Funny?

PAUL   She's always giving me food in tupperware, like she thinks I'm starving. It's like, "Eat! How are you? Eat!" My mom passed away about ten years ago. When I started coming to your mom's church, she kind of adopted me. She's really sweet.

EUNICE Are we talking about the same person?

PAUL   Don't be so hard on her.

EUNICE Am I? Hard on her?

PAUL   Kind of.

EUNICE She never mentioned you.

PAUL   Well, from what I gather, you two don't talk very often. She says you're off traveling a lot.

EUNICE Yeah.

PAUL   You don't remember me at all, do you?

EUNICE What?

PAUL   We went to the same church, back in junior high.

EUNICE I don't think so.

PAUL   No, I'm pretty sure.

EUNICE Really?

PAUL   Yeah, we all knew who you were. All the kids. We'd talk about you and be like, "That damn Eunice Kim!" I still remember the day your picture was in the paper, on the front page. My dad came to me with the paper folded in half, with your face big as that. And you had all these medals draped around your neck—I thought you were going to fall over. You were holding this trophy that looked to be about a foot taller than you. My dad goes, "Look at this!" And he rattles the paper in my face and says, "Eunice Kim's parents, very proud." Then he looked at me accusingly, narrowed his eyes and just said, "Electric guitar."

EUNICE   You play guitar?

PAUL   I tried. My parents hated it, they never even learned the terminology. My mom kept referring to my amp as "the loud thing"—she'd be like, "Turn off that loud thing!" And my dad, my dad usually referred to my guitar as "the devil's instrument." That gave me immense satisfaction.

EUNICE   I can't believe I don't remember you.

PAUL   About this high? Bowl haircut? It was not a good time in my life.

EUNICE   I guess I didn't know that many kids my age.

PAUL   Ah, you were busy practicing and winning. I mean, I guess that was the thing. I wanted to hate you, but I couldn't. I heard you play once.

EUNICE   You did?

PAUL   My younger sister, poor thing got drafted to play the viola. She started competing and of course the whole family got dragged out to support. I remember sitting there, just wanting to slit my wrists. I mean, the kids were good, but classical music makes me feel like I'm listening to one long Suzuki lesson on tape over and over again, you know?

And then you came out. I can't even remember what you were playing, but it was stunning. I felt like you were slowly hammering these little nails in my heart one by one. It was amazing.

EUNICE   Wait. You were Hannah's brother, weren't you?

PAUL   Yup. Still am.

EUNICE   She was good. Nice too, would say hi and smile.

PAUL   You don't play anymore, do you?

EUNICE   No.

PAUL   I always wondered what happened. Why'd you stop? Was it the pressure?

EUNICE   No, no one ever made me play. I wanted to. I loved it.

         (An uncomfortable pause.)

PAUL   I'm sorry, I really don't mean to pry. Man, if Emmy were here, she'd kill me. She always says I'm too nosy.

EUNICE   Who's Emmy?

PAUL   My fiancée.

EUNICE   You're engaged?

PAUL   Two months.

EUNICE   Wow.

PAUL   How 'bout you?

EUNICE   Oh, it was an immaculate conception. He's long gone.

PAUL   I'm sorry.

EUNICE   Yeah. Why do you think you got the dinner invite?

PAUL   Oh, man. No *wonder* you looked at me like you wanted to kill me.

EUNICE   Nothing personal—

PAUL   Are you kidding? I'm flattered that your mom thinks I'm good enough for you.

EUNICE   I think if you're Korean with a pulse you're good enough.

PAUL   No, your mom thinks the world of you.

EUNICE: She does?

PAUL: Yeah, she's always like "Eunice is so bright, so smart, she could be anything if she just put her mind to it . . ."

EUNICE: That does sound like her. When did you know? I mean, how did you know she was the one?

PAUL: I don't know. I mean, I've been in love before where I'm just so excited whenever that person walks into a room that it's like they *are* the room. But with Emmy, it's kind of different. Calmer. Better. I mean, the way she explains it, you don't marry someone because you're in love. You marry someone because it's a good match, because you make a good team.

EUNICE: Sounds unromantic.

PAUL: What's romantic? Being swept off your feet and then having it burn out in a year? Didn't your parents ever tell you about chung?

EUNICE: What?

PAUL: It's a form of love. But it's not like our idea of love. It's like care . . . I don't know how to describe it. In fact, Emmy says I really don't understand what it is and that I can't because I'm not really Korean—you know, born there and everything.

EUNICE: You mean, you can't feel it if you're not?

PAUL: Well, if you don't have a word for something, then how can you? I have to admit, when your mom offered me dinner, I was hoping you'd be here. It's nice to finally meet you.

EUNICE: Disappointing, huh?

PAUL: Not at all. You know, after that competition where I saw you, I went home and dug up that newspaper. I put your face up on my wall.

EUNICE: You're kidding.

PAUL: I mean, it wasn't like a creepy stalker thing, I just liked it. Liked your smile. Because you know what? You had every right to smile and be proud of your medals and trophies. You were good, really good. I've never been half as good as that at anything.

EUNICE   I bet you're a good doctor.

PAUL   As a matter of fact, I am. *(A small and comfortable silence.)* Here. It's the last one. Eat.

(He takes his chopsticks and puts food on her plate. PAUL *disappears.)*

EUNICE   Also on the reading list: Tennessee Williams's *The Glass Menagerie*. Pay special attention to The Gentleman Caller: the long-awaited and hoped-for someone that is never quite what we expect, and is never something we can have.

*(*SAH-JIN *is clearing the table angrily.* EUNICE *helps her.)*

EUNICE   It's not my fault.

SAH-JIN   You didn't even try. Don't you see? It could be the perfect solution to everything. He is what you need, someone steady and secure. And then you could keep the baby, Eunice. Just think—

EUNICE   Is that what this is about?

SAH-JIN   I just thought that maybe if you had a husband, then you could— You wouldn't have to hide anything, Eunice, and the baby wouldn't be ashamed—

EUNICE   You mean, *you* wouldn't be.

SAH-JIN   I only try to do what's best for you. What your father would want. My intentions, they are good.

EUNICE   I know. That's always been the problem.

SAH-JIN   I'm just saying, you could've been nicer.

EUNICE   Ma, he's engaged.

SAH-JIN   It's not serious.

EUNICE   He *loves* her, they've got chung, or whatever.

SAH-JIN What?

EUNICE Chung. Chung!

SAH-JIN Oh, *chung*.

EUNICE Yeah, that. So what is it?

SAH-JIN It's impossible to explain. You wouldn't understand.

EUNICE It's love, right?

SAH-JIN Puh! What's love? Love is nothing.

EUNICE Is it commitment? Devotion? Destiny?

SAH-JIN Stop talking nonsense. You don't have to love someone to have chung with them. You don't even need to like them to have chung with them. Put it this way: you could have chung with someone you hate.

EUNICE That doesn't make sense.

SAH-JIN Think about it: you hate someone, he's like a shadow that falls across your life. Now take that person away. You feel this emptiness, this feeling that something in your life, something is missing. Where's your shadow? What's proving you are there? Something that helped make you who you are is gone. That's chung. It's love, but not quite love. Love, but more than love.

EUNICE That's not chung, that's co-dependency.

SAH-JIN No. Chung is when you give the other person whatever it is in your power to give them. Whatever they ask. Because you care for them so much.

EUNICE Can you feel it for someone instantly? Like chung at first sight?

SAH-JIN It's not passion. Chung takes time.

EUNICE Have you ever loved anyone, the way I mean?

SAH-JIN Like love you fall in? I don't think so.

EUNICE Really? Never? Not even once?

SAH-JIN   So what. You have.

EUNICE   Yes.

SAH-JIN   And has it helped you?

           (EUNICE *makes no attempt to answer.*)

           Love goes, passion goes. But chung stays.

SCENE 4

EUNICE writes the letter.

EUNICE   My parents were old when they met. Old for their day and time. He was thirty; she was twenty-nine. A year after they married, they came here with nothing and opened and closed every kind of business you can think of. Liquor store, dry cleaning.

           And then they opened a convenience store, open from eight to eleven, six days a week. They worked together in that store for five years until the day my father was shot. My mother, to this day, has never talked about what happened. Even though she was the one who called the ambulance and sat with my father as he died.

           When I was in junior high, I saw that famous film of Kennedy's assassination in history class. And ever since then, in my head, when I think back on that day, I imagine my father is Kennedy and my mom is Jacqueline.

           (*As* EUNICE *talks, dim lights come up on two vague figures dressed as Jacqueline and John F. Kennedy. They are sitting as if in a car. They reenact the shooting from the Zapruder film, soundlessly, over and over again. Underneath the following, the sound of whispering begins to rise but it is impossible to make out the words.*)

           When the bullet strikes him, he has no idea what has happened. He is more surprised than in pain. When he falls over on her, she screams over and over again. His blood stains her pink suit. His blood stains her hands. And she will never be clean again.

(Lights on the figures snap off as lights go up on the GIRL. She holds her head in her hands and rocks. Her words are still whispered, but now are audible.)

GIRL   Get up please please please just get up and say something please just get up and do something get up please please please just get up GET UP.

(Lights go out on the GIRL and simultaneously up on SAH-JIN, who is in bed.)

SAH-JIN   Who's there? Eunice?

(EUNICE stands at SAH-JIN's doorway, hesitating.)

EUNICE   Can I sleep here?

SAH-JIN   What's wrong?

EUNICE   Bad dreams.

SAH-JIN   Come.

(EUNICE dives into SAH-JIN's bed like a little girl.)

Bad dreams about?

EUNICE   I don't remember. Just bad. I don't want to stay in that room, Ma.

SAH-JIN   Don't be silly. Bad dreams can't hurt you. Here, scratch my back.

(She turns her back towards EUNICE. EUNICE begins scratching it.)

EUNICE   Ma, why'd you come here? You and Dad?

SAH-JIN   What kind of stupid question is that? You wish you had growed up in Korea? You know over there, department stores, whole department stores, just fall down for no reason. And on the street, no one stops for red lights, it's true. If there's no one around, they just go right through. Is that the kind of country you want to grow up in?

EUNICE   That's not what I mean. I just wonder sometimes why you came here. I don't think Dad even liked it here. I remember how it felt after the store, after—

(SAH-JIN *moves away from* EUNICE.)

SAH-JIN Why are you thinking of that?

EUNICE I don't know, I—

SAH-JIN Eunice, you weren't even there. You have no idea how terrible, if you did, you wouldn't be bringing it up.

EUNICE But maybe if we talked about it, it wouldn't be so—

SAH-JIN What good does talk do? Doesn't bring anyone back. Doesn't change anything. Why don't you go back to your room. I can't sleep with you in my bed. You kick me in your sleep.

(SAH-JIN *gets up.*)

Here. I'll make you some tea. You want some tea?

(EUNICE *notices something in the corner of the room.*)

EUNICE What is that?

SAH-JIN Oh, I took it out of your room. Before you came.

(EUNICE *gets up and looks at it. It's a cello case.*)

What's wrong with you? It doesn't bite.

EUNICE I thought you got rid of it.

SAH-JIN I tried to. I couldn't.

EUNICE I was talented, wasn't I?

SAH-JIN You were the best.

EUNICE Better than . . . better than . . .

SAH-JIN Yes. You were.

(SAH-JIN *leaves.* EUNICE *goes to the cello case and looks at it for a moment. Then she picks it up and stuffs it into* SAH-JIN's *crowded closet. A box falls down and* EUNICE *picks it up. It falls partly open.* SAH-JIN *enters.* EUNICE *hides the box behind her back.)*

SAH-JIN   Water will be done soon.

EUNICE   I don't want any. I'll be fine.

SAH-JIN   Where's the . . . ?

EUNICE   I put it away. In there. *(She starts to leave.)* G'night.

SAH-JIN   Char-ja. Eunice? *(*EUNICE *turns.)* Just go to bed. All this thinking . . . I tell you too much is no good.

SCENE 5

Eunice's room. EUNICE *examines the box. It's made of a dark, glossy wood. There's an ornate latch that has grown dull with age.* EUNICE *opens the box.*

WOMAN   A photo of a young woman.

        (The WOMAN *appears. Flash.)*

EUNICE   Oh my God. Ma.

WOMAN   One watch with a faded face and a gold band. Stopped at 11:22.

        (She holds up a watch and then slips it on.)

        One scarf, square, colorful.

        (She holds up the scarf and ties it around her head.)

DANIEL   A photo of a young man.

        *(*DANIEL *appears. Flash.)*

        A book of postcards of California. Blank. Never sent.

        (He holds up the book and lets it fall open. It's folded like an accordion.)

WOMAN   And a book.

DANIEL	*Letters to a Young Poet* by Rainer Maria Rilke.
WOMAN	Signed:
DANIEL	Daniel.

SCENE 6

Lights up on SAH-JIN, *in the kitchen. She is peeling garlic in a bowl of water.* EUNICE *has the box open in front of her.*

EUNICE	I don't understand why you're getting so upset.
SAH-JIN	I am not upset.
EUNICE	You were so beautiful.
SAH-JIN	I was okay.
EUNICE	Look—who's that? The guy.
SAH-JIN	The name, I can't even remember.
EUNICE	Try Daniel.
SAH-JIN	What?
EUNICE	He signed this book—see?
SAH-JIN	Yes, Daniel. That was it.
EUNICE	He gave you a book and his photo and you don't remember?
SAH-JIN	It was a long time ago.
EUNICE	I know you don't have Alzheimer's, Ma, so stop acting like you do. *(She points to the photo.)* Look at him. Look at his face. I know you remember.
SAH-JIN	He was an American. I think. Come to our village.
EUNICE	Were you seeing him?
SAH-JIN	Don't disrespect your father.
EUNICE	I'm not. I'm just asking.

SAH-JIN	I hardly knew him.	
EUNICE	But you were friends.	
SAH-JIN	Everyone knew him, who he was. He was with the church. And he was the strangest-looking man we'd ever seen. So tall and all arms and legs and. He'd stop by every once in awhile, that's all. Say hello.	
EUNICE	So why keep the book?	
SAH-JIN	You think I don't read or something?	
EUNICE	Could you stop peeling garlic for just one second? You know they have whole jars of ready-peeled garlic at the supermarket.	
SAH-JIN	You think that makes food taste good?	
EUNICE	Look. *(She puts her hand on her mother's to make her stop.)* What does this say? *(She points to the title page of the book.)* The Korean.	
SAH-JIN	It says "To Teacher," okay?	
EUNICE	So was he one of your piano students, back in Korea?	
SAH-JIN	Yes, that's how we knew each other. I taught him a little piano. He taught me a little English. Like a trade. That's why he gave me the book. He was only there for five or six months. Then he left, went back to the States.	
EUNICE	How come you never mentioned him before?	
SAH-JIN	What are you, some pot calling bigger pot black?	
EUNICE	What?	
SAH-JIN	You never mention who is the one— *(She nods meaningfully at EUNICE's stomach.)*	
EUNICE	That's different. I don't talk about it because it's not important.	
SAH-JIN	Exactly. Same thing. What I don't say, I don't say because it is not important.	

SCENE 7

EUNICE   Rilke's *Letters to a Young Poet*. Written by the great German poet to a young man who is now forever known as "My Dear Mr. Kappus."

When she was young, my mother was the most beautiful woman our family had seen in generations. Her hair wasn't like mine; it wasn't a thin and mousy brownish, a black that hadn't quite made up its mind yet; her hair shone the deepest, quietest black imaginable. She used to wear it down all the time . . . when I was a child, she'd let me brush it and I can still feel it, how it slipped through my hands and crackled with static.

(SAH-JIN appears, partly in shadow, her back to the audience. Little by little she takes down her hair.)

After my father died, my mother started wearing her hair pulled back and it was like she had grown old and ageless at the same time. To this day, she has almost no wrinkles. I'm convinced it is the sheer tension of that bun that gives her a permanent face-lift. I used to go into the bathroom in the evening, after she'd already gone to sleep and see a huge pile of black hairpins on the sink. It was like she was held together by them. All of her, held together by little pieces of twisted and bent steel.

(The WOMAN has taken SAH-JIN's place. She turns and faces the audience. EUNICE looks at the book carefully. She turns it in her hand and looks closer.)

EUNICE   And . . . margin notes?

EUNICE *and* WOMAN   Say you hate me say

you do

stop here

and I lost my

WOMAN   You must not understand me.

(As the WOMAN speaks, she slowly moves forward and the bedroom is transformed.)

Say you hate me

must not

must not

must not

must not

Do Say you do

Good day

A day

Goodness

Goodness

Memory

Memory

I will

So much

(The walls become white and opaque, illuminated by a soft glow, so that they look like rice paper walls. There is a small piano. There are flat, square pillows on the ground and a short dark red table. The WOMAN keeps speaking the margin notes until the set is complete.)

EUNICE   Where are we?

WOMAN   Look around. Somewhere between the historical TV dramas you've seen and modern soaps set in Seoul, you have conjured up this place. Somewhere in the middle of five thousand years, there is this room.

EUNICE   Is this where you grew up?

WOMAN	Yes, but look outside.
EUNICE	It looks like . . . Southern California.
WOMAN	Where *you* grew up. What you imagine is always from what you know.
EUNICE	Aren't rice paper walls medieval?
WOMAN	Yes, but they look so nice and you can't help it: you like things zen.

(The WOMAN sits at the piano and starts playing.)

This is the story of the what happened, or even better, of the what never happened—which, I might add, is far more interesting.

(DANIEL appears outside the house. He hears the piano and stops and listens.)

EUNICE	Who is that?
WOMAN	Daniel.
EUNICE	Who is *that*?
WOMAN	You'll see.
EUNICE	He's beautiful.
WOMAN	So am I.

(DANIEL approaches the house as the WOMAN plays. In the following scene, when DANIEL speaks, he speaks hesitantly and awkwardly. The WOMAN speaks perfectly. They are speaking in Korean.)

DANIEL	Hello? Person home is?

(He stands at the doorway, listening. The song ends.)

DANIEL	Please. Don't stop. It is too pretty.

(The WOMAN stands up, startled. She bows.)

WOMAN	Is there something I may help Mr. Merritt with?

DANIEL: I come to learn. *(He gestures to the piano.)* You teach, yes?

WOMAN: Yes, but only to children.

DANIEL: Teach me.

WOMAN: I'm sorry, I can't. Now if Mr. Merritt will excuse me. . .

DANIEL: Please. I will pay.

WOMAN: I couldn't possibly—

DANIEL: Not with money. With English.

WOMAN: English?

DANIEL: Yes. I will teach you. For piano lessons, I am happy. Start now?

(A long pause.)

WOMAN: What does Mr. Merritt know already?

(He smiles.)

DANIEL: Not a thing.

(He sits at the piano.)

WOMAN: All right then: this is middle C. Every key is a different note. C-D-E-F-G-A-B-C. Eight notes make a scale. And it repeats itself, all the way up the keys.

(She plays a C major scale for DANIEL, crossing over so that she goes across several octaves.)

DANIEL: I see. Like English alphabet.

(The WOMAN repeats just the eight-note scale, playing it up and then down.)

WOMAN: C major scale.

(She gestures for him to try it. DANIEL slowly and awkwardly plays the scale.)

DANIEL: Do you know writer, Virginia Woolf? She writes human mind is made like a thing, like one of these. Like a piano. Except it goes

A to Z. How to say? You can go easy from A to R, maybe S, these notes our mind can reach. But more difficult with every next letter.

WOMAN   What do the notes represent?

DANIEL   Anything. If C-scale is A, then the song you play when I come in, maybe M or N. And someday I reach, can play that song, but then there is still harder and harder songs. X is maybe Chopin or Rachmaninoff. See?

WOMAN   And there's always some point farther away. Like chasing the horizon.

DANIEL   Yes. Z, no one ever reach. Impossible to reach.

(He slowly plays the scale up and down, then chord progressions, arpeggios—all the standard piano lesson fare.)

WOMAN   *(To EUNICE.)* I'd never had a more diligent student. Or seen anyone with hair so light. In the sun, his arms were dusted with gold.

It wasn't until much later that he told me that he never cared to learn the piano at all. He just wanted to be close to me because my hair was the most beautiful thing he had ever seen.

(She reaches over DANIEL's shoulder to correct his hand position. He stops playing and turns toward her.)

DANIEL   Why do you tie back?

(He loosens her hair and lets it fall forward. He takes it in his hands, slowly feeling its texture. He gathers some of it and shapes it into a brush which he then runs along her arm.)

WOMAN   Tickles.

DANIEL   Don't move. I painting your hand. And your arm. Your face.

(He runs the pointed tip of her hair lightly along her face. She closes her eyes.)

WOMAN   Don't. Daniel. Don't.

(She opens her eyes.)

DANIEL: You should wear down. Always.

(DANIEL is still and the lights on him dim.)

EUNICE: Were you in love with him?

WOMAN: That's not the right question.

EUNICE: What is the right question?

WOMAN: Some people, you meet them and they take your whole world and do this: *(She holds her hands out as if she's holding something and tilts it askew.)* He came, took my world, the world that had always felt wrong, and he did this: *(She rights her hands.)* That's the answer.

EUNICE: But what's the question for that?

(DANIEL steals up behind the WOMAN and puts his hands over her eyes.)

WOMAN: Hello, Daniel.

DANIEL: How you know?

WOMAN: Because of how you smell.

DANIEL: I do? Bad?

WOMAN: Just different. Like *(Sniffs him.)* wood. Right . . . *(Stops near his face.)* there.

DANIEL: Oh, aftershave.

WOMAN: After what?

DANIEL: Put it on after. *(Mimes shaving.)* Every day.

WOMAN: *(In wonder.)* Every day.

DANIEL: Look.

(He takes out the book of postcards from his bag and shows them to the WOMAN.)

	Hollywood. See? And Santa Monica Pier. That is big wheel. Person ride. You can see forever.
WOMAN	Say the names again.
DANIEL	Bel Air. Malibu. Santa Monica. Brentwood, Beverly Hills . . .
WOMAN	Beautiful.

(The WOMAN looks at the postcards again.)

This is California?

DANIEL	Yes.
WOMAN	And is it really this beautiful?
DANIEL	*(Looking at her.)* Yes. I brought something else. For you. To thank. For lessons.

(He takes the book out and gives it to her.)

WOMAN	*Letters to a Young Poet?*
DANIEL	From more old and more great poet. You will like.
WOMAN	Will you sign it for me?
DANIEL	Of course. *(He takes a pen out and signs the book.)* To Teacher. Daniel.

(He is gone. EUNICE takes the scarf and puts it into her hair.)

EUNICE	For everything there is a reason.
WOMAN	If you just go back far enough, you can find it.
EUNICE	He said,
WOMAN	Come with me.
EUNICE	I said, Yes.
WOMAN	Even though my mother says:
EUNICE	These Americans have big noses and they smell like milk. Even though everyone says:

WOMAN   This is infatuation. Your life with him will be built on air.

EUNICE   I don't listen. I don't care.

         The new world, bright like Sundays, vast as water. Oh, I can hardly wait!

WOMAN   He fills my emptinesses

EUNICE   and I know we love each other.

WOMAN   So much.

EUNICE   And we have chung?

WOMAN   Maybe.

         Yes.

         We were

EUNICE   I was—in love.

         My whole life, I held myself apart. I thought I was not capable or worthy—

WOMAN   Or ready.

EUNICE   And then it came to me.

         (The WOMAN disappears into the dark. JOE emerges holding a long box, the kind that looks like it holds long-stem roses.)

JOE   Open it.

EUNICE   Please tell me you didn't.

JOE   It's not a big deal. Just open it.

EUNICE   You can't keep giving me gifts like this. *(EUNICE opens the box and gasps.)* Oh my God.

         (She lifts out a drapery rod.)

JOE   You've had that string with a blanket over it hanging in front of your window ever since I've known you. It's time you had a real window treatment.

EUNICE   I can't believe you even know the term, "window treatment."

JOE   I'll help you put it up.

EUNICE   Where have you been all my life?

JOE   In Vermont, mainly.

EUNICE   I'll cherish it forever, or at least until my next apartment.

JOE   Actually, I wanted to talk to you about that. My lease is up in a few months; I just know they're going to crank up the rent.

EUNICE   I hate that.

JOE   Yeah, but I was thinking that maybe I'd try to find another place. I feel like I've kinda outgrown that little studio anyway.

EUNICE   But there's no way you can afford a one bedroom.

JOE   I could if I split it with someone.

(Pause.)

EUNICE   You want to move in together?

JOE   You know, when I rehearsed this scene beforehand, I imagined those words coming out of your mouth with a much more upbeat tone.

EUNICE   I just. Didn't see it coming. Moving in. I never had anyone before, or even came close to — Wow.

JOE   So does that mean . . . yes?

EUNICE   Joe, how well do you think you know me?

JOE   I know it's you on the phone in half a word. I know you hate shellfish. I know you keloid. What else is there?

EUNICE   I don't want to move in with you.

JOE   That's okay. You don't have to. It was just a thought. But. Do you mean now or ever?

EUNICE   Why would you want to move in with someone like me?

JOE   Someone like what?

EUNICE   Someone who, someone who doesn't know how.

JOE   What are you talking about?

EUNICE   It's like . . . I want to, and it's there, but I can't, I can't—

JOE   Can't what? Do you love me?

EUNICE   You know I do—

JOE   No. You always say, "I love being with you." Or "You make me so happy." But you never just say it. Can't you just say it?

(Silence.)

EUNICE   Joe. It's not that I don't want to settle down, it's just that I can't picture myself—I mean, I don't think I'm built for that.

JOE   Well. I am.

(JOE is gone. EUNICE slips the scarf out of her hair. She is alone. No more imaginary Korea.)

SCENE 8

EUNICE   Another item for the reading list, D. H. Lawrence's story "The Rocking Horse Winner." A little boy lives in a house that whispers, *Money, there must be more money.* In order to stop the whispering, he takes to riding his rocking horse endlessly, hours and hours each day. Well, I'm going to tell you a story about a girl. Her house had whisperings of its own, and her rocking horse was her cello. She was six when she touched it for the first time and as soon as she touched it, she was good. And then with time, she became great. The life she had before she began playing is silent, unremarkable. But when she played . . . *(The GIRL appears. She begins playing.)* When she played, she was extraordinary. Nothing was beyond her reach. She wasn't afraid of anything. Ten years old and she didn't even know what fear was. After her father died, she started playing the cello as she had never played before. By the age of fifteen, she was a champion.

(The music stops. The GIRL stops, frozen, completely lost in her own thoughts.)

And then. Everything. Changed.

(SAH-JIN appears. The GIRL doesn't even look at her.)

SAH-JIN	Eunice. Eunice, it's me.
GIRL	I know who you are.
SAH-JIN	I brought you food.
EUNICE	I don't want it.
SAH-JIN	You're hungry, I know you are. Why won't you eat?
GIRL	Might be poisoned.
SAH-JIN	How can you even think that?
GIRL	I'm just being careful. After all, how do I know you aren't working for them? They didn't shoot *you*, did they?

(SAH-JIN slaps the GIRL.)

GIRL	They said you'd do that.
SAH-JIN	"They" don't exist! If you say the word "they" one more time, I'm going to scream.
GIRL	Then scream.
SAH-JIN	I brought you your medicine, if you just take the pills, you'll see—

(The GIRL bats the pills out of SAH-JIN's hand. SAH-JIN scrambles to collect them.)

GIRL	Those pills make me stupid! So that I won't suspect, won't be on to them.
SAH-JIN	On to what? None of this is real. You are just imagining.

GIRL   Oh, Ma. Reality is like an onion. There are so many layers. You have no idea.

(Lights shift. SAH-JIN is gone. The GIRL turns toward EUNICE.)

GIRL   And then—you remember this part, don't you? And then what happened?

EUNICE I don't know, it was a long time ago—

GIRL   *(Mimicking EUNICE.)* I know you don't have Alzheimer's, so stop acting like you do. C'mon.

EUNICE He spoke to her, to me. I thought God, or something, was speaking to me.

GIRL   You found God, or He found you. And He said that they were after you. The men who killed your father,

EUNICE They were going to kill me.

GIRL   And you believed Him. So for six months you lived out there in the wilds of L.A. County suburbia. Hiding behind the Alpha Beta. Roaming the La Puente Hills mall. Like a latter-day John the Baptist. L.A.'s a good place to be a runaway. No fear of freezing to death, that's for sure. But you never strayed very far from home. Why is that?

EUNICE Because He told me not to.

GIRL   And what else? What else did he tell you to do?

EUNICE I don't remember.

GIRL   Yes, you do.

EUNICE He said:

GIRL   Go to the house. Go when it's quiet.

EUNICE Why should I go back there?

GIRL   So that I can take the pain from you. That's what you want, isn't it?

EUNICE I don't know.

GIRL   All you have to do is go back there and finish what has already begun.

EUNICE   You want me to—?

GIRL   Think about it. She's miserable and unhappy anyway. Hasn't she been through enough pain? Really, you'd be doing her a favor. Heaven is paradise, Eunice. Don't you want your mom to be with your father in paradise?

(The scratchy sound of a recorded cello rises. Lights go up on SAH-JIN. She is sitting, listening to the music.)

EUNICE   I go to the house.

GIRL   That's right. Go on.

EUNICE   I go from window to window and no one seems to be home. And then I find her in the living room. Listening to some old Casals record. She looks old and tired and oh my God she is beautiful in that room. I see a hand on the windowsill. It moves the curtain. And then I realize, it's my hand.

(The GIRL enters the room.)

SAH-JIN   Eunice!

(SAH-JIN goes to the GIRL and embraces her. EUNICE remains in the dark, absolutely still.)

You scare me to death. What's wrong with you, you're not dressed for the cold at all! Don't listen to me, I don't care, I'm just glad you're home.

(The GIRL disentangles herself from her mother's arms.)

GIRL   I'm not home to stay. I just needed something.

SAH-JIN   Temperature's getting lower. You should just stay here. At least for the night.

GIRL   You're not listening to me. I'm not staying.

SAH-JIN   Then what? Are you hungry? Do you need money?

(The GIRL is clearly distracted, but she struggles to act as if everything's normal.)

GIRL *(Low.)* Sshhh!

SAH-JIN What?

GIRL No, not money. What are you listening to?

SAH-JIN Oh, this . . . it's silly, I know. But it helps me not to miss you so much.

(SAH-JIN lifts the needle off the record and the cello music stops.)

House gets so quiet. You can't imagine. Without you playing. It's been so long. I keep the cello right where you left it, but now, it just collects dust.

(The cello is propped up in the corner of the room. The GIRL walks over to the cello. She slowly sits and begins playing, uncertainly at first, and then with more speed and fluidity. She plays the prelude to Bach's first cello suite in G. The GIRL suddenly stops. She looks at her hands. EUNICE looks at her hands.)

SAH-JIN What is it?

GIRL *(Touching her fingertips.)* Hurts.

SAH-JIN Keep playing. It will go away.

GIRL I sound awful.

SAH-JIN You sound beautiful.

GIRL Bach would turn over in his grave.

SAH-JIN Someday you will be better than Bach.

GIRL Don't be ridiculous.

SAH-JIN Better than Casals. Better than Yo-Yo Ma.

GIRL Maybe.

SAH-JIN You can be anything you want. If you don't get what you want . . .

SAH-JIN *and* GIRL   . . . it just means you didn't want it bad enough.

SAH-JIN   Then again.

> (*The* GIRL *continues playing. She starts to near the end of the prelude and the music begins to crescendo. The notes climb higher and higher. But this time she struggles. One wrong note shrieks out and then another.*)

SAH-JIN   Eunice?

> (*The music gets more and more jarring, more and more violent.* EUNICE *and the* GIRL *both clasp their hands over their ears.*)

GIRL   NO. Shut up!

SAH-JIN   What, what is it?

GIRL   Stop it. LEAVE ME ALONE.

SAH-JIN   I don't see anything, I'm—I don't understand. Who's there—who are you talking to?

> (*The* GIRL *stands, knocking the cello to the ground. It falls with a terrible clatter.*)

GIRL   Can't you hear them, Um-mah? Make them stop!

SAH-JIN   Just tell me who, who's hurting you?

> (*The* GIRL *seems to be struggling with herself.*)

EUNICE   No I won't No I won't No I won't No I won't

> (EUNICE *continues speaking under the* GIRL, *getting louder and louder.*)

GIRL   No I WON'T.

SAH-JIN   Eunice, what's happening? WHO'S HURTING YOU?

> (*The* GIRL *lifts her bow with one hand high over her head, her fist tightly encircling it. Her other hand she lays flat on the ground. She drives the end of the bow down into her hand and cries out.*)

SAH-JIN   EUNICE.

(Blackout except for one faint light on EUNICE. *She is still crouched over. Beat. She slowly uncurls and sits up. She raises her hand and looks at it.)*

—— END OF ACT I ——

ACT II

SCENE 1

An office. PAUL *is examining* EUNICE'S *arm.*

EUNICE   Thanks for squeezing me in like this.

PAUL   No problem—today's not so busy. This looks fine. If it gets fuzzy around the edges, then let me know. You've probably had this mole for years. What made you want to get it checked out now?

EUNICE   Oh, I don't know.

PAUL   Because as long as you don't notice any—*(He looks at her face.)* This isn't why you're here, is it?

EUNICE   Well, it's not the *only* reason why I'm here—

PAUL   You know, normal people just call and say, "Hey, want to have coffee?"

EUNICE   I know.

PAUL   Is everything okay?

EUNICE   Yeah. It's just that I don't have my check-up until next week and there were just some questions I had now. And I thought maybe you could. Illuminate them.

PAUL   All right. Shoot.

EUNICE   Are there any diseases that are, you know, hereditary?

PAUL: Well, sure. Lots of them. I mean it ranges from semi-hereditary, like psoriasis or something, to—

EUNICE: But is there any way to know what the probabilities are? Exactly? Like say I had a history of diabetes in my family. Could I calculate the chances of my baby having diabetes?

PAUL: But there's no sure thing. I mean, some of it is genetics, yes. But a lot of it is environment. It's not smoking, it's exercising, it's the choices you make.

EUNICE: Right.

PAUL: You're just getting nervous, it's natural. It's going to be fine. Your baby's going to be fine.

EUNICE: It's just there're so many factors . . .

PAUL: Listen to the worrier. Sound just like your mom.

EUNICE: Bite your tongue.

PAUL: Just enjoy it, will you? Go buy stuff. I don't know. Baby stuff, walkie-talkies, teething toys, whatever.

EUNICE: Oh, I'm not. I'm not keeping it.

PAUL: What?

EUNICE: I'm putting it up for adoption. That's why I came home.

PAUL: But your mom—

EUNICE: My mom what? Did she tell you I was keeping it?

PAUL: No, she didn't say anything. She just seemed so. Happy.

EUNICE: She did?

PAUL: Well. Yeah. Anyway. It's funny.

EUNICE: What?

PAUL: That you—I mean, Emmy and I, we can't have kids. And we want them. And here's you . . . Anyway.

EUNICE   You can't?

PAUL   Well, she can't . . . no.

EUNICE   I'm sorry.

> (PAUL *shrugs.*)

PAUL   What're ya gonna do? You love who you love, right? So. Gotta get back to the suffering masses. Take two pills and call me in the morning.

EUNICE   Thank you.

PAUL   For what? Tell your mom I said hi, okay?

EUNICE   Hey, Paul?

PAUL   Yeah?

EUNICE   Just out of curiosity, what could leave a scar, like a star-shaped one? Here?

> (*She touches her throat.*)

PAUL   Sounds like a trache.

EUNICE   A what?

PAUL   A tracheotomy. Your airway gets blocked so they have to put a hole in you.

EUNICE   What?

PAUL   Don't look so horrified. You talking about your mom's scar? That's ancient.

EUNICE   What do you mean?

PAUL   Probably a childhood bout with pneumonia or something. I wouldn't worry about it. Remember: normal people: phone, coffee. Much easier.

SCENE 2

SAH-JIN is sitting with a tape player on her lap. Her eyes are closed and she's listening to a piece of cello music. EUNICE enters.

EUNICE   Ma? What're you doing?

SAH-JIN   Nothing. How was the mall? Find anything good?

EUNICE   No.

SAH-JIN   Are you sleeping okay? I can hear you at night. Tossing, turning.

EUNICE   If you can hear me, then it means you're not sleeping well either. *(She stops the tape.)* Ma. Can I ask you something? How'd you get the scar? The one on your throat?

SAH-JIN   Why're you asking about that?

EUNICE   Just curious.

SAH-JIN   I told you.

EUNICE   No, you didn't.

SAH-JIN   I got sick, they put a hole in so I could breathe.

EUNICE   How old were you?

SAH-JIN   I don't remember.

EUNICE   Someone puts a hole in your throat and you don't remember?

SAH-JIN   Maybe eight. Maybe nine.

    (Pause.)

EUNICE   It's not you, is it?

SAH-JIN   What?

EUNICE   In that photo. She doesn't have your scar. You just said that you were—

SAH-JIN   Oh, Eunice, I'm too tired for this.

EUNICE   Why did you tell me that woman was you?

SAH-JIN	I didn't tell you, you *wanted* to think it, so I let you.	
EUNICE	What?	
SAH-JIN	You get to be my age and it doesn't matter so much anymore. Who said what, who did what, who is who . . .	
EUNICE	That's bull. Facts are facts. This woman, is she a relative?	
SAH-JIN	No, just a friend of the family.	
EUNICE	But she looks like you. Like us.	
SAH-JIN	We all look alike a little.	
EUNICE	I'm serious. Who is she?	
SAH-JIN	No one.	
EUNICE	She is NOT no one. That's a horrible thing to say.	
SAH-JIN	Why are you get so excited? It seem to make you upset and I told you, that's no good for the baby.	
EUNICE	*Stop saying that.* I don't care what's good for the fucking baby!	
SAH-JIN	What is wrong with you? Calm down.	
EUNICE	I'm not a child.	
SAH-JIN	Then stop acting like one! Look at you: so irritated, moody. Like you used to be—	
EUNICE	I am NOT like that anymore.	
SAH-JIN	I just meant you shouldn't think so much. This woman, she was a friend of the family. A good friend. She looked after me when I was young. That's all. Her family move away and then we lose touch. But I keep the photo because it reminds me of her. And I keep it in the book because it's around that same time that I know her and I know Daniel. That's all it is. Sometimes the answer is that easy. Things don't have to be mystery. You look for things that aren't there.	
EUNICE	Really?	

SAH-JIN Really.

(Pause.)

EUNICE You're lying.

SAH-JIN I do not lie, I NEVER lie—

EUNICE ALL YOU DO IS LIE.

(EUNICE *grabs the tape player and takes out the tape.*)

You want the tape? Huh? Then tell me what this is all about.

SAH-JIN EUNICE.

EUNICE I'll rip it out, so help me God.

(SAH-JIN *hesitates and* EUNICE *quickly pulls out some of the tape.*)

SAH-JIN DON'T!

(EUNICE *throws the tape down.* SAH-JIN *retrieves it.*)

SAH-JIN This is the only tape I have, the only one. Why are you like this?

EUNICE Bitter?

SAH-JIN Cruel. You don't tell me everything. I don't expect you to. You need somewhere to stay, you come home. You need food, I feed you. You are pregnant, I don't ask questions. I let you be a stranger to me because I know that's what you need.

EUNICE You have no idea what I need!

SAH-JIN What about me? Since the moment you walked into this house all you care about is how bad *your* life is, how much *you've* suffered. And you come here and expect me to give you everything, as usual, no matter what it costs me.

EUNICE I LOST EVERYTHING.

SAH-JIN And what do you think I have? I lost more. I lost MORE. Because at least you have yourself. I never had myself. I just had you.

EUNICE   That's not my fault, you can't blame me for that.

SAH-JIN   And here you are, digging into my life, not caring what it means to me, at the same time, you conveniently forget everything that happened to you in this house, pretending like it happened to someone else, in another life, not brave enough to look at it for what it is, to look at yourself for what it is.

EUNICE   And what is that, Ma, what am I?

SAH-JIN   I don't know. Not anymore. I don't know where you've gone. *(She looks at the tape in her hands.)* I miss what you were so much, you don't know how much I miss it. When you played it was like something inside me—the wrong things breaking apart and coming together right. I see that in you, that girl inside you and you never let her out.

EUNICE   I can't. Don't you understand?

SAH-JIN   I only ever want to make you happy. But sometimes, I think that you don't know how to be happy. That you never choose it. It's right there, but you don't choose it. Instead, you choose the difficult thing, the hard thing. Like the past. The past is a hard thing.

EUNICE   Then let *me* choose. Don't decide for me.

    (Pause.)

SAH-JIN   That woman is my sister.

EUNICE   You told me she died when she was a child.

SAH-JIN   She got sick. It was not like here. No good hospitals, no good medicine, no good anything. The war left nothing. What they could not heal, they took away.

EUNICE   Where?

SAH-JIN   To a home. And then no one ever spoke of her again. When I think of her, I think of fruit. One, a pale yellow fruit with ridges the length of your hand. She would peel it so quickly, long, see-through strands of skin. She would slice it into long thin canoes for me because she knew I liked it. Fruit never tasted as good as when it came from her hand. And the last time I saw her, she gave me a red, orange fruit, that had leaves on it like a little hat. Something like a tomato. Not much juice, a hard sweetness. After eating it, my fingers were coated with a powder that had tiny edges. Like sand. Like glass. I waved good-bye to her with glass on my hands.

Not everyone's like you, Eunice. Not everyone gets better.

EUNICE   What are you saying, that she was—? Was she. Was she like me?

SAH-JIN   Yes. No. You're different.

EUNICE   Ma, all this time, why didn't you ever say anything?

SAH-JIN   Why? What good does it do?

EUNICE   Ma. Were there others? Before her? Before me?

SAH-JIN   I don't know.

EUNICE   Yes, you do—

SAH-JIN   I'm not lying, honestly I do not know. We didn't talk about it like that. My mother, she died when I was young and I never knew *how* she died. Do you understand? No one would ever tell me. They just never said.

EUNICE   But it's possible that there were others. We don't know for sure, but there could have been—

SAH-JIN   Oh, Eunice, say it like that, *anything* is possible—

EUNICE   So even if Dad hadn't died, even if everything had been different, I would've still—?

(EUNICE *starts laughing.*)

SAH-JIN   Stop.

EUNICE   Oh, come on, this is irony at its richest! Two parents who sacrifice everything for their child, who strive to give her only the best.... And I don't inherit language or culture, hell, I don't even inherit your *hair* or your looks. I inherit a *disease. (EUNICE swallows her bitter laughter.)* That's my heirloom.

SAH-JIN   Do you think that's all we gave you?

EUNICE   What does the rest matter?

SAH-JIN   One time, when you were still just a very little girl, I got up late in the middle of the night and found you in the living room. I tried to be angry, but you look so small, sitting in the glow of the TV, your nightgown all blue. Like the little girl in that bad movie you made me watch.

EUNICE   *Poltergeist.*

SAH-JIN   Except no ghost, just a little Japanese girl playing the violin. She's not much older than you. She finishes and there's so much applause. And you turn and say to me, I'm going to be better than that. I'm going to be better than anyone. And for a while, you were. That is part of you.

(EUNICE holds up her hand and flexes it stiffly. She shows SAH-JIN the scar.)

EUNICE   So is this.

SCENE 3

SAH-JIN is at the locked door of Eunice's room.

SAH-JIN   Are you hungry? I made food. Not bought. Your favorites. Eunice? What's wrong with you? Open the door. You have to eat. You don't have to talk, but you have to eat. It's been three days and you haven't eaten a thing. Eunice. Eunice? *(Softly.)* You're scaring me.

SCENE 4

EUNICE   When week two hit with no period in sight, I bought eight tests from the Duane Reade. I drank a pot of coffee and did them all in a row. Ate up an entire Sunday. And still I couldn't believe it. So

I went to the clinic so I could be positive and as it turned out . . . I was. The nurse asked if I'd need a counselor. She didn't find it funny when I said, "Fuck the counselor—I need a drink!"

For two days, I felt . . . I was terrified, but there was this kind of amazement. I had felt so empty for so long and suddenly . . . I was a vessel. And I knew what it must have been like to be—not Columbus—but one of his ships, carrying all that hope, carrying all that expectation to the New World. But there is no New World. And I'm no Columbus. I want you to know, it's not that I didn't want you. But long after you leave my arms, everything in you will bear you back towards me. My dust on your heels, my . . . in you, rotting you from the inside out . . . And I won't. I won't do that to you.

Because I did. I do. Love you, I mean. In my own way, I do.

It's just that there is no one in my heart. Not even me.

SCENE 5

EUNICE is in the kitchen, standing before a pile of lemons on the table.

> (SAH-JIN *walks into the kitchen, sees* EUNICE, *and freezes.*)

SAH-JIN   There you are. I was looking for you.

EUNICE   So you found me.

SAH-JIN   What's all this?

EUNICE   The tree out back is bursting with them. They're dropping on the ground and rotting.

SAH-JIN   But what are you going to do with all of them?

EUNICE   I don't know. Make lemonade, I guess.

> (EUNICE *starts cutting the lemons in half and squeezing them into a glass.*)

SAH-JIN   Your father planted that tree.

EUNICE   Don't know why. He didn't even like lemons.

SAH-JIN   He meant to plant something else, a different fruit. But they sold him the wrong tree and he didn't know it until the fruit came out.

EUNICE   Poor Dad. Always getting shafted by life.

SAH-JIN   Don't say that.

EUNICE   Why not? It's true. I guess you never know what you've planted until it comes up.

>   *(She pounds the glass of juice back and sucks her breath in loudly through her teeth.)*

(Exhaling.) Sheee-uh!

SAH-JIN   *(Overlapping.)* Eunice!

EUNICE   Goddamn, Ma, that's some bitter fruit!

SAH-JIN   Drink some water.

>   *(She gets EUNICE a cup.)*

Crazy girl.

EUNICE   Don't call me that.

>   *(Pause.)*

SAH-JIN   After I saw your door open, I start to look for you everywhere. Then I look for you in the garage. The car was warm. Did you go somewhere?

EUNICE   Uh huh.

SAH-JIN   Where?

EUNICE   To the doctor's. Had my check-up.

SAH-JIN   Why didn't you say so? I could've driven you. What did they say? Baby healthy?

EUNICE   Yeah.

SAH-JIN   Then why do you look like that?

EUNICE	Well. I don't have AIDS.
SAH-JIN	Eunice, what is it?
EUNICE	I changed my mind. I'm not doing adoption.
SAH-JIN	What?
EUNICE	I checked and I'm still within the safe time.
SAH-JIN	What do you mean?
EUNICE	Well, after the first trimester, the procedure isn't as—
SAH-JIN	*Procedure?*
EUNICE	It's really for the best, when you think about it, given the chances of—
SAH-JIN	No, you CAN'T. I won't let you. Adoption is one thing, but this—
EUNICE	Ma, do you know the statistics? Do you have any idea?
SAH-JIN	I knew and I still wanted you.
EUNICE	Who's going to want a baby like this?
SAH-JIN	Then keep the child! Keep it like I kept you.
EUNICE	Why couldn't you have been brave and just gotten rid of me?
SAH-JIN	There was always a chance you wouldn't have it, just like I didn't.
EUNICE	*(Overlapping.)* But I did.
SAH-JIN	*(Overlapping.)* I was not afraid. Not of having you. Not of raising you.
EUNICE	I was sick. I could've hurt you. Don't you understand?
SAH-JIN	But you got help—
EUNICE	If that's what you want to call it. They carted me away and pumped me full of drugs and this stupid body of mine just kept going—
SAH-JIN	And you got better. And now you're fine—

EUNICE   Look at me, Mother. Look at my "*fine*."

SAH-JIN   But it's in you, it's all in you—

EUNICE   No. That girl's gone. Do you know why she was so good?

SAH-JIN   What do you mean?

EUNICE   Do you remember when I started becoming a champion?

SAH-JIN   You were twelve.

EUNICE   It was the year after Dad died.

SAH-JIN   That year, you won every contest you entered. Every tournament. Every competition.

EUNICE   I did nothing but play. Eight hours a day.

SAH-JIN   You went from being a good player to being a great one. Juilliard wanted you. Everyone wanted you.

EUNICE   When I played, I thought of nothing. Cared about nothing. Saw nothing. Heard nothing. I was going to make his sacrifice worth it.

SAH-JIN   He didn't die for you.

EUNICE   No, it was worse. He *lived* for me and only me. You know when I played, it was the only time we ever talked. There are so many different kinds of languages that exist between a father and daughter. And we didn't know any of them. I used to watch him in the evenings, writing out the checks for my lessons, my bows, my music. I was horrified by the large amounts. Those dollars represented his minutes, hours . . . his whole life trickling down into units of cash that brought me teachers, instruments, accessories. It felt like blood money. What kind of world, Ma?

SAH-JIN   What do you mean?

EUNICE   I was there. At the store.

SAH-JIN   What are you talking about? *(Pause.)* You were at school.

EUNICE   No, I was there.

SAH-JIN	Eunice.	
EUNICE	I remember: It's a half-day, a sunny half-day and I'm flying home so fast I don't even stop at the ice cream truck.	
SAH-JIN	I was in the back . . . I didn't even hear you come in.	
EUNICE	I'm going to spring out and surprise Dad because I've made it to state. The highest honor for someone in my age bracket and I know he'll be happy. He'll smile, he hasn't smiled in so long.	
SAH-JIN	No.	
EUNICE	He's helping a customer. Two men—no, they seem young, bodies like boys. They bark, they splinter, they break, and my father he is—and I don't make a sound—and my father he is—nothing has sound—The men run out and—My mother—	
SAH-JIN	I heard, I saw, I saw him fall—	
EUNICE	Nothing has sound—You claw by the counters towards him and—Hold his head, hold his head—	
SAH-JIN	Just hold his head—I hear someone wailing—And it's me—	
EUNICE	*(Fast and whispered.)* Get up please please please just get up and say something please just get up and do something get up please please please—	
SAH-JIN	But he doesn't—	
EUNICE	And I run, as hard and fast as I can

still no sound

everything quiet

I run away and I don't look back.

The quiet . . . I tried to fill it with music. I thought I could push out all the sadness like it was so much dusty air. . .

I came so close, Ma. | |
| SAH-JIN | To what? | |

EUNICE To being someone. Who mattered.

SAH-JIN You think the cello was what made you matter?

EUNICE What else was there?

SAH-JIN Eunice-ya. Listen. I told you I was never in love, not like you mean. And it's true. I know for sure that I never been falling in love with anyone. Not your father even. I loved him, but a different way. Not like how it is on TV where you have a deep love for someone and they are like your best friend, they go with you like a companion through your whole life. Kind of depressed me, you know? I thought, I will never know a great love. How sad, to go through your whole life and never experience a great love. But then I realize *you* are my great love. Because you are me, you are in me. And everywhere you go, it's like I'm there too. And my love for you is so big, sometimes I don't even know what to do with it. It's like my heart is beating outside my body and it's terrible not knowing how to keep it safe. That's what the ribcage is for, but what to do when your heart is walking all over the world without you? And I love you like this not because of anything you did. Not because you were talented or good at something, no. I loved you like this as soon as you were born. I loved you like this *before* you were born. I loved you like this before I even knew what you were. You didn't have to earn it. Or repay it. It was always already there. You just had to see it.

(A moment.)

Seems funny to think now . . . Did I ever tell you? Tell you why I wanted you to play the cello?

EUNICE What?

SAH-JIN I chose it for you.

EUNICE No, I chose it. I remember the room you took me to. How there were all of those instruments and you let me go one by one and choose the one I wanted. And it felt right, that's why I chose it.

SAH-JIN It was just a kind of whim. I heard it for the first time when I was just a child. I'd never seen or heard anything like it before. It was from another world, a better one, the one, more than anything, that I wanted to see. And I did. For better or worse, I did.

SCENE 6

Korea. DANIEL *sits playing the cello. He is smoking while he plays. The smoke curls up in opaque tendrils around him. A girl opens the door of the house and listens until he finishes. She is twelve.* DANIEL *stops and takes a drag of his cigarette. He puts it out.*

DANIEL Hey. Come here.

    (She hangs back. DANIEL *fishes out a pack of gum from his pocket.)*

  You like gum, don't you?

    (She quickly moves forward and snatches the gum from his hand. She chews a stick greedily.)

  Hey, hold on, you got to take the wrapper off first.

  I've seen you before, hanging around. Sah-Jin, right?

    (The YOUNG SAH-JIN *nods.)*

  Boy, you sure look like her. Know who I am?

YOUNG SAH-JIN *(With a strong accent.)* Daniel.

DANIEL That's right. And I'm your sister's friend. *(Hopefully.)* Do you know where they've taken her? *(Pause.)* Didn't think so.

    (She quietly approaches the cello.)

  Go on, you can touch it. It doesn't bite. This is the bow. Hold it like this. No straight, the bow has to be flat on the string. And then you draw it across.

    (He puts his hand on hers and guides the bow over the strings. A rich note pours out and she smiles for the first time.)

There. See? Not so hard.

(*She draws the bow and a note squawks out.*)

Okay, a little hard. I used to play for your sister all the time. Talk about music appreciation. I'd sit out here and play to her window—God, your parents hated me for that.

(*He hands her the whole pack of gum.*)

Here, have it all. I don't need it. I'm leaving tomorrow to go back to the land of gum. But will you do something for me? Stand in her room and let me play to you. It'll be like it used to be, like I'm playing for her. Will you let me do that?

(*She nods. She goes inside, and sits down. Outside* DANIEL *plays.*)

SCENE 7

EUNICE   We took pictures of the wrong things

and we recorded the wrong events.

We told the wrong stories

and we remembered the wrong memories.

What has lasted is sadness; it will outlast flesh.

What has lasted is forgetfulness; it wins over memory every time.

But sometimes, in the blue hour, between midnight and dawn, I'll wake up and my hands will be alive, moving over an imaginary cello all by themselves. That's how strong the muscle memory is. And then I feel such loss . . . but as Rilke would say, "[Y]ou must not be frightened, dear Mr. Kappus, if a sadness rises up before you larger than any you have ever seen; if a restiveness, like light and cloud-shadows, passes over your hands and over all you do. You must think that something is happening with you, that life has not forgotten you, that it holds you in its hand; it will not let you fall."

(EUNICE *sits with the cello, holding it like it's an old, fragile friend. She holds the bow and draws it over the string. At first it squawks and then a pure, rich note rings out. She starts playing a simple melody, like someone rusty and out of practice. But the song still holds together, revealing something of the player she once was.* SAH-JIN *comes to the door and listens. She holds a photo.* EUNICE *stops playing but doesn't look up.*)

EUNICE   I can't remember the rest. My hands . . . they shake.

SAH-JIN   Still sounds beautiful to me.

(She holds up the photo.)

Look. I found. This is you.

EUNICE   I'm not even in it. It's just you and Dad.

SAH-JIN   Look harder. You were inside me then. In this *(She makes a motion back and forth between herself and* EUNICE.*)* there was you.

(SAH-JIN *kneels in front of* EUNICE *and puts her ear to her stomach. She listens closely.*)

It's a girl.

EUNICE   How can you tell?

SAH-JIN   I can hear her singing.

EUNICE   A girl. What's she singing?

SAH-JIN   Very old song. About mountains and rain.

EUNICE   Yeah, right.

(SAH-JIN *begins to hum a melody.* EUNICE *begins to hum it with her.*)

EUNICE   I didn't even know . . . that I knew that.

SAH-JIN   Exactly.

EUNICE   Is mother's love a kind of chung?

SAH-JIN   Yes, a kind. Maybe the strongest kind. When you are with someone, first there is love. And time passes and then there can be hate. But after that, what is left, is chung. You can't have chung with someone you've just met. There is memory in chung. There is time.

EUNICE   Is there history?

SAH-JIN   Mm hmm. Memory plus time.

(SAH-JIN sees the box on EUNICE's desk. She looks in it and takes out the watch. She holds it carefully. EUNICE watches her. SAH-JIN winds it up and puts her ear to it.)

Hunh. Still works.

EUNICE   What's this thing in your hair? Is that a . . . ?

SAH-JIN   They call it a hairdini. I order off TV.

EUNICE   You're kidding.

SAH-JIN   Just twist it and you have a bun. No more hairpins. Saves a lot of time.

EUNICE   Oh, Ma.

(SAH-JIN goes to the mirror.)

SAH-JIN   Feh. I've gotten so old.

EUNICE   I think you're beautiful. After all, aren't all the women in our family beautiful?

(Lights dim. SAH-JIN disappears. We hear the Bach prelude. EUNICE gathers together her letters. She puts them into the box.)

One hope chest.

(The WOMAN and GIRL appear. The music continues. It reaches the point where the music crescendos, but this time, instead of falling apart, the music effortlessly climbs and climbs. The WOMAN begins speaking and then gradually the GIRL and EUNICE join in.)

WOMAN		
Good day		
A day	GIRL	
Goodness	Good day	EUNICE
Goodness	A day	Good day
Memory	Goodness	A day
Memory	Goodness	Goodness
Memory	Memory	Goodness
Memory	Memory	Memory
Memory	Memory	Memory

(End to the prelude of Bach's first cello suite in G.)

—— **END OF PLAY** ——

AMERICAN HWANGAP
Lloyd Suh

Lloyd Suh. Photo by Jeanie Lee Suh.

Lloyd Suh was born in Detroit, Michigan, in 1975 and raised in Indiana. As a young boy he wanted to become a novelist but developed an interest in playwriting in college. The collaborative nature of theater inspired him to enroll in the Actors Studio Drama School at New School University in New York and become a professional playwright. His plays include *The Children of Vonderly, Happy End of the World, The Garden Variety, Masha No Home, Great Wall Story, Jesus in India*, and several short plays, including *Happy Birthday William Abernathy, Not All Korean Girls Can Fly*, and *With a Hammer & a Nail*. His work has been seen at the Ojai Playwrights Conference, Ensemble Studio Theatre, East West Players, and Ma-Yi Theater Company. He has received grants and awards from the Dramatists Guild, Jerome Foundation, South Coast Repertory, New York State Council on the Arts, New York Foundation of the Arts, and the Lark Play Development Center. He has served as the artistic director of Second Generation and the co-director of the Ma-Yi Writers Lab. Since January 2011, he has served as Director of Onsite Programs at the Lark Play Development Center. *American Hwangap* (2007) was inspired by two anniversaries, the sixtieth birthday of Suh's father and the sixtieth anniversary of Korea's independence from Japan, which, for Suh, symbolically represents another sort of *hwangap*. *American Hwangap* is primarily about the human experience in the most intimate sense, but it also reflects Suh's thoughts on Korea's fractured history.

American Hwangap was developed at the Ojai Playwrights Conference (Robert Egan, artistic director) and originally presented by New York Stage & Film Company and the Powerhouse Theater at Vassar on July 27–29, 2007. It received its world premiere at the Magic Theatre (Loretta Greco, artistic director) in San Francisco on April 11, 2009. It was directed by Trip Cullman; the set design was by Erik Flatmo; the costume design was by Brandin Baron; the lighting design was by York Kennedy; the sound design was by Fitz Patton; the assistant costume designer was Antonia Gunnarson; the assistant sound designer was Matt Stines; and the production stage manager was Briana J. Fahey. The cast was as follows:

Min Suk Chun . . . . Keone Young
Mary Chun . . . . Jodi Long
Ralph Chun . . . . Jon Norman Schneider
Esther Chun . . . . Angela Lin
David Chun . . . . Ryun Yu

The play received its New York premiere on May 17, 2009, in a co-production by Ma-Yi Theater Company (Ralph B. Peña, artistic director; Jorge Z. Ortoll, executive director) and the Play Company (Kate Loewald, artistic director; Lauren Weigel, managing director) at the Wild Project. It was directed by Trip Cullman; the set design was by Erik Flatmo; the costume design was by Junghyun Georgia Lee; the lighting design was by Paul Whitaker; the sound design was by Fitz Patton; and the production stage manager was Jenn McNeil. The cast was as follows:

Min Suk Chun . . . . James Saito
Mary Chun . . . . Mia Katigbak
Ralph Chun . . . . Peter Kim
Esther Chun . . . . Michi Barall
David Chun . . . . Hoon Lee

The play was also produced at Tanghalang Pilipino in the Philippines in 2010. The three productions were part of the Lark Play Development Center's "Launching New Plays into the Repertoire Initiative" supported by the Andrew W. Mellon Foundation.

CHARACTERS

MIN SUK CHUN, 59, a Korean immigrant to the United States, returned to Korea and now back again. Probably either tall, large, or otherwise imposing. His English is actually quite good though rusty, it comes and goes, but he speaks quickly, often, and confidently even when he doesn't have the words.

MARY CHUN, 58, his ex-wife. Reinvented. A modern Asian American woman. Speaks proficient English, though may be tinged with only a slight accent.

RALPH CHUN, 29, their youngest son. Brilliant, damaged. Lives in his mother's basement.

ESTHER CHUN, 31, their daughter. Twice divorced, a perpetual student. Unsettled.

DAVID CHUN, 35, their eldest son. An investment banker. Away.

SETTING

Suburbs. Texas.

TIME

2005

SCENE 1

RALPH wears a traditional Korean hanbok. He holds a small cup.

RALPH   I wrote a poem for you, Dad. It's called "American Hwangap."

I'd recite it for you but I put it in my pants pocket and when I changed into this thing I forgot to transfer it from the other pants and it was kind of long so I can't remember how it goes. But um.

I don't know you very well. But I mean I like you and stuff. When I picture you away from home, you're in the desert with a knapsack over your shoulder, you have a grizzled beard with the mud of the earth on it, you're alone and undaunted by the distances from you to everyplace else.

That bigtooth maple out in back of the yard, that's the one we planted, all those years ago. It's a climbing tree now. If you climb

James Saito (right) and Peter Kim (left) in the New York City premiere of *American Hwangap*, co-produced by the Play Company and Ma-Yi Theater Company. Photo by Matt Zugale.

the tree, Pop, the leaves will spill and I'll rake them. You should climb it. Its roots are down.

I hope you stick around this time, Dad. That'd be pretty cool.

My prescription says that I'm not allowed to consume alcohol which sucks, so I guess I'm just gonna pretend I'm drinking it.

(*He pretends to drink.*)

Happy Birthday.

(*Lights.*)

SCENE 2

Afternoon. DAVID *at an office, suit and tie.* RALPH *in the basement of the Chun house, wearing pajama pants and a T-shirt. His arm is in a cast. They phone.*

RALPH   We went shopping and I got a birthday present, guess what I got.

DAVID   Birthday present for Dad?

RALPH   It's a book about birthdays. It has all famous people's birthdays and you can look up your birthday and find out what famous people were born on your same birthday as you.

DAVID   Oh yeah?

RALPH   I was born on the same day as Florence Nightingale and Katherine Hepburn and Yogi Berra and Emilio Estevez and Tom Snyder who I don't know who that is and skateboarding legend Tony Hawk and Kim Fields who was Tooti on *Facts of Life*.

DAVID   Great.

RALPH   Dad was born on the same day as Sean Diddy Combs Ralph Macchio Laura Bush Will Rogers Walter Cronkite and Matthew McConaughegehey or however you pronounce it.

DAVID   Okay.

RALPH   When's your birthday David and I'll look it up.

DAVID   You don't know when my birthday is, champ?

RALPH   If you tell me I'll remember because I just forgot for a second.

DAVID   September 14.

RALPH   Right September 14 just a sec I have the book here let me look.

(RALPH *fumbles to read the book while still on the phone.*)

September 14 is Sam Neill and Joey Heatherton and Harve Presnell and Clayton Moore.

(*Silence.*)

DAVID   That's everyone?

RALPH   Well and you too, David.

DAVID   Right.

RALPH: David I don't know who those people are.

DAVID: Clayton Moore, that sounds familiar, was he an astronaut or something?

RALPH: No it says he's the Lone Ranger.

DAVID: Oh, the Lone Ranger.

RALPH: Yeah.

DAVID: I guess that means I gotta get to work getting famous, huh champ? Us September 14thers are slacking off some, I gotta carry the load and get real famous, right?

RALPH: Oh yeah David you can get famous and then you can be in the book. But then I have to get Dad another book because then this one will be old.

DAVID: Hey, is Mom around?

RALPH: Mom yeah no, she's still at work and then she had to go to the grocery she said but she'll be back by six.

DAVID: Grocery, huh?

RALPH: Yeah she's gonna get a cake for the party and like some food and stuff. She's gonna make a big *dduk-gook* and some *gahl-bee*.

DAVID: So this is really happening.

RALPH: You're coming home, right, for Dad's birthday?

DAVID: We'll see, champ. How you doing anyway?

RALPH: How am I doing, I'm doing great.

DAVID: That's great, I heard you broke your arm though.

RALPH: Yeah I got it in a cast, what happened was I clumb a tree and I fell.

DAVID: Clumb?

RALPH: Yeah I saw a tree and I clumb it.

DAVID: I think you mean climbed there, champ.

RALPH	Right yeah climbed.
DAVID	Yeah it's climbed if you want to be correct about it.
RALPH	Oh well then I definitely clumb it then 'cause there was nothing correct in how I did it.
DAVID	I see.
RALPH	You wanna sign my cast?
DAVID	Sure thing.
RALPH	Okay so then come home for Dad's birthday and then you can sign it.
DAVID	How's your nerves?
RALPH	Oh they come and go.
DAVID	You taking your meds? Whadda they got you on?
RALPH	Something called Triloramine. You know something about pharmaceuticals, David?
DAVID	Yeah I know something about everything. You like that stuff?
RALPH	I guess so, I don't want to talk about it anymore. Except don't worry about me, you should just come down home for the party.
DAVID	Yeah well I'm working on it, kid.
RALPH	It's actually kind of a sweet deal. I get to sit around with my butt hanging out of my pants all day, I don't have to have a job and people let me get away with stuff like at the hospital when my arm was broke the doctor was all hesitant to shoot me up with painkillers on account of my nervous situation and it sucked really so I called him a fucking cunt. And no one got mad. So it's like I'm a short bus kid only nobody thinks I'm stupid, they actually treat me like I'm supersmart or some kind of genius, which I guess is technically true if you want to break it down in terms of standardized psychoanalytic testing methods, but that's ultimately not very helpful on account of me most of the time feeling like I'm teeter-

ing toward a very nearby precipice beneath which is untold personal misery and psychological disaster.

(Silence.)

DAVID   We all of us live every day on that precipice, buddy.

RALPH   Cool.

DAVID   Just bear that in mind for comfort.

RALPH   I talked to Dad you know.

DAVID   No shit.

RALPH   No shit.

DAVID   What did you guys, I mean what did he say?

RALPH   Well the conversation was basically broken up into two main categories, the first being his plans for his visit and the second having more to do with like feelings.

DAVID   Ah.

RALPH   So he's here now, he's landing at the airport and then meeting up with Esther and she's going to drive him up here for tonight and then tomorrow we're gonna have a party.

DAVID   Did he say anything about me?

RALPH   Um. About you David?

DAVID   You know what, forget it. Just tell Ma I called, 'kay?

RALPH   I've been writing poetry David.

DAVID   Say again?

RALPH   The kids in the neighborhood they have a band called The Love Song of J. Alfred Punk Rock and they want me to be in it or something so I've been writing songs and occasionally lyrics which is like poetry, mostly it's blank verse except for some of them which rhyme only not in a corny way.

DAVID   Blank verse is great. So Mom'll be back by six, huh?

RALPH   You want me to read you a poem David?

DAVID   What's that?

RALPH   I said yeah Mom'll be back at five, in the meantime you want me to read you a poem?

DAVID   Okay sure, but wait five, or did you say six?

RALPH   This one's my best one it's called "Weazleton."

DAVID   That's an ace title, champ.

RALPH   Weazleton is my dog's name.

We live in my mother's basement

playing ping pong and the daily crosswords.

His nerves are a tatters from a fall

last fall or the fall before.

A dog never knows his father

because puppies are litter,

sold before they're old and gray,

some stray,

given away.

It's a dog's life.

If I could talk to Weazleton

I would ask if it bothers him

that a dog never knows his father.

In fact I can,

so I ask

and he licks my hand

and poops.

             This must be an answer.

             (Silence.) That's the end.

DAVID   That's a tops poem there, champ.

RALPH   You like it David?

DAVID   I like it more than you can know, buddy. I like it a lot.

RALPH   It's autobiographical.

DAVID   Yeah, buddy. I know.

RALPH   Cool.

DAVID   I know.

             (Lights.)

SCENE 3

Dusk. CHUN and ESTHER at a diner, window seat. Beyond them, mountains and desert. CHUN eats, ESTHER drinks coffee.

CHUN   I remember well this desert. So different so same is with Korea, mountain here like mountain there only so apart and lonely or things of this nature. In Korea see mountains, cannot help but dream of going to top of mountain but here is almost like hope for hop from one mountain to another, learn to fly or dream of wandering one to the next instead, strange how different mountains can be.

ESTHER   Um hey Dad?

CHUN   Mm.

ESTHER   Could we maybe just have some silence for like two seconds?

CHUN   Yeah okay.

             (They sit in silence for like two seconds.)

             You are have some boyfriend?

ESTHER   Dad.

CHUN   What?

ESTHER   No, I don't have a boyfriend.

CHUN   Oh. Because on purpose or because nobody wanting be boyfriend for you?

ESTHER   Heh. Uh, I you know, I really don't know.

CHUN   This something maybe you need to know.

ESTHER   I can handle it Dad, thanks.

CHUN   If you're in need of advice from Daddy, I have advice to give.

ESTHER   Yeah no I don't need any advice.

CHUN   Okay.

(ESTHER drinks her coffee.)

Thing about boys, Esther, is that sometimes man is need to feeling like he is so important or have so much freedom or something, maybe boys certain age not good for appreciate things woman are having, type of nurture and good feeding and things of this nature.

ESTHER   Dad, please.

CHUN   But after certain age man is begin to understanding need for good woman, *cham-han ah-gah-shee*, who can taking care of things for man, not just crazy wild hoochie time.

ESTHER   Okay.

CHUN   Maybe it's good thing you don't settle for man who cannot appreciating you.

ESTHER   That's really not the problem, Dad, thanks though.

CHUN   You know Kim Jong Il?

ESTHER   Do I uh, Kim Jong Il, well yeah.

CHUN	He has nuclear weapon now.	
ESTHER	I know, I read the paper.	
CHUN	Is unexpected situation.	
ESTHER	Yeah I guess so.	
CHUN	In Korea maybe you know maybe don't know, but Kim Jong Il he is kind of weird guy.	
ESTHER	I understand that.	
CHUN	Still so complicate you see, many people in Korea want reunification, but so divide so many years, hope for together but philosophy so different. Has been so long divided, so now they spend one whole lifetime apart.	
ESTHER	Right.	
CHUN	You date Korean man?	
ESTHER	I said I'm not dating anyone, Dad.	
CHUN	Hypothetically. You are date somebody, is he Korean?	
ESTHER	I don't know.	
CHUN	Because I think is important for you to knowing, Korean people are kind of fucked up.	
ESTHER	Yeah I already know that.	
CHUN	So enough about me, tell me a story about you.	
ESTHER	Uh . . . what?	
CHUN	What is a day in the life of Esther?	
ESTHER	I uh what?	
CHUN	You are in school.	
ESTHER	Yeah. I have classes.	
CHUN	You're too old for school.

ESTHER   Thanks.

CHUN   How many school you've been to?

ESTHER   This is my uh, third, maybe fourth — depends on how you look at it, fifth degree.

CHUN   Why? This is satisfy you?

ESTHER   Not really.

CHUN   Mm.

ESTHER   It fills the day.

CHUN   Mm, fills the day, okay. Can I just give you one little advice? I am sixty soon, used to be for Korean people this means entire life, somebody is become sixty years old he better get ready for die soon. But now sixty of course is not so old, after all Clint Eastwood he is probably like eighty years now, so this is okay. But how much time left? Hm? Life is short time for to do something filling days.

ESTHER   Um.

CHUN   When your turn at end of life, Esther, you should be unencumbered of regret.

ESTHER   Okay.

CHUN   Regret, wasted time, when mountains surround us.

ESTHER   Look, Dad.

CHUN   Mountains I never clumb.

ESTHER   Never what?

CHUN   Clumb? Climbed?

ESTHER   Mountains you climb.

CHUN   In any case Esther, don't waste time.

ESTHER   Dad, why are you here?

(*Silence.*)

CHUN   Well, reason I went to Korea, you know, is because when I lost my job I lost everything here, American new life was lost and I could only think this west was not for me. I lost my . . . I lost my ride. You know?

ESTHER   No.

CHUN   Okay.

ESTHER   Explain it.

CHUN   You know what is planned obsolescence?

ESTHER   What?

CHUN   Planned obsolescence, important concept. Engineer of products understand that part of job is to make sure one day it's gonna stop working, why? Because manufacturer want to make sure you buy another. This is American way, you buy say stereo system, sound good look sexy or whatever, then one day kerplooie, stereo system breaks, Americans say oh well, this is the way of things, go buy new stereo. So engineer is create flaws, we plan demise of product to sell more stereos, and I think you know where I'm going with this.

ESTHER   Um.

CHUN   My American life had planned obsolescence. Company gets what it need from me, technology changes, young kids know new things, old guys go by the side, fall off, die or whatever, just die, I became obsolete.

ESTHER   So then what'll you do now?

CHUN   Relearn cowboy way.

ESTHER   You were never a cowboy.

CHUN   I was.

ESTHER   No, Dad.

CHUN   I was.

    (Silence.)

    But also in Korea, I was there one lifetime too late. Try to order banana from grocer, I say "banana" instead of "bah-nah-nah," and this Korean, to him I am not Korean. I turn TV and Smurfs you know Smurfs, they talking Korean!, and I say hey this is not Brainy Smurf voice, Brainy Smurf voice up high, not this crazy Korean Brainy Smurf voice. And then when *hwangap* is coming, they are make such big deal, my brother he says big party to have, remembering lifetime of Chun Min Suk, but Chun Min Suk life was not in Korea, was here, Mommy here, David, Esther and and and what is third one?

ESTHER   Ralph.

CHUN   Ralph yes. Thinking of you here, American *hwangap* maybe would be *hwangap* for me.

ESTHER   Oh.

CHUN   This is why I am here.

ESTHER   For your birthday party.

CHUN   For my life, Esther.

ESTHER   Right.

CHUN   For my life.

    (Silence.)

ESTHER   I don't know what to say to you.

CHUN   Okay.

ESTHER   You left us.

CHUN   Okay.

ESTHER   You know what, let's just pay up and head out, they're waiting at home.

CHUN   Yes.

ESTHER   Can I just say, Dad, can I just say . . . ?

CHUN   Anything you want.

        (Silence.)

ESTHER   We should pay now.

CHUN   How much is it?

ESTHER   Never mind, I got it.

        (She takes the check and her purse. Lights.)

SCENE 4

Evening. MARY *on the phone. Dining room.* RALPH *over a laid-out newspaper, ripping the tails off of soybean sprouts and placing them in a bowl.* DAVID *in his office. They phone.*

DAVID   So I don't get how it works.

MARY   Well *hwangap* just means a sixtieth birthday. The ceremony is the *janche*, and the *hwangap janche* is a celebration of the life. A man turns sixty, his zodiac cycle is ended, so we celebrate the occasion. Of a lifetime lived.

DAVID   Yeah, I still don't get how it works.

MARY   Well in the olden days you'd prepare a banquet, and there would be speeches and tributes from family and friends, usually formal but ours won't be.

DAVID   I hear you're making tons of food.

MARY   Ralph's helping.

RALPH   Tell him I'm here if he wants to talk to me.

MARY   He says he's here if you want to talk to him.

DAVID   So what do you want from me?

MARY: It's not a complicated thing, David, all you have to do is show up and see the man, I have a feeling it'll be good for you.

DAVID: Is there supposed to be a bunch of bowing?

MARY: Well that's how it usually works, but you don't have to do anything you don't want to.

DAVID: Oh alright, then I'm not coming.

MARY: David.

DAVID: You know what your problem is?

MARY: Oh do I have just one?

DAVID: You're a pushover.

MARY: Oh is that right.

DAVID: Looks that way from where I sit.

MARY: Well you can't see anything from that far away, kid, I'll have you know that I share a birthday with Rosa Parks, Oscar de la Hoya, and Lawrence Taylor.

RALPH: And Charles Lindbergh and Alice Cooper.

MARY: Yeah.

RALPH: Did he hear me?

DAVID: So where's he gonna stay? At the house?

MARY: If he has to.

DAVID: Yeah, that doesn't sound like a good idea.

MARY: He'll sleep on the couch.

DAVID: And where am I supposed to sleep?

MARY: You can sleep in the basement maybe.

RALPH: Yeah, he can sleep in the basement.

MARY: Ralph doesn't mind.

RALPH	Tell him it's gonna be awesome.	
MARY	Esther in the other bedroom, you and Ralph in the basement, your father on the couch, sounds reasonable to me. Ralph says it's gonna be awesome.	
DAVID	Just lemme understand what's expected here: are you planning on a series of weepy hugs? Is all forgotten? Or is there recrimination involved, a little weekend of arguments and fistfights?	
MARY	Which would you prefer?	
DAVID	Well, obviously I'd most prefer not to drop everything and just rush down for some supplication congratulation situation.	
MARY	Don't you have anything you want to say to him? To ask?	
DAVID	Not so much, no.	
MARY	Oh I don't believe you. I'm sorry, David, but I don't.	
DAVID	Just don't go to bed with him.	
MARY	Oh give me some credit.	
DAVID	Just don't.	
MARY	Come home, alright?	
DAVID	We'll see.	
MARY	We're all here, David. The whole family, together. You shouldn't leave us waiting for you.	
DAVID	Oh yeah, why not? Isn't that what he did?	

(Silence.)

MARY   I suppose it is, David, yes. In which case you can choose to do the same or else be quite unlike him in that.

(Silence.)

RALPH   Does he want to talk to me now?

DAVID   I gotta go.

(David hangs up.)

RALPH   Can I talk to him real quick?

MARY   He had to go. We'll try him again later.

RALPH   Oh.

MARY   I think that's plenty of *kong-namul*.

RALPH   Can I keep shucking anyway, Ma?

MARY   Oh I think we have more than enough there, Ralphie.

RALPH   But I like it and I wanna keep shucking.

MARY   Okay.

(They shuck together. Lights.)

SCENE 5

ESTHER holds a small cup.

ESTHER   Funny thing about birthdays. You left just before I turned sixteen, I remember you sent a card. It says "Isn't It Great, You Just Turned Eight." I got nothing the year after, but you did send a Sweet Sixteen card when I turned eighteen. So I actually sent you a sixtieth birthday card about ten years ago, maybe you got it, I don't know, but I thought at the time you might find it funny. You weren't there for either one of my weddings, but I did get the toaster you sent after my first divorce.

And you know, I kind of loved that. I kind of loved wondering if and when something might randomly appear in the mail, even after anything had long since stopped arriving.

I guess that means a part of me has always wanted this. A second chance. But now that you're back, Dad, I'm not so sure I really want it anymore.

Maybe I should just get on a plane and head to Korea. Maybe that's the only thing that makes sense. The missing of you, the leaving of you, the back and forth away and away and away from you.

I don't know, Dad.

I didn't get you a card.

Maybe I'll send you one next year.

Wherever you are.

(She drinks, holding the cup with two hands.)

Happy Birthday.

(Lights.)

SCENE 6

Night. RALPH *in the basement.* ESTHER *enters from the stairs.*

ESTHER	So you still live down here.
RALPH	For now.
ESTHER	I could really use a drink.
RALPH	I have Juicy Juice juice boxes.

(Silence.)

ESTHER	What flavor?
RALPH	Grape.
ESTHER	Yeah, I'll have one of those.

(RALPH gets juice boxes for the both of them.)

ESTHER	This is some serious work you've done down here.
RALPH	Yeah every month or so I try to do a significant upgrade and/or renovation.
	How was the trip?
ESTHER	Dusty. Your fly is open.

RALPH	I don't mind.
	You wanna sign my cast?
ESTHER	How long are you gonna live here?
RALPH	As long as I can I guess. Here's a pen.
ESTHER	Who are all these signatures from?
RALPH	Kids in the neighborhood.
ESTHER	Frank Paul Peter Hazel Jeff?
RALPH	Yeah they all signed it.
ESTHER	How old are these kids?
RALPH	Frank twelve Paul nine Peter eighteen Hazel seventeen Jeff I think he's eight.
ESTHER	Ralph you're thirty years old.
RALPH	Twenty-nine.
ESTHER	Is that your guitar?
RALPH	Yeah. You want me to play you a song?
ESTHER	No.
RALPH	Okay. Hey did you get Dad a birthday present?
ESTHER	No.
RALPH	When's your birthday?
ESTHER	January 24.
RALPH	I have a book!
ESTHER	Did you get Dad a birthday present?
RALPH	Just a second.
ESTHER	You seem excited about this thing, huh, Ralphie?

RALPH   Ernest Borgnine, Aaron Neville, Neil Diamond, Yakov Smirnoff, and Mary Lou Retton.

ESTHER   That's a weird thing to say.

RALPH   Those are people whose birthday is the same as yours.

ESTHER   Ah, yes, I knew about the Borgnine.

RALPH   Oh you knew?

ESTHER   Hard not to know about the Borgnine, it follows you, a thing like that. Yakov Smirnoff, that's news to me.

RALPH   I don't know who that is.

ESTHER   Sure you do, unfunny Russian cold war crossover comedian.

RALPH   Nope.

ESTHER   "Wadda country"?! Really no? Dad was way into that guy.

RALPH   Wait, he was, really?

ESTHER   Oh yeah, he would do impressions. "Ung. Wadda country!"

(Smirnoff laugh.)

RALPH   Wow.

ESTHER   Yeah.

RALPH   I wish I remembered that.

ESTHER   No. You don't.

But it is nice to know that I share a birthday with such notaries of lame.

RALPH   Totally.

ESTHER   What's it mean, you think?

RALPH   Well there's evidence to support a truly scientific basis for astrology, keep in mind. That the phases of the moon, earth's rotation and the placement of the stars all correspond to tides and directly affect human and animal biorhythms, even weather, and have been known to wreak havoc with everything from natural disaster to the schedule of women's menstrual cycles, so the kind of thing has merit. Although in the east it's the year as much as the time of year, so maybe that's how Mary Lou broke out and won the gold.

(Silence.)

ESTHER   What's the secret, Ralphie?

RALPH   Secret to what Esther?

ESTHER   You got it all figured.

RALPH   No.

ESTHER   You got the bean bags, Ralphie, you got the bean bags and the basement, and I wanna live your life.

RALPH   Okay.

ESTHER   Not just the basement, I wanna live in your head; how did you get this way?

RALPH   What way?

ESTHER   You're faking. Tell me you're faking.

RALPH   Um faking what?

ESTHER   This really doesn't bother you? Dad back after years of nothing and Mom all of a sudden fixing *dduk-gook* and *gahl-bee*, trotting out the old wares like it's a hero's welcome?

RALPH   I'm confused here.

ESTHER   *(Pokes him.)* This doesn't bug you? What he did?

RALPH   *(Forceful.)* Hey cut it out, alright?

(ESTHER backs away.)

ESTHER   Sorry.

RALPH   I mean *fuck*.

ESTHER   Sorry, Ralph.

    (Silence.)

RALPH   *(Sunny.)* It's cool.

    (Silence.)

    You want me to play you a song on the guitar?

ESTHER   No.

RALPH   Okay.

    (Lights.)

SCENE 7

Night. CHUN and MARY in the dining room. He carries a small bag.

CHUN   Your English so good.

MARY   Thanks. That's all you brought?

CHUN   Don't need much.

MARY   Okay.

CHUN   So how's David?

MARY   He's well.

CHUN   He's coming?

MARY   I think so.

CHUN   He's where?

MARY   New York.

CHUN   No shit.

MARY   No shit.

CHUN   What he is doing there?

MARY   He's an investment banker.

CHUN	Investment banker no shit.
MARY	No shit.
CHUN	What is investment banker?
MARY	I'm still not so sure myself.
CHUN	I like your hair.
MARY	I didn't fix it.
CHUN	Looks good the natural.
MARY	Well, my friends told me to doll it up, but I didn't.
CHUN	Doll it up?
MARY	To look all desirable for your return, some sort of visual ex-wife tactic of trying to look dazzling, I don't know what purpose it'd serve.
CHUN	You always look dazzling.
MARY	Shut up.
CHUN	I should maybe have combing my hair.
MARY	We've seen each other at our worst. There's no need for that crap.

(Silence.)

CHUN	I'm off the sauce, by the way.
MARY	Oh.
CHUN	Four years.
MARY	That long.
CHUN	Okay three weeks. But I were quit for real for four years ago, just had a bad few weeks I'd rather not talk about that one, anyway wasn't my fault.
MARY	Sure.
CHUN	So what should I calling you?

MARY   Huh?

CHUN   *Yuh-boh* I can't anymore calling you, Myung-hee seeming so wrong so long time ago, Mrs. Chun you are not anymore, you are have new name?

MARY   My name is Mary.

CHUN   Okay then Mary.

MARY   Yes?

CHUN   I love you, Mary.

MARY   Shut up.

CHUN   Okay.

MARY   You have a place to stay after the party?

CHUN   Yeah no problem.

MARY   Okay.

CHUN   I'll go to hotel or something.

MARY   You have money for a hotel?

CHUN   No.

MARY   Well, I guess you can stay here.

CHUN   Oh okay thanks. Such the unexpected. Where?

MARY   Couch.

CHUN   Oh.

MARY   When Esther goes you can take the other room.

CHUN   So then no man will coming middle of night, nobody to worry about?

MARY   Huh?

CHUN   I don't know, maybe if you are have some man who maybe is coming around sometime, maybe you do maybe you don't. Just you know want to make checking sure not have to worry about something like that.

MARY   What's the question?

CHUN   So no man I am have to worry about.

MARY   No, there won't be any men over.

CHUN   I see.

MARY   I stay at his place when I see him.

CHUN   Ah.

MARY   There's linens in the laundry room.

CHUN   'Kay.

MARY   You wanna clean up a little first?

CHUN   No I like the dust. America soil on my hands, I like the dust on me.

MARY   Yeah okay.

CHUN   Hey check out my pjs.

MARY   Yeah those are real sexy.

CHUN   Long shorts.

MARY   Okay goodnight!

(She starts to go.)

CHUN   Going to bed already?

MARY   Yeah, well, big day tomorrow, we should get some rest. You need anything first?

CHUN   Um.

MARY   Toothbrush? Razor? Book to read?

(Silence.)

CHUN   Can I get a hug?

	(Silence.)
MARY	Yeah okay.
	(They hug. It lasts a while. It's good.)
CHUN	Yeah okay.
MARY	Right.
CHUN	Is that bedroom?
MARY	No. I mean yeah, I think so.
CHUN	What?
MARY	I mean yeah. You uh wanna . . .
CHUN	Maybe okay.
MARY	Have a look at the place, I mean.
CHUN	Right no hanky panky.
MARY	Yeah.
CHUN	Because kids downstairs.
MARY	Just for a second.
CHUN	Right.

(They work their way to the bedroom. They barely make it there. Clothes in the hallway. Lights.)

SCENE 8

Early the next morning, same. MARY, *fully dressed, stands in the doorway, talking into the bedroom.*

MARY	The kids are downstairs asleep. They wouldn't have seen anything. Come on, up up.
CHUN	Uh?

MARY   I don't need this kind of weird this weekend. You can't be in my bed.

CHUN   *Jahn-kah-mahn.*

(CHUN *enters, wearing long pajama shorts.*)

Good morning.

MARY   Nice pants.

Alright, I set up the couch so it looks like you were on it, mussed up the sheets and threw around towels and stuff. Pop on the TV, I'll make some eggs.

CHUN   Was fun last night.

MARY   Shush.

CHUN   Sorry if I fall asleep too fast after.

MARY   Oh I was expecting that.

CHUN   Anyway yeah.

MARY   Now look, I'm not saying that what happened doesn't mean anything, but it also doesn't mean *everything*.

CHUN   Uh-huh.

MARY   Do you understand?

CHUN   No.

MARY   We're not gonna make a habit of this.

CHUN   Oh.

MARY   Maybe once or twice more, but that's it.

CHUN   Okay.

MARY   I mean from time to time, just not a regular thing.

CHUN   What is mean regular thing?

MARY   I'm not the woman you knew, maybe last night was familiar, but

	I live a different life here, without you, I'm nimble and I'm out in the world, I have a *life*, do you see? Ask anyone in the local real estate game and they'll tell you, that Mary, she can head 'em up and move 'em out.
CHUN	Uh-huh.
MARY	I'm not at home in the wait with a hot meal and a pair of slippers. I take flamenco lessons, I drive stick, I got an ever growing set of friends and associates and when we play bridge they say I'm the one to partner with.
CHUN	Wow.
MARY	If you think you can just roll up in here lookin' all sexy and turn me back into some do-it-all darn-your-socks kimchee-burying melon-cutting *ah-joo-mah* well you've got another thing coming, understand?
CHUN	I'm not sure.
MARY	This old house might seem familiar, but it's mine now, see? We paid the mortgage you left us with, me and the kids, so it's our roof you're under, and you don't get to just jump in and suddenly call this home.
CHUN	Okay.
MARY	And the kids are not to know this happened. Tell me you understand.
CHUN	Yup.
MARY	We're not together.
CHUN	Uh-huh.
MARY	That's never gonna happen again, I'm no sucker. Now what do you think of that?
CHUN	Um.
MARY	Answer fast, the kids'll wake soon.

CHUN	I think . . .
MARY	Yeah?
CHUN	I think you gonna change your mind.

(Silence.)

MARY	Don't count on it.
CHUN	I love you, Mary.
MARY	Shut up and put your pants on.
CHUN	I love you.

(She goes. Shouts from off.)

MARY	And wipe that grin off your face, old man.
CHUN	You bet.

(He doesn't. Lights.)

SCENE 9

Morning. ESTHER *on the phone, basement.* RALPH *sits on a beanbag, playing video games.* DAVID *at his office. They phone.*

ESTHER	Mom and Dad are having sex.
DAVID	Say again?
ESTHER	I said Mom and Dad are having sex.
DAVID	What, right now?
ESTHER	Last night. Mom took a quilt and she flung it around all over the living room couch to make it look like they hadn't, this morning I woke up and Dad was sitting there wearing socks and slippers and it was all over their faces.
DAVID	Oh.
RALPH	Ask him when he's coming.

ESTHER   Why do I have to be here and you get to be so far?

RALPH   Ask him when he's coming.

ESTHER   Are you coming?

DAVID   The flight's long and I got piles on my desk.

ESTHER   Bring a laptop.

DAVID   Maybe.

RALPH   What'd he say?

ESTHER   So it doesn't freak you out that they're . . . you know?

DAVID   Heh heh. Well. Wanna hear something funny?

ESTHER   Yes please.

DAVID   I must have been about twelve or so, it's when the three of us shared a room in that second floor alcove, and every night there were sounds of thumps and moans all through the house. You thought a Demon Gnome had taken lodge in our floorboards with bad teeth and claws, you remember any of this?

ESTHER   Um no.

DAVID   One night I got up to investigate. This was during my Encyclopedia Brown phase, so I picked up my Sherlock hat and a magnifying glass, and I told you I was off to slay this Demon Gnome and bring you its head for proof.

ESTHER   I wanted the head?

DAVID   Yeah you were obsessed with severed heads, kiddo, I don't know what to tell you.

ESTHER   Gross.

RALPH   Hey what are you guys talking about?

DAVID   So anyway, it became pretty instantly clear that the gnome wasn't in our lawn or in our halls, but right in the middle of the master bedroom.

RALPH   Hey Esther what are you guys talking about?

ESTHER I don't need to hear the rest of this, David, thanks.

DAVID   Oh but you do. Because at that moment I had a realization that there was no gnome, that the penile head shape of my Sherlock hat was of some deep psychological symbolism, and that the magnifying glass held in my sweaty, shaking palm also portended my prepubescent shock into manhood.

ESTHER Shut up.

DAVID   Now I'd never seen an image of what a man and woman do together before. I'd heard stories, of course, but they got a lot wrong—like Jacob Cross who said the guy sticks it in and then pees to make a baby. And yet, I could picture every thrust, and every grind, he was on top of her, her legs bent up and forward with her ankles around his shoulders.

RALPH   Is he coming?

ESTHER I'm gonna hang up now.

DAVID   No you won't.

RALPH   Don't!

DAVID   You won't and I'll tell you why. It's the same reason I opened the door.

RALPH   Hey Esther?

DAVID   I knew what was behind it, and I opened it anyway.

ESTHER No!

DAVID   I sat there quite a while in fact, studying the shadows. Eventually, they slept, and I watched their spent bodies heave in time with the guttural snore of the old man's satisfaction, his exhausted exhilaration (or was it mine?), but before I returned to bed I went into the kitchen and selected the most twisted raw oxtail from the fridge in order to present it to you as the severed head of the now-slain Demon Gnome.

ESTHER   What the why?

DAVID   You'd already fallen asleep, so I just tucked the oxtail gently into the overalls of the Teddy Ruxpin you were cradling, and whispered a secret in your ear before saying an audible goodnight to you, to Ralph, to Teddy and my then defunct innocence, but most of all to the oxtail Demon Gnome, who headless and bloody would inevitably rise again.

ESTHER   What did you whisper?

DAVID   "Don't open the door."

    (Silence.)

ESTHER   You totally just made all that up.

DAVID   Yup.

ESTHER   I hate you!

DAVID   You *were* obsessed with severed heads though, that part was true.

ESTHER   Come home, David.

DAVID   We'll see.

ESTHER   Fine.

RALPH   What'd he say?

DAVID   Don't open the door.

ESTHER   What?

DAVID   Huh?

ESTHER   Did you just say something?

DAVID   Who, me?

ESTHER   Yeah.

DAVID   Nuh-uh.

ESTHER   You didn't?

DAVID   Nope.

           (Silence.)

RALPH   Hey.

ESTHER   That story, David?

DAVID   Yeah?

ESTHER   You *didn't* make it up, did you?

           (Silence.)

DAVID   Just the part about the severed head.

           (Silence.)

ESTHER   Please come home.

DAVID   I'll call you later.

           (They hang up. ESTHER looks at RALPH, who says nothing, and just goes back to his video game.)

ESTHER   Oh, sorry Ralph, he got tied up, he'll call again later.

RALPH   He's not coming, is he?

ESTHER   I don't think so.

RALPH   Mm.

ESTHER   How's your game?

           (Abruptly, he drops his video game controller, picks up the console, and throws it in a violent motion to the ground. Destroys the thing. He walks calmly out of the room. ESTHER sits alone, stunned still. Lights.)

SCENE 10

Afternoon. ESTHER *in the basement, reading a worn composition book.* MARY *enters.*

MARY I'm about to roll the dumplings, you wanna help?

ESTHER Nope.

MARY What are you reading?

ESTHER Ralph's poems, compositions, doodles and stuff. Have you seen these?

MARY Only what he reads to me aloud, I never wanted to snoop.

ESTHER The centerpiece is an ongoing series of epic poems. In iambic pentameter. All about this mutant space alien child trapped on earth with an assortment of special abilities, but he can't figure out how to use them.

MARY Sounds pretty interesting.

ESTHER Yeah the first couple hundred pages or so focus mostly on the kid's fish-out-of-water-type misadventures where he just doesn't fit into the world, but more recently he's gone off though the galaxy in search of his father.

MARY Huh.

ESTHER The space alien doesn't have a sister.

MARY Does he have a mother?

ESTHER He does, actually. An adoptive Asiatic earth mother who discovers him in a rice paddy as a foundling infant to raise him as her own. She's benevolent and moral, a nurturer.

But ultimately quite permissive.

To his detriment, I think.

MARY I see.

ESTHER "And once the Nub did find his way to earth" . . .

that's what he calls the kid, he calls him a "Nub."

"And once the Nub did find his way to earth,

He fell upon a field of rice and wood.

An earthling woman brought him home and hearth

This foundling super Nub who could be good."

MARY   Can I see?

ESTHER   I thought you didn't want to snoop.

MARY   Oh, right.

ESTHER   How long are you gonna let him live down here?

MARY   As long as he needs to.

ESTHER   What about Dad? Are you gonna what, let *him* stay in the basement too, live rent-free and act like a baby, become a science fiction poet himself?

MARY   Esther.

ESTHER   They just get to break things and break things, don't they? And then you just make them sandwiches, let 'em go off in my car to go have fun, so now what am I supposed to do?

MARY   What do you want to do?

ESTHER   I wanna go home.

MARY   Isn't this home?

ESTHER   Not really, Mom, no.

I shouldn't have come.

MARY   I'm glad you did.

ESTHER   You seem to have found a way to occupy yourselves without me.

MARY   What's that supposed to mean?

ESTHER: One of my therapists once told me that I lack a definable pattern, I've just hopped from one set of obligations to the next, so I don't mind if you oblige me to behave a certain way, I'll try it, just tell me what I'm supposed to do.

MARY: You can do anything you want.

ESTHER: Oh really? Anything, well, wouldn't that be nice? Okay, great, you think I wouldn't have loved to drive up to the airport in a decent car? With a husband who could be appropriately polite and tell Dad a bunch of nice stories about all the great stuff I've done, how I, just . . . Just, forget it.

(Silence.)

MARY: You know, when your father left, *my* mother was furious with me for not going with him.

ESTHER: What?

MARY: Well, that's what I was supposed to do, after all.

My husband was going home, I was supposed to go with him, and take you kids with me.

ESTHER: Wait.

MARY: Of course I didn't want that. It wasn't the best thing for you, either, you were still in school, it was an easy decision to make at the time, but after a while . . .

I mean, Esther, I can't tell you what's best for you.

But you don't have to just do what you're supposed to, don't you know that?

ESTHER: Well gee, Mom, I don't know, because right now it looks like you're just doing what he tells you. He comes wandering back through the dust and guess what, he gets a party.

MARY: Oh Esther. You think I'm just doing this because he told me to?

ESTHER: Well, yeah.

MARY No, I asked him to come.

ESTHER Wait, what?

MARY I asked him. This isn't just for your father, don't you understand? It's for you. Ralph and David. I mean, you've read these books, Ralph's poems, you see what's in these. He has powers, things inside him that he doesn't know how to use, and needs to find his father to show him how.

Alright fine, I've read them. I wasn't snooping, he wanted me to see them, I mean he lays the notebook on the kitchen counter open to specific pages.

He wants me to help him find his father. To help him find himself. And when a boy can say that, and feel that, and put it face up on the countertop for everyone to see, well doesn't it make you think you might want that for yourself?

ESTHER Want what?

MARY To face the thing that made you. To make it see you.

(Silence.)

Think about it.

Anyway, come help me roll the dumplings, alright?

(Silence.)

You like dumplings, don't you?

ESTHER Stupid.

Everybody likes dumplings.

(MARY goes up the stairs. ESTHER stays looking at the staircase. Linger. Lights.)

SCENE 11

MARY holds a small cup.

MARY   We've all done things we're proud of, and things we're not.

Today, I hope you can reflect on the best of times—like our first years in America, so suddenly arrived. We were around the same age as our children are now, so we had the luxury then of imagining we might make of our lives whatever we dared to.

It's been a long time. I'm glad we could be together on such a meaningful day. One that allows you to consider not just where you've been, but where you are, right now.

And right now, you're here with us.

I'm proud of the fact we're still here, in this house we used to share.

I'm proud of our children.

Look at them.

And let yourself be proud too.

And if there are things you're ashamed of, well then let yourself be ashamed as well.

And we'll go from there.

Hwangap chook-ah hab-nee-dah.

    (*She drinks. Lights.*)

SCENE 12

On a lake, in a fishing boat. Probably about an hour from sunset. CHUN *and* RALPH. *Lines in the water.*

CHUN   Good to sometimes coming here and fishing, line in the water. Eat sandwiches from plastic baggie, put on unusual hat for sunblocking, things of this nature. I used to do this after work sometimes, your mother at home and me so stress out from the bastards in engineering, the HR fuckwads, out here this is nothing like this.

	Out here is just self and artificial catgut fishing line, water away from desert, fish don't talk back or nagging, so good for calm.
RALPH	It's nice.
CHUN	Is important to be calm.
RALPH	I know.
CHUN	You scared your sister, you know, with this throwing video games into crashing on floor and everything.
RALPH	Yeah, I'm sorry Dad.
CHUN	You know what Ralphie, I think is okay. Sometimes is not big deal to scare Esther, she maybe kind of a little how you say tightass.
RALPH	Yeah.
CHUN	What a man does, Ralph, what he does is okay sometimes to say hell with it, I am what I am.
RALPH	I am what I am.
CHUN	There are things man is have to do that woman is know nothing about.
RALPH	Like what?
CHUN	Like you know, carry things on his back and and, yes and things of this nature.
RALPH	Uh-huh.
CHUN	Man must be strong. Be unafraid of anger if he is have it. I don't criticize what you did by throw video games this afternoon, I think sometimes video game machine or whatever is in your way, sometimes objects such as this, they have it coming.
RALPH	I can see that.
CHUN	You were angry.
RALPH	I was upset I guess.
CHUN	You were mad about something particular?

RALPH	Sometimes I do things and I don't remember why I did them, know what I mean?
CHUN	Yeah.
RALPH	You do?
CHUN	It happens.
RALPH	I guess it does.
CHUN	How long have you living in Mommy basement, Ralphie?
RALPH	Um. I guess since my nervous situation. You know about my nervous situation?
CHUN	Hard not to notice, Ralph.
RALPH	Right.
CHUN	What happened to you?
RALPH	I just kind of cracked out I suppose, I'd just as soon not talk about it.
CHUN	Why?
RALPH	Important to be calm and it riles me to talk about it, I'd rather keep my focus on the fishing.
CHUN	I see.
RALPH	They're not biting, are they?
	(Silence.)
CHUN	Do you think is my fault, Ralphie?
RALPH	Sometimes I just, I have so much feeling, Dad. I get this head full of much too much, and I lose control. I'm like some kind of werebeast. Or a mutant child with an empathic superpower, I can harness the pain and the joy of the entire world. A type of lycanthropy controlled by the moon or the tides, like I'm the devil. I can be so good but oh man I can be so bad as well.
CHUN	I don't understand.

RALPH	I'm an engineer.	
CHUN	No shit.	
RALPH	I have a Master's in Nanotech.	
CHUN	You wanted be like me?	
RALPH	No.	
CHUN	Oh.	
RALPH	After grad school I tried to get a job, but one day I woke up from this dream in which a girl I was apparently seeing (but only in the dream, I had no girl at the time), woke me from another dream to tell me she had been back from a trip to Ecuador. It really bothered me that I had missed it, and I got so angry at this fictional girlfriend that when I woke up for real I went to the airport and flew to Ecuador myself.	
CHUN	Wait, in a dream?	
RALPH	No, this was real, this part. I flew to Ecuador.	
CHUN	You did this really?	
RALPH	I did. And only after the long flight did I realize I'd lost my way.	
CHUN	I know this feeling.	
RALPH	You do?	
CHUN	Oh yeah.	
RALPH	Mom had to fly down and get me. I've been in the basement ever since. But I wish I'd stayed in Ecuador, you know. Because when I think about it Dad, I think about it and I wanna live in the world.	
CHUN	Yeah.	
RALPH	Dad I want you to know who I am!	
CHUN	I want to know that too.	
RALPH	I'm trying to tell you who I am!	

CHUN I'm listening, Ralphie.

RALPH Do you understand?

CHUN Ralphie, I . . .

RALPH Do you?

CHUN . . . No.

>   *(Silence.)*

>   Ralph. Do you like living in Mommy basement?

RALPH Well yeah.

CHUN Really?

RALPH Well yeah, I mean, no not so much, really I guess, no.

CHUN What do you like?

>   *(Silence.)*

RALPH I like this fishing.

CHUN You do?

RALPH I wish we'd come here sooner.

>   *(Silence.)*

CHUN There's no fish.

>   *(Silence.)*

RALPH It doesn't matter.

>   *(They sit, lines in the water. Linger. Lights.)*

SCENE 13

Front porch swing. Around sunset. ESTHER *stands, leaning and smoking a cigarette.* CHUN *enters. A silence.*

ESTHER I know you and Mom've been hittin' it.

CHUN   What?

ESTHER   Hittin' it. I know you've been like, you know, *together*.

CHUN   Oh.

ESTHER   So what's that about?

CHUN   You shouldn't smoke.

ESTHER   I know you want one.

CHUN   Can I?

ESTHER   No.

(Silence. She gives him the pack, he takes one.)

CHUN   Can I get a light?

ESTHER   You can suck my butt.

(She hands him her lit cigarette butt, he uses it to light his. Hands it back, a silence as they smoke.)

ESTHER   You wanna know what else I found out?

CHUN   What?

ESTHER   All that crap about you coming home to repair your obsolescent ass, turns out that was all lies.

CHUN   What are you talking about?

ESTHER   You didn't come back for me, didn't come back for your family, you came back because Mom told you to. Didn't you?

CHUN   So what?

ESTHER   What do you mean, so what?

CHUN   I came back for *me*, Esther. You have to understand. I came for myself.

ESTHER   Yeah I got that.

CHUN   Can I ask you something?

ESTHER Don't ask me if you can ask me something. I hate that.

CHUN What?

ESTHER If you ask me if you can ask me something, then you're already asking me something. If you were really worried about whether or not asking me something was somehow an inconvenience or presumptive, then you wouldn't ask me the question of whether you can ask, would you?

CHUN You get upset, Esther, about strangest things.

ESTHER Yeah well.

CHUN Yell at me about ask question, what's the matter with you?

ESTHER What's the matter with you!

CHUN Such a child.

ESTHER Oh am I.

CHUN You are.

ESTHER Alright, drop it then.

CHUN Fine.

ESTHER What's your question then?

CHUN Never mind.

ESTHER Just ask the question.

CHUN No.

ESTHER What's the question?

CHUN I forgot.

(They smoke.)

Oh okay, I remember now.

ESTHER So?

CHUN — Are you angry because I left, or because I come back? Which one is worser one?

ESTHER — That's a stupid question.

CHUN — Is it?

(ESTHER *puts out her cigarette.*)

ESTHER — You know, the second man I married, Dad, he was just like you.

CHUN — Was he.

ESTHER — We had a baby.

CHUN — You . . . ?

ESTHER — We had a baby and I didn't want you to know, you didn't deserve it.

CHUN — Esther.

ESTHER — I lost that baby, Dad, and I lost my fucking mind.

That baby came out of me cold, do you get it? I lost him and I know that happens, couples lose babies and I know that.

But I'd already given him a name.

I'd bought sheets, toys, books, and a car seat, BabyBjörn and all that bullshit for the little guy and he was gone.

And we were gonna try again, because that's what you're supposed to do is try again, but I couldn't touch my stupid husband. I didn't want him near me. He smelled like you. And he walked like you. This husband and surrogate you.

So which was worse, the coming or the going? That was the question, right? Well it's actually a good question now that I think about it.

I wasn't unhappy when you left Dad, truly.

I wasn't unhappy until I realized what it meant that you left.

Because I wanted a family so badly.

And couldn't get one.

And you had it all the time.

Had it right here.

And you didn't care.

(She goes back into the house. Lights.)

SCENE 14

Night. CHUN *in the dining room.* DAVID *in his office. They phone.*

CHUN	Had hoped you would come around.
DAVID	Well, Dad, things are pressing here.
CHUN	We have cake.
DAVID	I heard.
CHUN	You do okay up there, New York?
DAVID	Well, we do our best.
CHUN	You are have some girlfriend?
DAVID	Yeah I have some of those.
CHUN	Oh good.
DAVID	Wish I could be there, Pop, really do.
CHUN	Still time.
DAVID	How's that?
CHUN	We had looking it up on Internet. Flights from New York still coming, redeye for way back too possible, one at 8:15 arrive here just before 11, there is time difference so is okay.
DAVID	8:15's not a good time, Pop, I can't squeeze in a redeye tonight.
CHUN	Then maybe next week I can come to New York.
DAVID	Yeah maybe you can. How's the weather down there, fella?

CHUN	Dry.
DAVID	Should be good, should be good.
CHUN	How is job?
DAVID	It's righteous, Pop.
CHUN	What's that?
DAVID	It rules. I'm King of the World six days a week, I got money falling out of my asshole, that's what you want to hear?
CHUN	I want to hear you are happy.
DAVID	Happy, what's that?
CHUN	I wish I could see your face, can't uh decipher your, your tone.
DAVID	My tone is on purpose evasive, Pop, that's one of my trade skills.
CHUN	Oh.
DAVID	See, I'm wearing a robe of red Italian silk right now, smoking Cuban cigars with some leggy blondes who wanna get up on this.
CHUN	That doesn't tell me anything. Think of me, David. I have no home, no car no horse. I have a bag of belongings that wouldn't hurt your shoulders were it strapped to your back for days, and yet I'm happy.
DAVID	Oh are you?
CHUN	A little.
DAVID	I'm not so sure I get the concept.
CHUN	I know this tone now.
DAVID	Is that right.
CHUN	I know this tone you speak with me, it is pretend to be cold.
DAVID	Wait you think I'm pretending?
CHUN	Afraid to see me.

DAVID   Oh I see.

CHUN   Afraid to come see me, afraid to speak on phone, this is why finally you are call back after so many yes I'll try to and probably I will be there but now finally you are call too late to arrive but this is not talking. Come home, David.

DAVID   No thanks.

CHUN   I need to explaining more better to you, everybody coming to me, telling me of their disappointment, their upset, but I need to telling myself too.

DAVID   I got another call here, Dad.

CHUN   One second. Because you see. My brother, he is big man in Korea, making buildings, apartment and shopping stores, and when he were sixty like me now, his *hwangap* was massive with buildings he had constructed, markings on the earth, he can say *I built this*. Engineer he was too, like I was engineer, but I had build only tiny cogs in tiny machines, not by my blueprint. I look at *janche* and who is there? I have only thing to show for this life, what I have made, just you David. I made you, to become what I could not be. Come home. David. Come home. Come home. Come home.

DAVID   You made me?

CHUN   Yes.

DAVID   Well, yeah, Dad, but by your blueprint, you made me to leave you.

CHUN   . . . What?

DAVID   No, Dad, I'm not happy. But I don't hate you, I just don't fucking care. Okay? Because when you left I learned to be a man. I guess you changed since then, chief, but I didn't. I'm not sure if it's really what you wanted me to be, but I know what I became.

CHUN   Come home.

DAVID   I became this.

CHUN   Come home.

DAVID   I became this.

>   (DAVID *hangs up.* CHUN *puts the phone down, does not hang it up. The bleat of the disconnect.*)

SCENE 15

> CHUN *stands in a suit and tie.* RALPH, *in his hanbok, sits with* ESTHER *and* MARY *at the dining-room table, each with a small cup. A birthday cake, plates, dishes, and a bottle of soju.*

CHUN   I thank you my family for wonderful *hwangap janche*. Thanks Ralphie for wonderful birthday book, which talking about astrology, you know. And this book such beautiful book because it is tell story all about who we are.

You know I was born sixty years ago. Same also is Korea. This is year of Korean independence, so like me these are countries sixty years old, one whole lifetime. And same as with me this country was create division within itself, broken to two separate countries in which family was divided.

But now I have come back. When first I left, I was maybe little bit . . . I left because things were taken from me, small things, my job, my pride, but when I left I lost much bigger thing. I see now that I left behind much better life here that I could have lived.

I was not allowed *hwangap janche* in Korea. My brother tells me I cannot have *janche* without wife, without children, in Korea I cannot stand up and say I lived a life when was fill so full of shame. I cannot call myself a man.

But when you are sixty you can have much bigger party than what I have now. I want you each of you children when you are sixty to stand in real your home, with family you desire, to look back on sixty years you lived and feel proud, okay? Not like me.

And to my oldest son David, who is not come to me, well maybe I will come to you. If there is a way to prove myself to you, then I will do this way.

But I thank you for spending such a day with such a man.

(He picks up a small cup.)

First drink in long time.

(MARY picks up the bottle of soju, pours with both hands.)

Thank you my family.

(He drinks. He takes the bottle from MARY; she doesn't stop him. She turns back to the table and begins to clear the plates. RALPH and ESTHER help her, in no rush. CHUN turns his back as they exit. He drinks straight from the bottle now. Lights.)

SCENE 16

Night. ESTHER outside, keys in one hand, phone in the other. She talks to DAVID.

DAVID	What'd you eat?
ESTHER	At least one of everything on the table, damn that woman can cook.
DAVID	Mother's milk.
ESTHER	I wish you'd been here.
DAVID	Chin up, sweetheart. You made it through, birthday's over right? They say the ones still standing after, you know what they call 'em?
ESTHER	What's that?
DAVID	The "winners of the party."
ESTHER	Hooray.
DAVID	Means you can go home now.

(Silence.)

Head held high, you can go home with dignity.

(Silence.)

	Esther? You still there?
ESTHER	Yeah I'm still here.
DAVID	Oh, thought I lost you for a second.
ESTHER	I'm feelin' kinda funny.
DAVID	Yeah, too much Korean food'll do that.
ESTHER	Can I call you back later, David? I think I need to get out of here.
DAVID	You sound a little iffy there, sweetie, why don't you tell me what's up?
ESTHER	I'll call you in the morning.
DAVID	No, don't.
ESTHER	What?
DAVID	Morning's no good, I got you know meetings and shit, let's just talk now.
ESTHER	I was just getting in the car when you called, I feel like I wanna like go somewhere.
DAVID	You sound a little down, tell me what's on your mind.
ESTHER	I'm not down.
DAVID	Are you sure?
ESTHER	Yeah.
DAVID	Really?
ESTHER	Yeah.
DAVID	Good.
ESTHER	Well see ya later then.
DAVID	Yeah okay.
ESTHER	Alright.

DAVID   G'bye.

(Silence.)

ESTHER   You still there?

DAVID   Yeah.

ESTHER   Yeah me too.

DAVID   Wanna hear something funny?

ESTHER   I guess.

DAVID   You know when I got out of college, I went off for some internship, before you married that guy Richard?

ESTHER   Yeah.

DAVID   I gave you some excuse when I got to the wedding, the reason I missed your rehearsal dinner and barely showed up in time.

ESTHER   I was just glad you were there, I don't remember the excuse.

DAVID   You wanna know what really happened?

ESTHER   Do I?

DAVID   Well, I left the office on my last day and went to the airport to fly home, but when I got there I had an idea. I traded in my ticket for a roundtrip overnight to Seoul.

ESTHER   Hold on.

DAVID   The best wedding gift an older brother could give. I was gonna find the old man and bring him home, bolt through the doors of the church and let him give you away.

ESTHER   David—

DAVID   That would've been something, huh?

(Silence.)

ESTHER   It would have.

(Silence.)

DAVID   So anyway I land in Seoul and look up our cousin Sunman, you know the one who speaks perfect English?

ESTHER   Oh yeah, the fat one?

DAVID   Yeah, figured he could help me track the old man down, but it wasn't quite that easy.

ESTHER   What do you mean?

DAVID   When he told me where your father was, I beat the living shit out of him.

ESTHER   Oh.

DAVID   Your father was in prison. He wasn't working for his brother like he said. He was doing six months, for doing the same thing I did.

ESTHER   What?

DAVID   I ended up in prison myself until that fat fucker Sunman dropped the charges. And as I sat there in a South Korean jail cell, I said look at me. My father is in jail. I'm in jail. And I will not become my father.

ESTHER   David, you didn't.

DAVID   I will not become my father.

(Silence.)

Esther, are you still there?

ESTHER   Yeah I'm still here, David, I just, I don't know what to say.

DAVID   You still feel like going somewhere?

ESTHER   I don't know.

DAVID   Where do you want to go?

ESTHER   I thought something might occur to me if I just started driving.

DAVID   Feel like going further?

ESTHER   Where?

DAVID	New York maybe?	

(Silence.)

ESTHER	Yeah.
DAVID	Yeah?
ESTHER	I'll go to the airport.
DAVID	You don't have classes?
ESTHER	I'll take the absences.
DAVID	I'll totally pay for the flight, take a cab when you touch down, you know the address?
ESTHER	Of course.
DAVID	Oh. Good. And don't worry either, I'll be here when you land. I don't really have meetings in the morning.
ESTHER	Yeah.
DAVID	I made all that up.
ESTHER	I know, David.
DAVID	Cool.
ESTHER	I know.

(They do not hang up. Lights.)

SCENE 17

CHUN in a tree. It's late. His tie is loosened, his shirt untucked. He's singing, probably something traditionally Korean, and drinking from a fifth of Jim Beam. He's having a great time up there. MARY enters.

MARY	So there you are.
CHUN	Saw the tree and I clumb it. Wanna come up too?
MARY	Why don'tcha come down.

CHUN   Hell no, is nice up here.

MARY   Really.

CHUN   Best tree ever.

MARY   You sure I can't convince you to come down?

CHUN   Actually I been wanting get down for about an hour now but I don't think I can.

MARY   Is that bottle empty?

CHUN   Nope little bit left.

MARY   Maybe I'll have one with you.

CHUN   Up in tree?

MARY   No I'll stay down here, just pass it to me.

(He screws the lid on it, throws the bottle down, she catches it. Doesn't drink, just sets it on the ground.)

CHUN   Oh. Okay.

Good party.

MARY   Yeah, you clean up alright.

CHUN   Pants a little tight for some reason.

MARY   Well, they hung in my closet fifteen years, I guess you've put on some baggage.

CHUN   Fuck it.

(He takes off the pants and throws them out of the tree.)

MARY   Nice.

CHUN   Wooot!

MARY   Hey, you're gonna wake the neighbors, you know.

CHUN   How old you are?

MARY   You don't know how old I am?

CHUN   Fifty-nine.

MARY   Fifty-eight.

CHUN   Ah, almost like me.

MARY   Oh I don't know about that.

CHUN   Pretty fucking cool to be sixty. Look at me here, no pants full of Jim Beam and sitting in tree, night Texas wind all around and still can see mountains though it's dark.

MARY   You're old.

CHUN   Bullshit. Because sixty years is rebirth, when Zodiac ends is a baby born anew. You know I'm Year of the Cock. Wood Cock.

MARY   I'll bet you are.

CHUN   No really, Year of Wood Cock and then twelve years of each every animal, five elements Wood Cock twelve years then Earth Cock twelve Fire Cock Metal Cock Water Cock twelve each and this is first year in all whole sixty my life is Wood Cock again.

MARY   Okay then.

CHUN   I'm reborn!

MARY   Oh?

CHUN   First day of new my life!

(He almost falls out of the tree.)

Oops.

MARY   I really think you should get down from there.

CHUN   Marry me, Mary.

MARY   What.

CHUN   Marry me, alright?

MARY   Shut your drunk face.

CHUN   If I were earthbound I would fall on my knee, I want you be my wife again.

MARY   I'm gonna go get you a ladder and some coffee, okay?

CHUN   Check left-hand pocket of pants down there.

MARY   No.

CHUN   Check it.

MARY   Why?

CHUN   Just check inside the goddamn pocket.

(She does, inside is a ring box, she opens it. A ring.)

MARY   What the hell is that.

CHUN   It's a ring.

MARY   Yeah I can see that.

CHUN   So now you know this is not just stupid drunk question, but whole thing quite premeditated.

MARY   I'm not gonna marry you, idiot!

CHUN   Yes you are.

MARY   This isn't cute.

CHUN   Yes it is.

MARY   You don't know what you're talking about!

CHUN   Yes I do. Because I was so broken in Korea. Whole time I wanted to come back, but I didn't want you see me so full of shame. But now, after this *hwangap* I am happy again.

MARY   You're happy after that?

CHUN   Almost. Because when you said to me this is not my home. Yes. But I have a plan.

MARY   A plan.

CHUN   Mm. Step one, you marry me.

MARY   Wow.

CHUN   Step two is I will be such best husband this time. We can do whatever you want, like this flamingo dance or whatever, things we did when first we married, like um, like you know things of this nature. Holding hands and watching sun set, sit on front porch every nighttime forever till we die.

MARY   That's romantic.

CHUN   Oh yeah. You'll see. Together all the time, I'll be hanging around you constantly. Always talking talking talking, no matter what you're doing, you will never be alone. I'll be talking talking talking all the time.

MARY   Oh my god you poor man.

CHUN   Why, whatsa matter?

MARY   What do you expect me to say to this?

CHUN   I hope that please you can just say yes, yes, you will marry me. Mary.

Because you are most number one best thing for me.

When you said to me, come back. When you told me this, it means we can start over, not from when I left, not from when I became bad husband, bad father, but to beginning of America when still we had all whole world in front of us, because sixty years is rebirth! Step three of plan is I'm a baby now! Waaah!

MARY   I don't wanna hear any more of this plan.

CHUN   Okay, well that was last step of plan anyway.

(MARY goes to the bottle of Beam, picks it up.)

You know, I am okay to try different plan. If maybe this one you don't like.

(She unscrews the cap on the bottle.)

Um. Is there anything about it you like?

(She takes a drink.)

MARY: I like the notion you're a baby.

CHUN: Wah.

MARY: Yeah.

(She sets the bottle on the ground.)

You'd almost make sense if you were somehow still an infant.

CHUN: You can be a baby too, we can each be each other's baby.

MARY: Oh no. Not for me. I did what I needed to, when I hit sixty I get to be *old*. I'm looking forward to that. But you, you have to try again.

Here's a place to start: The only thing a baby needs to know is who loves them. Not who they love, but who loves them.

(She stands on tiptoes and holds the ring box out to him.)

CHUN: Maybe I'll just hold on to it a while.

MARY: Alright.

(He takes the ring.)

CHUN: In case you know, you change your mind.

MARY: You want a ladder now?

CHUN: In a minute.

(She sits, her back at the root of the tree.)

What do you want to talk about now?

MARY: Let's just sit. Let's don't talk.

(They sit. Don't talk. Lights.)

SCENE 18

The wee hours, basement. CHUN *still in his suit, shirt untucked, tie loosened. No pants, but the long Korean pjs. He's playing videogames.* RALPH *wakes.*

RALPH   Whatcha doin', Dad?

CHUN   Saving humanity from resurrected dead people bodies.

RALPH   Oh. What time is it?

CHUN   Dunno.

RALPH   So how's it, I mean how's it going?

CHUN   I think zombies gonna win.

RALPH   Yeah that's a hard level.

CHUN   Shit I died.

RALPH   Yeah that'll happen.

           (He sets the controller to the machine on the couch beside him.)

CHUN   Had fun tonight?

RALPH   Yeah, good party.

CHUN   I could use a drink.

RALPH   I have Juicy Juice juice boxes.

CHUN   What?

RALPH   Here.

           (RALPH gets juice boxes, gives him one.)

CHUN   How do I do this?

RALPH   Yeah you gotta pop the straw in the hole.

CHUN   Strawinthahole?

           (RALPH does it for him.)

CHUN   Oh.

(They drink.)

RALPH: You want me to play you a song on the guitar?

CHUN: No.

RALPH: Okay.

CHUN: Son?

RALPH: Yeah, Pop?

CHUN: How well you are know your mother?

RALPH: Pretty well I guess.

CHUN: Mm. Okay. Well maybe you can helping me.

RALPH: With what?

CHUN: I have idea on maybe how to make your Mommy marry me.

RALPH: No shit.

CHUN: Need some advice. So. What kind of things your mother like?

RALPH: Like what do you mean?

CHUN: Go to movie, basketball game or things of this nature, what kind of things I can doing to you know wooing her?

RALPH: Oh.

CHUN: Whatever you can helping with I am appreciate.

RALPH: Well she likes cooking shows.

CHUN: What shows?

RALPH: Cooking shows. TV programs with average looking people in a kitchen sharing recipes.

CHUN: They are just cook?

RALPH: It seems to make her happy when I eat a lot. It's an easy way to make her happy, she makes the food and I eat it, works out good for everyone.

CHUN	So just I eat and this is make her happy?	
RALPH	There was a guy I think his name was Norman, I think he was like a white guy. He tried to take her white water rafting once and she came back all mad and I never saw him again after that, so my advice is to not take her white water rafting.	
CHUN	Okay good to know.	
RALPH	So you're going after Mom then, huh?	
CHUN	Gonna try.	
RALPH	Where you gonna stay?	
CHUN	Well thought I might wanna talk to you about this, Ralph.	
RALPH	Yeah?	
CHUN	I think you need to moving out of Mommy basement, okay?	
RALPH	What?	
CHUN	Okay?	
RALPH	You mean like now?	
CHUN	Yeah. Because I'm gonna need to living in Mommy basement now, okay?	
RALPH	Wait.	
CHUN	What do you think?	
RALPH	You're gonna live down here?	
CHUN	That's my plan. Try to work my way up.	
RALPH	That sounds awesome.	
CHUN	Maybe hopefully.
	But you gotta go.
	(Silence.)
	When does cast come off?

RALPH   Ten to fourteen days.

CHUN   Okay this is good timeframe.

RALPH   Wait what?

CHUN   After ten to fourteen days, you should find your own place.

RALPH   Okay.

CHUN   What?

RALPH   I said okay.

CHUN   Really?

RALPH   I can do that.

CHUN   Wow.

RALPH   What?

CHUN   That was easier than I thought would be.

   (Silence.)

   Wait, are you sure?

RALPH   Yeah.

CHUN   Wait but hold on Ralphie, I don't know about this.

RALPH   What's the problem?

CHUN   I mean look at you, where you gonna live, what you're gonna do?

RALPH   Well I'm gonna be in this band called The Love Song of J. Alfred Punk Rock.

CHUN   Huh?

RALPH   Peter's brother, he's the drummer, he has a house where the whole band lives, they practice there too, it's pretty cool and they said I could live there if I wanted but I guess I just wasn't ready or whatever.

CHUN   Oh.

RALPH: It's actually just down the street.

CHUN: Oh.

RALPH: But that's awesome 'cause I mean I'd like to like, see you, Dad.

CHUN: Okay.

RALPH: I mean I thought that if you were around and stuff, maybe you and I, we could maybe go fishing again or something.

(Silence.)

CHUN: Would like this too, very much, Ralph.

RALPH: You want me to play you a song on the guitar?

CHUN: No.

RALPH: Okay.

(Silence. They drink their Juicy Juice.)

CHUN: On second thought yeah.

RALPH: What?

CHUN: Play me a song, Ralph.

(RALPH runs to the guitar. He plays. CHUN listens. After a few bars, he starts to hum, maybe sing along, or clap in a steady rhythm. RALPH's playing might not be skilled, but it might be beautiful.)

— END OF PLAY —

HONGBU AND NOLBU
THE TALE OF THE MAGIC PUMPKINS
Jean Yoon

Jean Yoon. Photo by Tim Leyes.

Jean Yoon is an actor, playwright, and poet. Born in Champaign, Illinois, in 1962, she moved to Toronto, the city she now calls home, at age three. After receiving her degree in literary studies at the University of Toronto, she began her career in theater as an actor. Faced with inequity in theater, she became motivated to work toward improving opportunities for theater artists of diverse cultures. She worked for the Theatre Ontario and was the Co-Artistic Director of Cahoots Theatre Projects in Toronto. She served three years on the Second Advisory to the Canada Council on Racial Equality in the Arts. In 1995, she began to write plays and founded the performance group Loud Mouth Asian Babes, which Yoon described as "Kimchi-hot theatre for the culturally confused." Her plays include *Sliding for Home & Borders, Spite,* and the multimedia show *The Yoko Ono Project,* which was nominated for a Dora Mavor Moore Award for Outstanding New Play in 2000. She has an extensive list of acting credits and has worked with Tarragon Theatre, Crows Theatre, Theatre Passe Muraille, Cahoots Theatre Projects, Canasian Artists Group, Toronto Free Theatre, Civilized Theatre, Die in Debt, Necessary Angel, Factory Theatre, and Soulpepper Theatre. *Hongbu and Nolbu: The Tale of the Magic Pumpkins* (2005) started as a birthday gift to her friends' seven-year-old daughter, after which the story was further developed and commissioned by the Lorraine Kimsa Theatre for Young People (also known as Young Peoples Theatre) in Toronto. Yoon's desire was to create a play accessible to young audiences but that would also have a special appeal to both Korean Canadian and general adult audiences.

Hongbu and Nolbu: The Tale of the Magic Pumpkins premiered on the main stage of the Lorraine Kimsa Theatre for Young People (Allen MacInnis, artistic director) on April 14, 2005. It was directed by Allen MacInnis; the set design and the costume design were by Julia Tribe; the lighting design was by Lesley Wilkinson; the stage manager was Robert Harding; and the assistant stage manager was Patricia Levert. Debashis Sinha was the composer and percussionist; Charles Hong was the consultant for Korean dance and drumming; and Mike Petersen was the consultant for puppetry. The cast was as follows:

Mira / Farmer's Wife / Swallow / Story-Teller / Debt Collector / Mangy Monster.............. Nina Lee Aquino

Nolbu / Young Boy / Swallow Queen / Child / Architect .... Insurp Choi

Hongbu / Baby / Swallow Queen / Smelly Piggy Thief / Two-Headed Mangy Monster ..... Richard Lee

Myung-Mi / Old Man / Swallow / Story-Teller / Child................................ Jane Luk

This play was originally performed by four actors playing multiple roles, with two roles, the Swallow and the Swallow Queen, played by different actors in the first and second half. Many of the characters, such as the Old Man, the Farmer's Wife, the Swallow, and the Swallow Queen are delivered in mask, reflecting the style of the Korean Farmers Dance Dramas. The children are corn-husk dolls animated by the actors. The Two-Headed Mangy Monster is played by two actors who divide/share/overlap their lines.

The tone of the play is light, whimsical, and folksy.

Sound and music play a large role, with live sound effects throughout created vocally by the actors, and with instruments and toys such as drums, rattles, Korean violin, chimes, gongs, and flutes. Korean *Samul Nori* drumming serves as the base musical reference.

Wherever possible, techniques that children could themselves create are preferred over high-tech effects.

CHARACTERS

    NOLBU, the greedy elder brother
    HONGBU, the kind-hearted younger brother
    MIRA, HONGBU's wife
    MYUNG-MI, NOLBU's wife, a comical shrew
    SWALLOW
    SWALLOW QUEEN
    FARMER'S WIFE
    OLD MAN
    ARCHITECT
    SMELLY PIGGY THIEF
    DEBT COLLECTOR
    TWO-HEADED MANGY MONSTER
    CHILDREN

SCENE 1: THE HAPPY FAMILY

Korean drumming. A rousing upbeat rhythm.

Four actors emerge with drums onto an empty stage. They assemble on stage, then don masks. The actor playing MYUNG-MI *puts on an "Old Man" mask. The actor playing* MIRA *takes the "Farmer's Wife" mask. The actor playing* NOLBU *is in a "Young Boy" mask, and* HONGBU *chooses the "Baby" mask.*

OLD MAN	Hanna! Dool! Set! [One! Two! Three!]
	(The actors strike a tableau: the happy family.)
	A long time ago, in a little country called Korea.
	(The YOUNG BOY *pulls out a Korean flag.)*
YOUNG BOY	Tae Han Mingook! Tae Han Mingook! Tae Han Mingook!
OLD MAN	There was a little boy named Nolbu.
YOUNG BOY	Nolbu was a very happy little boy because anything he wanted, his Omma and Appa gave him.
FARMER'S WIFE	Have another yummy persimmon, sweetie.

Richard Lee (left) and Insurp Choi (right) in the premiere of *Hongbu and Nolbu: The Tale of the Magic Pumpkins*, produced by the Lorraine Kimsa Theatre for Young People, Toronto. Photo by David Hawe.

YOUNG BOY	Mmm, nummy, perfect persimmon-ee.
OLD MAN	Then, one beautiful autumn day, a baby brother was born.
FARMER'S WIFE	Oh! Oooohh!
	(*The fourth actor, HONGBU, slides out from under the FARMER'S WIFE's skirt and is "born," breaks into a newborn baby cry, then immediately coos and goos.*)
OLD MAN	He was a cute kid. Easy-going, good-natured.
FARMER'S WIFE	Oh my little goochie poopy doo! Look at your little wiggledy piggledees! Let's name him Hongbu, dear.
OLD MAN	Hongbu. That's a good name for such a good little boy.

YOUNG BOY	Nolbu was not happy.

(The YOUNG BOY removes his mask and becomes NOLBU.)

NOLBU	This situation sucks!
OLD MAN	Nolbu-ya! You're a big brother now. It's your job to take care of little Hongbu now, understand?

(The FARMER'S WIFE takes a ball from NOLBU.)

NOLBU	What? What are you—? That's mine!
FARMER'S WIFE	You have to share, Nolbu. That's part of being a big brother.

(She gives the ball to HONGBU, who coos happily.)

What a good boy you are, Hongbu! Nolbu, you watch your brother.

(The FARMER'S WIFE and OLD MAN exit. HONGBU plays contentedly while NOLBU looks on. Then NOLBU takes the ball back. HONGBU starts to cry.)

NOLBU	Okay, okay! Geez! Here.

(NOLBU gives the ball back to HONGBU, who is immediately thrilled. NOLBU storms off in frustration. HONGBU toddles after him.)

SCENE 2: STORM WATCHER

NOLBU is playing alone. HONGBU, age eight, runs on stage pulling a kite string.

HONGBU	Nolbu! Nolbu! Nolbu!
NOLBU	Hongbu! Would you like just quit bugging me!
HONGBU	Nolbu, you gotta check this out.
NOLBU	A kite!

HONGBU		I found it in a tree, just hanging there and it still works and everything! Look at it. It's awesome!
NOLBU		Let me try.
HONGBU		Sure.
NOLBU		I like the purple stripe. I'm gonna call it "Storm Watcher"!
HONGBU		Storm Watcher. That's an awesome name. Here, let me fly it for a bit.
NOLBU		No. If you fly it, you'll just wreck it and drive it right back into the tree or something. It's better this way.
HONGBU		But—
NOLBU		I'm your older brother. I know what I'm doing and you don't. Besides, you're supposed to do as I say.
HONGBU		But—
NOLBU		I'll let you *watch*, okay?
HONGBU		Okay.

(The two boys stare into the sky, watching the kite.)

NOLBU   Storm Watcher roves through the skies, dominating the heavens. He soars, powerful, magnificent and unchallenged—

(The SWALLOW sails into view and circles playfully around the kite.)

HONGBU   Look! A swallow! It's dancing with Storm Watcher.

NOLBU   Hey! Get away from my kite. Shoo! Scat! Scram!

HONGBU   No, don't make it go. It's beautiful! Come back Swallow, come back.

NOLBU   You're such a wuss.

HONGBU	Can I fly it now?	
NOLBU	No. Forget it. It's my kite now.	

SCENE 3: THE PROMISE

MYUNG-MI and MIRA enter and introduce their children, represented by rustic Korean dolls made of corn husks.

MYUNG-MI	Many, many years later, when the boys were all grown up, Nolbu married me, the bright, beautiful, and sophisticated city girl, Myung-Mi, and we had a smart handsome son.
MIRA	And Hongbu married me, Mira, and we had several children as well, and we all lived together in one house—
MYUNG-MI	One very small and modest house—
MIRA	—as all Korean families used to do.
NOLBU	Those are my chopsticks you're using.
HONGBU	Oh sorry. I—they all look the same to me.
NOLBU	Well, they're not. Those are mine.
MIRA	One day, when the sky was high and the horse was fat, when golden autumn leaves sashayed to the ground, after a huge meal of rice and kimchi and chicken and tender spinach and a whole bunch of other delicious and savory dishes, Appa lay down and called his two sons to his bedside.

(The OLD MAN lies down, weak and frail.)

OLD MAN	My sons, my sons. Listen carefully. You are brothers. Promise me you will take care of each other. Promise me.
HONGBU	I promise Appa.

NOLBU	I promise too, Appa.
OLD MAN	Good, good. You're good boys. If you take care of each other, I can sleep in peace.

(The OLD MAN pats both boys on the cheek, then lays down.)

NOLBU	Appa? Appa?
HONGBU	He's gone. Our Appa is gone . . .

(The "Old Man" mask slips off and the actor playing OLD MAN pulls away, leaving the mask, now the OLD MAN's emptied body. The actor transforms into the SWALLOW and sweeps down, dropping a flower on the OLD MAN's "body." The boys, weeping, gently remove the OLD MAN's "body.")

SCENE 4: FIGHT

MYUNG-MI, with a broom, sweeps the courtyard singing rowdily to herself. Children poke their heads from behind a wall, giggling.

MYUNG-MI   A few years later . . .

Arirang, arirang, ah-rah-ha-rii-yoh-ooo—ow!

(MYUNG-MI's been stung in the bum with a sling shot. She turns, annoyed, and the children duck, laughing.)

Aioo-cham. Kids!

(She resumes sweeping.)

Arirang, arirang, ah-rah-ha-rii-yoh-ooo—ow!

(And again, the children appear and she is struck in the bum with a slingshot. The children laugh and scurry.)

That's it. I've had it with you kids. Hongbu! Hongbu-yah.

(MYUNG-MI finds HONGBU and grabs him by the ear.)

HONGBU	Sister, sister, what's wrong?	
MYUNG-MI	I'm your older brother's wife. And that makes me boss over you. And right now, I want you, your wife, and your no-good kids out of this house right now. This place is barely big enough for one family, much less two. So pack up and ship out.	
NOLBU	Honey?	
MYUNG-MI	I've had it, Nolbu. Hongbu and his family have to leave. There's not enough room for four grown-ups, six kids, three cats, and a dog.	
NOLBU	But honey—	
MYUNG-MI	No buts! I can't take it anymore. I just can't take it. Oh honey, sweetheart, love of my life, you're the eldest son, you're the man of the house, your home is your castle. It's up to you to make the big decisions, and this is a big decision.	
NOLBU	That's right. This is a big decision. My home is my castle, I'm the man of the house, what I say goes. Hongbu, you're my brother, but let's face it, enough is enough. It's time for you and your family to leave. Sorry, but, well, you'll just have to find a new place to live.	

(MIRA *enters with the children and joins* HONGBU.)

HONGBU	Where? With what money? Where will we go? Everything we have is here.
NOLBU	That's just too bad. You have to go, Hongbu. There just isn't room for everybody. Just go on.
MYUNG-MI	You heard him. Go! Git! Scat and good riddance!

(HONGBU, MIRA, *and the children stand dejected.* MYUNG-MI *turns to her husband and begins to exit.*)

Oh my big man, you're such a hero-ey weeroh-wee!

SCENE 5: HARD TIMES

In the wilds. HONGBU, MIRA, *and the children enter now in rags.*

MIRA	Hongbu, how are we going to survive like this? We have no roof if it rains, no food, no protection from wild animals.
CHILD 1	I'm hungry, Omma!
CHILD 2	Me too! I'm cold and tired and hungry!!!!
CHILD 1	I wanna go home, Omma.
CHILD 2	Me too, I wanna go home! I wanna go home!
CHILD 1	Why can't we go home?
CHILD 2	I wanna go home. I wanna go home *now*!
MIRA	Hush, hush little ones. Yoboh?
HONGBU	It's all right, children. It's all right. This is home now. I'll build a fire and we'll be warm. I'll make a shelter from sticks, and we'll be safe. And even though we don't have real food we can always eat a delicious imaginary meal.
CHILD 1	An imaginary meal?
CHILD 2	What's that?
HONGBU	An imaginary meal. They're the best kind. To the untrained eye this is just a sack. But if you use your imagination this bag is really an entire pot of steaming white rice big enough to feed us all.
CHILD 1	Really? White rice?
MIRA	White rice. What I would do right now for a whole bowl of white rice.
CHILD 2	Me too. Me too. Me too. I want some too!

HONGBU: Here. Have some. Remember this is one great big mouthful.

CHILD 2: Mmmm. White rice.

CHILD 1: Mmm. Yummy rice.

(HONGBU *puts one grain into* MIRA's *mouth and into the mouths of each of his children.*)

HONGBU: Eat it slowly now. And as you're eating, imagine all the savory side dishes. Juicy bulgoki . . .

CHILD 2: Bulgoki . . .

HONGBU: Tangy kimchi . . .

CHILD 1: Oi kimchi?

HONGBU: Yes, Mom's special cucumber kimchi too.

CHILD 2: That's my favorite!

HONGBU: And a piece of fish that's so tender it breaks into little flakes.

CHILD 1: Oh boy oh boy oh boy!

MIRA: And tofu with shrimp, with my special garlic sauce. And glass noodles sauteed in sesame oil—

CHILD 2: And spinach! And bits of of of—

CHILD 1: Bits of carrots!

CHILD 2: And more bulgoki! Lots of it!

CHILD 1: Real sweet, juicy, bul-bul-bul-gogogo-waahhhh!!!! I want *real* bulgoki!

CHILD 2: Me too. Me too!!!! I want, I want, I want real rice!

CHILD 1: I want it now! I'm so hungry, Appa!

MIRA: Oh honey, this is hopeless. This imaginary meal is just

	making things worse. We're hungrier than ever. Imagination won't fill the children's bellies.
HONGBU	You stay here with the kids. I'll be back as soon as I can.
MIRA	Where are you going?
HONGBU	To find food. Real food to fill our bellies.

SCENE 6: HONGBU'S LONELY MARCH

HONGBU is walking alone, singing to himself. The SWALLOW flies by, a friendly presence.

HONGBU	In my hometown, there's food for all.
	The chopsticks are one hundred feet tall.
	No one goes hungry ever at all.
	No one is sad. Ever!
	Cuz we share all we have.
	Oh hello, Swallow. I wish I could eat insects too. Then I'd never go hungry.
	(The SWALLOW chirps and dances. HONGBU arrives at NOLBU's house.)
	Well. This is it. My brother's house. Wish me luck.
	(He peeks in the window.)

SCENE 7: THE HOUSE OF PLENTY

NOLBU and MYUNG-MI lounge after a very big meal.

NOLBU	Honey, that was delicious.
MYUNG-MI	There's still a whole plate of noodles left. I made it just the way you like it. Didn't you like it?

NOLBU   Oh honey, it was great, delicious. It just, well, I'm too full.

MYUNG-MI   You didn't like it.

                  (He slaps his belly. There's a huge resounding boom.)

NOLBU   You hear that? I'm stuffed.

MYUNG-MI   Have some more noodles anyway.

NOLBU   Just one more bite. Mmmm. Fantastic! Myung-Mi, darling, you're a culinary goddess!

MYUNG-MI   Ooo, now you're getting cheeky! I'll just clear the dishes, then . . .

                  (MYUNG-MI exits. HONGBU steps in.)

NOLBU   Honey, could you—. What the—! What are you doing here?

HONGBU   Nolbu, I—

NOLBU   Sneaking up like some kind of a thief—get out of here before I call my wife!

HONGBU   Nolbu, please, I've come a long way. My children are cold and hungry. I need food and money to buy them warm clothes. Please, if you could spare even a little? Just one bag of rice. Maybe a chicken so we can have eggs—

NOLBU   Food? You want food? Here, take these noodles. That's all you'll get. My wife cooked this. It's better than you deserve.

HONGBU   But Nolbu—

NOLBU   Do you want these noodles or not?

                  (HONGBU meekly takes the food and puts it in his sack.)

	Now get out, before my wife comes back and gives you the beating you deserve. Go on. Git!
HONGBU	You have so much, Nolbu, why can't you share?
NOLBU	I just gave you some noodles, what more do you want?
HONGBU	Forget it. Goodbye, brother.

(HONGBU *exits just as* MYUNG-MI *returns.*)

MYUNG-MI	Sweetheart, you finished the noodles!
NOLBU	How could I resist your kitchen-ry witchery. Come here you sweet thing, my special yummy wifey wifey.

SCENE 8: SWALLOW SHOWS THE WAY

HONGBU *makes the long journey back home. The* SWALLOW *follows along.*

HONGBU	What am I going to do? All I have to feed my family is this small pack of leftovers. It's barely enough for one meal for one person . . . And what about tomorrow and the day after that?

(HONGBU *sits down to rest. The* SWALLOW *alights at a distance and sings.*)

That's a pretty song, Swallow. If I could sing like you, I'd sing on the streets for money. Then I'd be rich for sure.

(*The* SWALLOW *sings and swoops with an odd urgency.* HONGBU *takes notice.*)

SWALLOW	(*Singing.*) Toragi, Toragi, To-oh-ra-gi . . .
HONGBU	What? What is it? Is something wrong?
SWALLOW	(*Singing.*) Toragi, Toragi, To-oh-ra-gi . . .

(HONGBU *rushes over to the* SWALLOW *and finds himself in a wonderful patch of wild vegetables.*)

HONGBU	Toragi!? Toragi! There's toragi everywhere!
	(The SWALLOW *flies to another area of the stage.* HONGBU *follows.)*
SWALLOW	*(Singing.)* Koguma, koguma, ko-gu-ma!
HONGBU	What?
SWALLOW	*(Singing.)* Koguma, koguma, ko-gu-ma!
HONGBU	Koguma!? Koguma! Wild sweet potatoes! This is what you were telling me. Oh thank you, Swallow! Thank you! With food like this my family can eat well, at least for tonight.

SCENE 9: HOMECOMING

MIRA and the children rush toward HONGBU, who shows all the food he has gathered. The family eats ravenously yet generously shares what little they have. They quickly finish everything.

CHILD 1	Mmmm! Koguma! And toragi!
CHILD 2	This is the best koguma ever in the whole history of the world.
CHILD 1	And the best toragi in the history of the universe. Ever. I could eat koguma and toragi all day long.
CHILD 2	Me too! All day. Deee-licious.
CHILD 1	Thank you, Mommy. That was so so yummy. Thank you Daddy . . .
CHILD 2	Thank you, Omma, thank you, Appa. Kamsahamnida.
CHILD 1	Komapsumnida.
MIRA	Here, let me wipe your face, little one.
CHILD 1	Mommy?
MIRA	Yes, dear.

CHILD 1	Mommy, is there, is there anymore?	
CHILD 2	Just a tiny little bit more?	
CHILD 1 and CHILD 2	We're still hungry.	
MIRA	There's no more today, little ones.	
CHILD 1	Oh.	
CHILD 2	Okay.	
MIRA	There'll be more tomorrow. I promise.	
HONGBU	Go to sleep now, little ones. There'll be more food tomorrow.	
CHILD 1	Okay. Goodnight.	
CHILD 2	Goodnight, Omma.	
CHILD 1	Goodnight, Appa.	
CHILD 1 and CHILD 2	Goodnight.	

(HONGBU and MIRA *exchange a worried look.*)

MIRA	(*Singing a lullaby.*) Cha-ah jang, Cha-ah jang
	Oori aeh-gi chajang . . . (*Whispering to* HONGBU.) They're asleep now . . .
	Your brother gave you nothing? No rice? No money to buy clothes for the children?
HONGBU	Nolbu has other worries.
MIRA	What worries? He has enough rice to last for years, and we helped plant and harvest it. Eugh! He's just a greedy, selfish goat.
HONGBU	Don't talk about him like that. He's my brother. He's family.
MIRA	Well, he should act like family, then.

HONGBU	I know, I know . . . But things are tough, Mira. I'll find a way, and we'll survive. We will. Mira, I love you.
MIRA	I love you too, Hongbu.

(As the family falls asleep, HONGBU sits up, worrying. He gathers his bags and goes out again looking for food.)

SCENE 10: THE WOUNDED SWALLOW

HONGBU is digging the earth, gathering wild yams.

HONGBU	Six, seven, eight. Eight yams. All this work, and only eight yams.

(The SWALLOW careens in, flying with reckless glee.)

SWALLOW	Wheehee! Look at me! Look at me! I swoop, I sail, I soar! I'm Super Swallow! Faster than a speeding mosquito! I swooo—woooo—woooohhh!!! Whoooaaaa!!! Ow!!!

(The SWALLOW loses control and crashes, breaking its wing. HONGBU spots the wounded SWALLOW, shaking and shivering on the ground.)

HONGBU	What's this?
SWALLOW	OH! Wahhhh!!! Ooooh!
HONGBU	A swallow. Poor little bird, are you all right?
SWALLOW	My wing! My wing! I've broken my wing!
HONGBU	It's okay. It's all right. Don't be afraid. Mira!
MIRA	What is it?
HONGBU	This Swallow is wounded. I need some rags for bandages.
MIRA	We barely have enough rags to clothe our children.

HONGBU		I only need a small scrap. Look at her, she's in pain.
SWALLOW		Ow! Oh! Easy! Oooo!
MIRA		Oh poor thing, she's shivering. *(She tears a piece of cloth off her skirt.)* Here, use this.
HONGBU		You'll be better soon, Swallow. You'll see.
SWALLOW		Every day, the whole family took care of the Swallow. They made a soft warm Swallow bed from leaves and moss. And every day they fed her all sorts of juicy insects. Ants, succulent flies, crispy mosquitoes, crickets, meaty beatles.
HONGBU		Eat well and you'll grow strong again.
MIRA		It's good to see *someone* eating well . . .
SWALLOW		Oh dear, I'm so rude. Cricket?
HONGBU		No, Swallow, we can't eat insects.
SWALLOW		Oh!
HONGBU		But thank you. I wish we could. Then we'd all be as fat as bears. No, no, eat some more.
SWALLOW		And after several weeks, the Swallow's wing was healed and her strength returned. She stretched her wings . . . Oh, that feels good! She rose into the air. Goodbye! I'm going South now to meet my Queen, goodbye!
HONGBU		Anyong! Anyong Swallow!

(HONGBU and MIRA watch the SWALLOW fly off, then turn to go home.)

Boy, I sure hope the weather holds up.

MIRA		She's got a long journey home. Oh, my koguma! I just found this great new recipe. Koguma casserole with kosari!

HONGBU	Sounds delicious.	
MIRA	I'm sure it will be. And very filling.	

SCENE 11: THE SWALLOW QUEEN

SWALLOW	And the Swallow flew south, over lush green rice paddies, over hills and thatched roofs, over crowded city markets, over a long dark ocean, south, south, south for days until she arrived at the palace of the Swallow Queen.
	(The SWALLOW arrives at the palace of the magnificent SWALLOW QUEEN, who is fretting royally.)
SWALLOW QUEEN	Ottokae yirokae neujeusoh wasoh?! Eunh? Omoni-ka olmana kokjong haeneunji arart-gee?! [Why are you so late? Do you have any idea how worried I've been?!] Keegeebaeh! Eunh? Eunh?!
SWALLOW	I'm sorry, Your Majesty—
SWALLOW QUEEN	Aiyoo cham! I am so worry! So so worry! I feel like to die. Chincha salsooka obsoh! Talkal dookae bak-ae do moht nasoh! Only I can lay two eggs! Two! Last time I made obah two hundred eggs!
SWALLOW	Your Majesty, I—
SWALLOW QUEEN	Aioo! I am anxious and so bloated. Look at me! The whole Swallow Kingdom, everybody is depend on me and I can't lay eggs. So much pressure. But I am Queen so I endure . . . So tell me why you are so late. Hangook-mal hae bah! Speak in Korean.
SWALLOW	Umh, okay . . . Ohn-jae, uhm, uhm, uhm, on, on, onjae . . .
SWALLOW QUEEN	*(Cutting SWALLOW off—to audience.)* Aigoo cham! Waekook-euroh yimeen-haet-duhni, kapjah-ki

hangookmal-eul hanado mot han-da. [Your kids move abroad, and all of a sudden they can't speak Korean anymore.] Okay, everybody suffer enough already! English is okay. But I warning you, dis better be very good or you are in big trouble.

SWALLOW: I broke my wing, your majesty. I couldn't fly.

SWALLOW QUEEN: What?!! Did you say you broke your wing?

SWALLOW: I broke my wing.

SWALLOW QUEEN: You broke your wing?!

SWALLOW: I broke my wing.

SWALLOW QUEEN: You broke your wing!

SWALLOW: My left wing. It feels pretty good now except when I do this—ow!

SWALLOW QUEEN: Den don't do dat. Why do you do dat?

SWALLOW: I just wanted to show you—

SWALLOW QUEEN: Who does dat? Nobody does dat!

SWALLOW: All the other swallows are doing it—

SWALLOW QUEEN: Do I do dat!? No. So you don't do dat!

(Beat.)

What are we talking about?

SWALLOW: **I BROKE MY WING!**

SWALLOW QUEEN: You broke your wing! And you are surviving?! But what about mengmengyi, wild dogs! Aiyoo cham! Horangi do ittgee! Tigah! Big tigah! They eat small birds. Omona! What about those bad bad boys? How is it possible? Midoolsooka obsohyoh, I've never heard of such a thing. You broke your wing, and you are surviving! Oori saeki-ya!

SWALLOW	A human saved me.	
SWALLOW QUEEN	A human?	
SWALLOW	A human named Hongbu. He and his whole family nursed me, and fed me for three weeks until I was better. They fed me the most tender insects. I felt guilty because they are so poor they themselves barely had enough to eat.	
SWALLOW QUEEN	Well, you don't have to eat all by yourself, I think. You should giving dem some too.	
SWALLOW	Humans can't eat insects.	
SWALLOW QUEEN	Oh yes, that's right, that's true. I forgot. Yijoh boriyoh soh . . . So, what is the name for this human?	
SWALLOW	Hongbu.	
SWALLOW QUEEN	Hongbu. Hongbu. Oh, *Heungbu*. Well, I think we must reward . . . Heungbu. So, okay, what do we have . . . Okay, let's see . . . Not this one . . . Oh, yes, this one is good, Cho-eun koshida. This is a magic seed. When you go back, give this seed to that human. He can plant it in the ground. After dat, I promise, he and his family, they will never never peel hungry again.	
SWALLOW	Thank you, your majesty. Thank you, your generosity is—	
SWALLOW QUEEN	Oh! I am laying an egg. What happened? Aigoo, dtalk-yal-yi wasohyoh! Aiyoo kopamda! Thank you heaven! I am laying an egg. I am laying an egg.	
VOICES	Royal Egg Alert! Royal Egg Alert!	

SCENE 12: THE SWALLOW RETURNS

SWALLOW	The next spring, the Swallow flew back north, carrying the magic seed. She flew over the wide waters of the

	ocean, over mountains and small towns, over rice paddies still flooded with water, she flew until she found the poor shanty where Hongbu and his family shivered through the long dark winter.
HONGBU	Look, children. A swallow! Our Swallow!
MIRA	Hello Swallow! Welcome!
SWALLOW	And the Swallow circled high above, then dropped the magic seed at Hongbu's feet.

(Sound of the Seed dropping from a great height.)

MIRA	What is it?
HONGBU	It looks like a seed.
MIRA	A seed?
HONGBU	Looks like it.
MIRA	Well, I guess we should plant it.
HONGBU	Right. Good idea.
SWALLOW	And they did. And every day Hongbu, Mira, and the children took turns watering the seed. And soon there was a green sprout, and the green sprout became a green vine, and on the green vine, three white flowers blossomed, and from the white flowers three great pumpkins grew and grew and grew.

SCENE 13: THE MAGIC PUMPKINS

HONGBU	Wahhh!!!! This is one big pumpkin.
MIRA	It's as big as a, as a, as a—
HONGBU	As a cow!
MIRA	Bigger than a cow.

HONGBU	As big as a house!
MIRA	Maybe a very small house.
HONGBU	It's pretty darn big. That's the biggest pumpkin I've ever seen, that's for sure.
MIRA	How are we going to cut this up?
HONGBU	I guess we'll need a saw.
SWALLOW	Hongbu took one end of the saw, and Mira took the other. Back and forth, back and forth they sawed.

(Sound of sawing.)

HONGBU	Oh boy. What a workout.
MIRA	My back is killing me.
HONGBU	Just a few more minutes, honey.
SWALLOW	Back and forth, back and forth, until— *(Boom!)* The pumpkin spilled open and tons and tons of rice spilled onto the ground!
MIRA	Rice! Look at all this rice, Hongbu! I've never seen so much rice in my life. Oh my god, I think I'm going to cry!
HONGBU	Where you going?
MIRA	I'm going to start the fire and cook some right now. Do you know how long it's been since we've had rice?
HONGBU	I'll start putting it away.
MIRA	*(From off.)* Good idea, sweetheart.
HONGBU	Thank you, Swallow! Wherever you are!

SCENE 14: BLISS

SWALLOW	A week later, Hongbu and his wife cut open the second pumpkin.
HONGBU	Ready, honey?
MIRA	Ready.
SWALLOW	Back and forth, back and forth they sawed until— (Boom!)
MIRA and HONGBU	WAHHH!!!!
HONGBU	Gold.
MIRA	Gold?! No. Gold?! Pinch me. Am I awake?
	(HONGBU *pinches her.*)
	OW!! It really is gold!
HONGBU	Thousands and thousands of pieces of gold!
MIRA	And beautiful fabric too. Silk and satin, embroidered with birds and flowers and dragons. I can't believe it. Oh Hongbu, we can all have new clothes.
HONGBU	And I can buy books and toys for the children.
MIRA	And we'll never be cold and hungry again! Hongbu, Hongbu, Hongbu, let's cut open the third pumpkin. Right now, please, oh please Hongbu, I can't wait.
HONGBU	Aren't your arms sore?
MIRA	Just saw, husband. Saw! Push, pull! Push, pull! Push, pull! Faster! Harder! Faster!
	(*There is a huge boom and cracking sound.*)
HONGBU and MIRA	HUNH????!!
	(*A distinguished* ARCHITECT *steps out of the pumpkin and unfurls blueprints for a house.*)

ARCHITECT	Sir. Madam. May I present you with drawings for your NEW HOME! I've designed a commodious estate for you and your family, with bright bedrooms for all the children, a playroom, a library, a bright kitchen for you madam—
MIRA	Oh, my!
ARCHITECT	And here, sir, you can see where I have done the drawings for a lovely garden and a fresh water well.
HONGBU	Gosh. I mean. Uhm. Is there, could you, perhaps add a birdhouse?
ARCHITECT	A birdhouse?
HONGBU	Yes, a birdhouse. A house for birds. For swallows. A very fine birdhouse.
ARCHITECT	A birdhouse. For swallows. Yes, of course, sir, of course. A wonderful idea. I should have thought of that myself.
	(MIRA *and the children hug and dance.* HONGBU *stares into the sky.*)
MIRA	Honey? What are you looking at?
HONGBU	Oh, I was just hoping our friend was around.
MIRA	I'm sure she'll come and visit soon.
HONGBU *and* MIRA	A New Home!

SCENE 15: NOLBU GETS JEALOUS

NOLBU is reading a newspaper. MYUNG-MI, who is now very, very fat, is eating candy.

NOLBU	That useless good-for-nothing brother of mine found a magic pumpkin seed and now he's filthy rich. And do you know what he's doing with his money? Donating it to charity. His picture's in the paper. Shaking hands

	with the mayor. "I want to share my good fortune because I know what it's like to be hungry."
MYUNG-MI	He's giving it away?
NOLBU	Can you believe it? Idiot.
MYUNG-MI	Well, if he's giving it away, he should give you some for all those years he lived in *your* house. Toffee? We can always use more money.
NOLBU	You know, if I asked, he probably would. He's like that. But no. Never! Not in a million years! I'll get my own magic pumpkin seed.

SCENE 16: NOLBU'S PLOT

NOLBU has a stick and a lantern. MYUNG-MI follows.

NOLBU	Be very very quiet. Remember the plan.
MYUNG-MI	We wait.
NOLBU	Very quietly.
MYUNG-MI	Very quietly. When the Swallow comes, you whack it with the stick. When I hear the bird fall, I walk over—
NOLBU	Real casual like.
MYUNG-MI	I remember! I walk over real casual like and I say, "Oh, you poor little thing!"
NOLBU	That was very good!
MYUNG-MI	Thank you, sweetheart.
NOLBU	Then you call me, and I'll rescue it. Got it?
MYUNG-MI	Got it. I love you, boogey bear.
NOLBU	I love you, too, snoogle-poogles. Now go.

(NOLBU crouches. MYUNG-MI hides at the opposite

end of the stage. The SWALLOW *flies in, humming a jingle.)*

SWALLOW   Meaty mosquitoes! Meaty mosquitoes. Munchable, crunchable meaty mosquitoes. Aghhh! I can't get this song out of my head. I hate when that happens.

(Spotting one.)

Oh! Meaty mosquitoes, I'm gonna getcha getcha getcha—

(Snaps down on it.)

Mmmm, very nice. Munchable crunchable meaty mosqitoes! The problem with catchy tunes is they're so darn . . . catchy! Advertisements. I should never watch television. Ohh!!

(Goes off in another direction.)

Meaty mosquitos, meaty mosquitoes, I'm gonna getcha getcha getcha—

(The SWALLOW *flies straight to where* NOLBU *is hiding, a stick in hand.)*

What the—?!

NOLBU   Oh mae!

(He whacks the SWALLOW *with the stick and the* SWALLOW *falls.)*

SWALLOW   Ow!!

*(*NOLBU *rushes off to remove his disguise and pushes* MYUNG-MI *forward.)*

MYUNG-MI   Oh, you poor little thing! Honey bunch! There's a wounded Swallow here!

NOLBU   A wounded Swallow! That's terrible. Don't worry, Swallow. We'll take care of you. You'll be flying in no time.

(He turns to MYUNG-MI, who acts as his E.R. nurse.)

Splint.

MYUNG-MI: Splint.

NOLBU: Bandages.

MYUNG-MI: Bandages.

SWALLOW: Ow, ow! Watch the feathers!

NOLBU: Tape.

MYUNG-MI: Tape.

NOLBU: There you go.

MYUNG-MI: Do you want the fresh insects now or later?

NOLBU: Now. Now, of course. Fresh insects. Bugs, flies, assorted insects. Eat up.

SWALLOW: No, I — mpphh!

MYUNG-MI: Come on, little birdie. Yum yum yum.

NOLBU: That's the way. The more you eat, the faster you'll heal. There, you're all better! Now fly south to that Swallow Queen of yours, and tell her Nolbu, Hongbu's Older and much Kinder Brother, helped you.

MYUNG-MI: That's Nolbu. N-O-L-B-U. I just want to make sure she gets it right.

NOLBU: Good thinking, sweetheart.

MYUNG-MI: Thank you, honey.

NOLBU: *(Showing his business card to the SWALLOW.)* Here's my card. Name, address, it's all there.

MYUNG-MI: And, oh, Swallow! If you bring us back one of those little pumpkin seeds —

NOLBU: *Magic* pumpkin seeds. *Magic* pumpkins.

MYUNG-MI	I remember! If you could bring us one of those *magic* pumpkin seeds, well, we won't say no!
	(The SWALLOW, bandaged but far from healed, limps off, cursing under her breath.)
MYUNG-MI	Well, I think that went rather well, don't you?

SCENE 17: THE SWALLOW, THE SWALLOW QUEEN, AND SWALLOW BABIES

SWALLOW	After several months, the Swallow finally arrived home, at the Palace of the Swallow Queen.
	Your Majesty? Your Majesty? I'm home. Your Majesty?!!
	(From off we hear a giant wave of sound, the mewling squeaking cries of newly hatched baby swallows. "Omma! Omma! Omma, omma, omma!" The SWALLOW QUEEN sweeps on stage, an armful of baby swallows in one hand, more chicks strapped onto her back, and a pram full of more baby swallows that she pushes before her. The SWALLOW QUEEN is a frazzled new mom, scattered but still awash with the ecstasy of early motherhood. The sounds of hundreds of hungry little birds continue to rise and fall like waves through the scene. Calls of "I'm hungry, Mommy, Mommy" in Korean. The SWALLOW QUEEN rushes from cluster of baby birds to the next feeding and wiping up.)
SWALLOW QUEEN	Here, hold babies.
	(She passes an armful of chicks to the SWALLOW, who awkwardly bounces them and begins feeding the others.)
	Osoh mogoh! Osoh mogoh! Aioo nomoo kiopda! So cute. Eat and grow big and strong for Mommy. Memmemememe me! So. How come you taking so long to come back? Again! You know new babies are hatch!

	You have duty and responsibility too. I am Queen and I can't do eberything all by myself?
SWALLOW	Ow! She bit me!
SWALLOW QUEEN	Omona, she's so hungry, that's why. Onnee-rul moolge ma! [Don't bite your big sister!] You did same thing, you know.
SWALLOW	I did?
SWALLOW QUEEN	Oh yes!
SWALLOW	I don't remember that.
SWALLOW QUEEN	And when you come out of egg, you are so excite, you choke on your own eggshell! I shake you upside down. Hard. Then pop! Shell comes out. Cham.

(The SWALLOW reaches out, then winces doubling in pain. The SWALLOW QUEEN notices.)

	Ommoh-na! What happened to your wing?
SWALLOW	I broke it.
SWALLOW QUEEN	Again?!!
SWALLOW	What?
SWALLOW QUEEN	How many times do I tell you, you flying too fast, eunh? Always look up down, den dis way den dat way den dis way, okay? You gotta be careful!
SWALLOW	Your Majesty, I *was* careful! I wasn't flying fast. I wasn't even flying. I was ambushed. Attacked! Mugged while munching mosquitoes!
SWALLOW QUEEN	Oh sure. Here, give me baby.
SWALLOW	A mean, greedy, nasty human snuck up behind me and whacked me with a stick. On purpose! And after he whacked me, he and his fat wife pretended to rescue me, and they stuffed me with stale crickets until

	I choked. It was horrible, your Majesty. Really, really horrible.
	(The baby birds begin wailing.)
SWALLOW QUEEN	Shhh, shhh! Oolgi-ma oolgi-ma! [Don't cry, don't cry!]
SWALLOW	It's all true, your Majesty. And they kept talking about a magic pumpkin seed. "And don't forget, bring us a magic pumpkin seed! Remember now, Magic pumpkin seed. Magic pumpkin seed!"
SWALLOW QUEEN	What? What did you say?
SWALLOW	They were horrible people, horrible—
SWALLOW QUEEN	No, after dat. After dat.
SWALLOW	They kept talking about a magic pumpkin seed?
SWALLOW QUEEN	Yah! Tashi hanbon. [One more time].
SWALLOW	They kept talking about a magic pumpkin seed. They want one really badly.
SWALLOW QUEEN	Magic pumpkin seed. *(To the baby.)* Oh, is that funny? Magic pumpkin seed, magic pumpkin seed!
SWALLOW	Your Majesty?
SWALLOW QUEEN	Eunh?
SWALLOW	He gave me his card.
	(The SWALLOW *hands the business card to the* SWALLOW QUEEN.*)*
SWALLOW QUEEN	His ka-teuh.
	(She pulls out reading glasses, reads the card. Beat.)
	"Nolbu. Older, much kinder brother of Hongbu." Keureun-ya. Well, I guess I give magic seed then.
SWALLOW	But, your Majesty! Your Majesty—

SWALLOW QUEEN		Reach over dere, no dere, in the—no, there, yes, yes, that's it. Oh. No. Not dat one. Next to it. YES! That one! Dat seed! Dat seed is just right . . . When you go back, give dat seed. He wants magic seed, okay, he will have magic seed.
SWALLOW		But your Majesty—
SWALLOW QUEEN		*(To audience.)* Kids! [in Korean: They think us parents are all fools!] *(To the SWALLOW.)* Come, come and help me feed babies. They growing up so fast!

SCENE 18: THE SECOND SEED

SWALLOW In the spring, the Swallow returned, swooped over Nolbu's house, and dropped the magic seed.

(Sound of the seed dropping.)

NOLBU Honey! It's here. Our very own magic pumpkin seed.

(MYUNG-MI rushes on with a shovel and a watering can.)

Hurry. Hurry. The sooner we plant it, the sooner we'll all be stinking rich.

MYUNG-MI Lots of water, we have to give it lots of water.

NOLBU I want someone guarding this seed twenty-four hours a day. Understand? Just in case someone tries to steal it. We'll divide up into three-hour shifts. Honey, you do the first shift. I'll come and relieve you in three hours.

MYUNG-MI Yes, dear. I just sit here?

NOLBU That's right. And fend off thieves. And dream about all the gold and riches we'll soon have.

MYUNG-MI Gold and riches . . . I'll hire a maid, no, three maids, three little maids. We'll eat chocolate-covered chocolates every day.

NOLBU	I'll build a bigger house. Bigger and more beautiful than Hongbu's. And I'll get the new Play Station Super Quantum X-12! Sweet!

SCENE 19: NOLBU'S PUMPKINS RIPEN

SWALLOW	Nolbu and his wife watered and guarded the seed jealously. Soon there was a green sprout, and the green sprout became a green vine, and on the green vine three white flowers blossomed, and from the white flowers, three great pumpkins grew and grew and grew.
NOLBU	Show me the money!
MYUNG-MI	Pay day!

(NOLBU *and* MYUNG-MI *grab a saw. Sawing noises.*)

SWALLOW	Back and forth, back and forth, back and forth they sawed.
MYUNG-MI	Big money big money big money!
NOLBU	Can't you go any faster?

(*Big huge booming sound. Something smells bad.*)

MYUNG-MI	Something smells like Pig. Pee.

(NOLBU *and* MYUNG-MI *are startled by the loud snorting sounds. A* SMELLY PIGGY THIEF *jumps out of the pumpkin.*)

SMELLY PIGGY THIEF	Damn, I'm hungry!
NOLBU *and* MYUNG-MI	A Smelly Piggy Thief!
SMELLY PIGGY THIEF	Yessir, that's me. The smelliest stinkiest piggiest thief of all time and, man, am I hungry! You got any food around here? Well, I'm going to eat it all! I'm going to eat, gobble, and devour everything in sight until there's

NOLBU | nothing but crumbs and wrappers. Whoohoo! How's do ya like them apples, hunh!

NOLBU | But, but why?

SMELLY PIGGY THIEF | You're not too bright, are you? I'm a Smelly Piggy Thief. I'm insatiable, gluttonous, and just generally rude. I eat 'n eat 'n eat! That's what Smelly Piggy Thieves do. Union rules. Oooo! Is this your lunch?

MYUNG-MI | No! Nolbu, stop him! Stop him, Nolbu! He's eating all our food.

SMELLY PIGGY THIEF | Mmmm, yum, rice, dumplings, pickles! Mmmm. Oooh! President's Choice, very nice. God, I love my job!

NOLBU | Get away from there! That's our food! That's ours!

SMELLY PIGGY THIEF | Oh yeah? Is your name on it? Didn't think so. Finders keepers, losers weepers!

(The SMELLY PIGGY THIEF suddenly stops, sniffs, then dashes toward MYUNG-MI, who is protectively clutching a large box.)

Gimme that!

MYUNG-MI | No! Never. Never!

SMELLY PIGGY THIEF | Gimme gimme gimme!

MYUNG-MI | No! Get your hands off me, you—you—you, piggy thing! Ahhhh!

(The SMELLY PIGGY THIEF wrenches the box from MYUNG-MI and opens it.)

SMELLY PIGGY THIEF | Ooooooohhh! Chocolates! With pretty red things in the middle. *(Reading.)* Belgian Truffles. Yummy!

(The SMELLY PIGGY THIEF gobbles up the chocolates.)

MYUNG-MI | Oh no! My beautiful melt-in-your-mouth dark choco-

	late truffles with cherry and brandy centers, decoratively dusted with slivered almonds. I was saving those!
SMELLY PIGGY THIEF	Deliciously decadent with the rich unmistakable savour of real butter! Delectable! Oh, gotta go.
NOLBU	You'll never get away with this!
SMELLY PIGGY THIEF	Oh yeah? Just watch me. Anyong! Adios! Chow for now kids! I'm pretty funny, eh? I crack myself up! See ya later alligator! In a while crocodile!

(The SMELLY PIGGY THIEF *exits laughing.* NOLBU *and* MYUNG-MI *are devastated.*)

SCENE 20: FROM BAD TO WORSE

NOLBU	That must have been a defective pumpkin.
MYUNG-MI	My chocolates. Devoured. Destroyed. Kidnapped! This is awful!
NOLBU	Oh, stop whining, Myung-Mi, and help me open this second pumpkin. There's probably gold in this one.
MYUNG-MI	Gold? I could buy more Belgian chocolates then?
NOLBU	As many as you want. Heck, we could go to Belgia.
MYUNG-MI	Belgium.
NOLBU	What?
MYUNG-MI	Belgium. Not Belgia. Belgian chocolates are from Belgium. Oh, forget it. Do you really think we could go?
NOLBU	Absolutely!
MYUNG-MI	Well, let's do it, then!

(NOLBU *and* MYUNG-MI *pick up the saw and begin sawing.*)

NOLBU	Push, pull, push, pull, push, pull, push, pull—
	(A big booming sound. The pumpkin cracks open. A miserable old DEBT COLLECTOR with an ominous looking abacus steps out.)
DEBT COLLECTOR	Nolbu. Is there a Nolbu in the house?
NOLBU	That's me. Nolbu. N-O-L-B-U. I'm the man.
DEBT COLLECTOR	Ah, yes, I see. Nolbu. Your grandfather borrowed three gold coins from me and he never paid them back. I'm here to collect.
NOLBU	What?
DEBT COLLECTOR	I calculate at an average annual cumulative interest rate of 18.9%, accrued hourly and factoring in a modest administrative fee of 20% per annum over 46 years, plus late charges, your total overdue balance is now 33,467 gold pieces and 68 silver coins.
NOLBU	What?—I don't have that kind of money.
MYUNG-MI	A Smelly Piggy Thief just ate us out of house and home.
DEBT COLLECTOR	Please, I'm a debt collector, not a therapist. Just give me what you have. Cash, stocks, or gold bullion. Quickly now, I don't have all day.
	(NOLBU empties his pocket. He has only four or five copper coins. The DEBT COLLECTOR is unimpressed. NOLBU signals to MYUNG-MI. MYUNG-MI reluctantly retrieves a hidden bag of money. The DEBT COLLECTOR continues to be unimpressed.)
	Remember, a penny unpaid today is just a dollar you'll have to pay tomorrow.
	(Panicked, NOLBU presents the DEBT COLLECTOR with a substantial bag of coins.)

	My my my my my my my, this is completely inadequate.
MYUNG-MI	What does that mean? Is that good?
DEBT COLLECTOR	It means, it's not enough! It's nowhere near enough. Debts are serious business, Nolbu. They are meant to be repaid! Don't you know anything about fiscal responsibility?
NOLBU	Fishy, fishy what?
DEBT COLLECTOR	Fiscal responsibility! Don't you know anything? If money is the master, then debt is the slave driver that keeps the engine turning. Fiscal responsibility, Nolbu.
NOLBU	Ow! That hurt!
DEBT COLLECTOR	Fiscal responsibility!
NOLBU	Ow!
DEBT COLLECTOR	If you can inherit wealth, then you can inherit debt also. You're poor!
NOLBU	You should watch where you—
DEBT COLLECTOR	You're impoverished, destitute, delinquent, and downright broke!
NOLBU	Ow!
DEBT COLLECTOR	You're a bad person, Nolbu! Bad! Very, very bad and very poor and very much in debt, and debt is bad!
NOLBU	Ow! Ow! Please stop. I'm bad, I'm bad. I understand.
DEBT COLLECTOR	I'll be back in two weeks. I hope you're ready to pay up then.
	(The DEBT COLLECTOR *leaves.* NOLBU *and* MYUNG-MI *are stunned.*)
MYUNG-MI	Honey? Are you alright?

NOLBU	Oh my God, what are we going to—Myung-Mi, Myung-Mi, Myung-Mi, we have to open the third pumpkin.
MYUNG-MI	I don't know if that's a good idea.
NOLBU	We have to. The third pumpkin. The third pumpkin. It's our only hope! There's bound to be something good in that third pumpkin.
MYUNG-MI	Honestly, sweetheart—
NOLBU	Myung-Mi, in two weeks when that horrible terrible withered-up little man and his abacus comes back, I have to have something. We're opening the third pumpkin.
MYUNG-MI	But honey—
NOLBU	No buts, Myung-Mi! We're opening the third pumpkin! And there'll be something nice inside—something especially nice to make up for all the other stuff. You'll see. Now saw, woman! Saw! Big money, big money, big money!

(Sawing sounds. Big booming pumpkin opening sound and a great TWO-HEADED MANGY MONSTER *steps out.)*

TWO-HEADED MANGY MONSTER	Wasseumnida!
MYUNG-MI *and* NOLBU	A Two-Headed Mangy Monster!
TWO-HEADED MANGY MONSTER	That's right. A Two-Headed Mangy Monster that smells like wet socks and rotting garbage! You got a problem with that?
NOLBU	No, no, not at all.
TWO-HEADED MANGY MONSTER	I'd rather be a big old Two-Headed Mangy Monster that smells like wet socks and rotting garbage than a meany who beats up on innocent little swallows.

NOLBU   Wha . . . wha? What are you talking about?

TWO-HEADED MANGY MONSTER   Oh, don't play all innocent with us. You broke that swallow's wing so you could get a magic pumpkin seed just like your brother.

NOLBU   No, no, I didn't do it. That wasn't me. I mean, it, it was an accident, it was dark and I thought, well, we've had skunk problems lately, and I'm sure you can imagine how in the dark it's easy to mistake a swallow for a— Look, I'm the good guy! I'm the good guy! I healed the Swallow. I made it better.

TWO-HEADED MANGY MONSTER   You're a really lousy liar, you know that? I suppose next you're going to tell us you didn't steal your little brother's kite when you were kids.

NOLBU   What? What kite?

TWO-HEADED MANGY MONSTER   What kite! Can you believe this guy? Liar, liar, pants on fire! Storm Watcher. Purple Stripe. Amazing awesome sky-roving kite.

NOLBU   That was my kite. Hongbu gave it to me.

TWO-HEADED MANGY MONSTER   Hongbu *would have* given it to you, but you took it first. Ah, just drop it, okay, we know the truth about everything, and it just makes us feel more, more, more monsterish when you lie to us like that.

NOLBU   I'm not lying.

TWO-HEADED MANGY MONSTER   You're so totally lying! You're a great big panty-pooping liar! With a stinky bum!

NOLBU   I am, I am not!

TWO-HEADED MANGY MONSTER   You are so! Yeah! You are so! Yeah! And you're a farty pantses too! You're both farty pantses!

MYUNG-MI   Farty pantses! Are you calling me a farty pantses?

TWO-HEADED MANGY MONSTER   Farty pantses! Farty pantses!

MYUNG-MI   Nolbu, are you going to let them get away with that? Nolbu! This is all your fault. Don't cut open the third pumpkin, that's what I said, but did you listen? No! And now this Mangy Monster is calling me a farty pantses!

NOLBU   Honey, honey, please, just calm down—

MYUNG-MI   I will not calm down! This, this Mangy Monster thing just called me a, a—I can't say it, it's so awful—and you're letting them get away with it!

TWO-HEADED MANGY MONSTER   Oh, stop your whining, noodle-nose.

MYUNG-MI   Noodle-nose! Well, I never!

TWO-HEADED MANGY MONSTER   Hey, is this your house?

NOLBU   Yes. I mean no. I mean, please not the house. I love this house, I grew up in this house!

TWO-HEADED MANGY MONSTER   Wanna bet I can knock it down with my head? Hey, what about me? Two heads are better than one. Wanna bet we can knock it down with our heads? In one go. You wanna bet?

NOLBU   No! I mean, I'm sure a big strong monster like you can do it, no problem. It'd hardly be a fair bet. No, no, please don't. I'm begging you, not my house. It's all I have left.

TWO-HEADED MANGY MONSTER   But I wanna! I wanna knock down your house! I wanna! We both wanna! It'd be so much fun. The sound of the wood cracking, the rumble of plaster crashing to the ground, the glorious cloud of dust and debris. There's nothing like it.

MYUNG-MI   Oh, well, the Kims down the road, they have a very nice two-story house with a real ceramic tile roof. Why don't you knock down their house?

(Beat.)

TWO-HEADED MANGY MONSTER   Nahhh. We wanna knock down this one. We wanna knock down your house. Not the Kims. We're gonna enjoy this. Ready? Ready. Hanna, Dool, Set!

(The TWO-HEADED MANGY MONSTER *rams his head into the house. There's a huge boom.)*

NOLBU   Oh no.

MYUNG-MI   My beautiful house . . .

TWO-HEADED MANGY MONSTER   There goes the roof!

(The house creaks ominously, rumbles, then collapses in a thunderous clap.)

NOLBU   Destroyed. Devastated. Demolished.

TWO-HEADED MANGY MONSTER   Well done! We still got the touch. Ready?

(The TWO-HEADED MANGY MONSTER *blasts* NOLBU *and* MYUNG-MI *with their killer bad breath.)*

Boo!

NOLBU   Ugh!

MYUNG-MI   Wet socks . . .

NOLBU   Rotting garbage . . .

MYUNG-MI   Oh. I feel sick.

*(*NOLBU *and* MYUNG-MI *pass out.)*

TWO-HEADED MANGY MONSTER   Gotcha! Nice one, dude.

(The TWO-HEADED MANGY MONSTER *laughs and laughs and laughs.)*

SCENE 21: THE BLAME GAME/SHAME GAME

NOLBU is in a state of shock—he's hearing things.

MYUNG-MI	*(Waking.)* Oh my head! I just had the most horrible dream. All these horrible things happened to us and—oh my God. It wasn't a dream? It wasn't a dream!
NOLBU	*(In shock.)* It's all my fault. I did this. Me. Nolbu. We've lost everything, and it's all my fault.
MYUNG-MI	Oh, sweetheart, you're talking crazy. Did you knock down our house? Did you devour my beautiful cherry and brandy Belgian chocolates? Did you tell that awful little Debt Collector, here, take all our money, take it all, take it take it take it. If it's anybody's fault it's that sparrow, that swallow, that that that bird. After all we did for her!
NOLBU	I'm a horrible person. I'm greedy and mean and selfish and mind-numbingly materialistic. That's why all this happened.
MYUNG-MI	Oh honey, oh sweetheart, you've lost your mind. It's the shock. Sit down, sweetheart. Breathe. In, out, in, out.

SCENE 22: RECONCILIATION

HONGBU and MIRA rush in.

HONGBU	Nolbu, sister, we came as soon as we heard.
NOLBU	Hongbu, brother, I owe you and your family an apology, a hundred apologies. I've been a horrible horrible brother to you. Horrible. I'm a horrible person and an especially horrible brother.
MYUNG-MI	Don't listen to him, he's lost his mind.
NOLBU	When we were kids, remember? I took your kite and wouldn't let you fly it. Storm Watcher. Remember? It

	was your kite and I took it. It was purple with a white stripe. Sweet sweet Storm Watcher.
HONGBU	It was just a kite, Nolbu.
NOLBU	And when you were poor, I didn't help you at all. I didn't even give you grocery money. A monster, that's what I am. A monster. And I'm sorry, Hongbu. I'm so so sorry. And Myung-Mi's sorry, too, aren't you, honey?
MYUNG-MI	Yes, of course. I'm, I'm, I'm . . . I'm very sorry.
NOLBU	Will you ever forgive us?
HONGBU	Nolbu, I'm your brother. I've already forgiven you. Come on. Let's go.
NOLBU	Go where? We have nowhere to go.
HONGBU	I'm taking you home.
NOLBU	Home?
HONGBU	There's more than enough room. Nolbu, you're my brother. Your home is with me.
NOLBU	But that's so nice.
HONGBU	I mean, if that's all right with you.
MYUNG-MI	Of course, it's all right! Isn't it, sweetheart?

(NOLBU *breaks down and collapses at* HONGBU's *feet, weeping.*)

NOLBU	Oh, Hongbu, I'll never be mean or greedy again. I promise. I promise, Hongbu.
HONGBU	Nolbu, geez. Come on, you're embarrassing me!
MIRA	I hope you like pumpkin.
MYUNG-MI	I'm sure I could get to like pumpkin.
MIRA	We eat a lot of pumpkin at our house. Pumpkin stew,

	pumpkin pancakes, pumpkin salad, pumpkin porridge, pumpkin cookies with raisins, the kids love those.
MYUNG-MI	How delightful.
HONGBU	Hey Nolbu, maybe later this week you and I could go do a little fishing, whaddya say? Remember we used to fish when we were kids?
NOLBU	Yeah, I forgot about that. That was fun. Remember how I used to steal your worms?
HONGBU	You stole my worms?
MIRA	And Nolbu and his family moved in with Hongbu, Mira, and their children, and their dog, chicken, pigs, and cows.
HONGBU	And they lived happily ever after, working and playing together, sharing everything they had.
NOLBU	Somehow, there was always enough to go around.
MYUNG-MI	Almost.

—— END OF PLAY ——

YI SANG COUNTS TO THIRTEEN
Sung Rno

Sung Rno was born in 1967 in Minneapolis to parents who introduced him to theater at an early age. He majored in physics at Harvard, but his desire to write led him to enroll in a postmodern drama class with Robert Brustein, which turned out to be an eye-opening experience. After receiving his BA from Harvard, he earned an MFA in creative writing from Brown University, where he studied both poetry and playwriting. He is also an alumnus of New Dramatists and a founder of the Ma-Yi Writers Lab. His plays include *Cleveland Raining*, *wAve*, *Behind the Masq*, *Weather*, *Gravity Falls from Trees*, *Drizzle and Other Stories*, *Infinitude*, and *The Trajectory of a Heart, Fractured*. He is also the co-author of *Balangiga* with Ralph Peña. His work has been produced at East West Players, Ma-Yi Theater Company, Thick Description, Asian American Theater Company, North West Asian American Theater, San Diego Asian American Rep, Dance Theater Workshop, Immigrants' Theater Project, and others. Honors include an NEA/TCG Playwriting Fellowship, the Whitfield Cook Prize, the New York Fringe Festival Best Overall Production Award, Van Lier Fellowships (with New Dramatists and New York Theatre Workshop), and first prize at the Seattle Multicultural Playwrights' Festival. In *Yi Sang Counts to Thirteen* (2001) Rno draws inspiration from the writings of the Korean poet Yi Sang to explore the idea of fractured language, psyche, and cultural identity.

Sung Rno. Photo courtesy of Sung Rno. This photo was taken during the shooting of the KYOPO Project. www.kyopoproject.com.

Yi Sang Counts to Thirteen premiered at the Seoul International Theater Festival (Yun-Tae Kim, executive director) on October 10, 2000. It was directed by Lee Breuer; the assistant director was Kang-Shin Lee; the set and costume designs were by Jee-Hee Paik; the lighting design was by Manuel Rukenhost; the sound design was by Tae-Hyung Im; the video design was by Kyu-Suk Park and Jong-Hyun Suh; the stage manager was Soo-Hun Lee; and the producer was Shin Lee, who also worked as a translator. The cast was as follows:

Blue. . . . . Kwang-Jo Ahn
Green . . . . Myung-Hee Hahn
Red . . . . C. S. Lee
Chorus . . . . Jun Ho Song, Mi Hwa Um,
                    Nam Hyung Kim, Ji Hyun Kwon, Jee Hee Kwon

The U.S. premiere was presented on August 10, 2001, at the New York International Fringe Festival, where it received a Best Overall Production Award. It was directed by Sung Rno; the set and costume designs were by Antje Ellerman; the lighting design was by Josh Bradford; the sound design was by Paolo Gomez; the stage manager was April Kline; the production manager was Vincent Hokia; and the producers were Sung Rno and Helen Yum. The cast was as follows:

Blue. . . . . C. S. Lee
Green . . . . Deborah S. Craig
Red . . . . Paul H. Juhn

The play has since been produced at the Kraine Theater in New York City in 2002 and revived in Seoul at the historic Changgo Theater in 2009. The revival production was presented in May to June 2009 as a 719 Production sponsored by Sam-il-ro Changgo Theatre. It was directed by Lee Breuer; the scenic and costume design was by Jee-Hee Paik; the lighting design was by Sang-Soo Lee and Chi-Sung Kim; the sound design was by Tae-Hyung Im (Sound Central); the video design was by Hong-Yeol Park; the choreography was by Jung-Yun Kim; the stage manager was Seul-Yae Jeon; the production manager was Mee-Young Son; and the

Paul H. Juhn (left), C. S. Lee (center), and Deborah S. Craig (right) in the U.S. premiere of *Yi Sang Counts to Thirteen*, directed by Sung Rno at the New York International Fringe Festival in 2001. Photo by Helen Yum.

producer was Kwang-Jo Ahn, who also translated the play. The cast was as follows:

Narrator . . . . Chang-Soo Lee
Blue. . . . . Dong-Ruk Shin
Green . . . . So-Jin Kim
Red . . . . Young-Jun Im

Special thanks to Lee Breuer, Walter Lew, Michael Shin, Mabou Mines, Shin Lee, Jee-Hee Paik, Kwang-Jo Ahn, C. S. Lee, Paul H. Juhn, Deborah S. Craig, Ron Domingo, Andrew Pang, Nancy Wu, Bruce Ostler, Ma-Yi Theater Company, and New Dramatists for both the water and Diet Coke needed for this play. And to my family for their inspiration and support.

A valuable resource for this play was Volume 1 of *Muae: A Journal of Transcultural Production* (Kaya Press), a portfolio of Yi Sang's translated writings edited by Walter K. Lew.

> *I stood my pair of lost arms up as candleholders to decorate my room with. The arms are dead but seem to show all the more nothing but fear of me. Such frail etiquette I consider more lovely than any flower basin.*
>
> —Yi Sang, Poem no. XIII (Shi che shipsam ho)

CHARACTERS

BLUE could be the Korean surrealist writer Yi Sang.

RED could be his best friend.

GREEN could be the woman both fall in love with. But these are just guesses.

TIME

Imagine, in a mathematical-theatrical sort of way, if you took the date 1937 and mapped it onto the present one.

PLACE

Imagine a similar mathematical-theatrical mapping in which Seoul circa 1937 was mapped onto New York City, with all the memories and nuances of Mr. Yi Sang's strange and twisted psyche.

1.0 NOODLES #1

Lights up on a pot simmering. We hear the sound of burning magnified.

> (BLUE *stares at the pot. He stares for a really long time. He glares out into the audience, then resumes his staring. He looks at his watch. He takes his watch off, listens to it, winds it.*
>
> GREEN *enters. They look at each other in surprise. Then they play it cool.*
>
> *With a flourish, she pulls out a package of instant ramen noodles.*
>
> *She peers into the pot.*)

GREEN You got no water in there.

BLUE   What do you mean, I got no water.

Dong-Ruk Shin (Blue), Young-Jun Im (Red), So-Jin Kim (Green), and Chang-Soo Lee (Narrator) in the 2009 revival production of *Yi Sang Counts to Thirteen*, directed by Lee Breuer at the Changgo Theater in Seoul, South Korea. In this production, the character Blue was split into two characters: Blue and Narrator. Photo by Seo Jong Hyun.

GREEN   Look.

            (He does a double-take.)

BLUE   Dammit!

GREEN   What?

BLUE   Someone stole my water!

GREEN   Stole?

BLUE   Yeah! Of all the low-down, dirty things someone could do.

GREEN   I think you forgot.

BLUE   Forgot? You think I forgot to put the water in? What kind of an idiot do you think I am? Don't answer that.

GREEN   Well, here're your noodles anyway.

(GREEN gives BLUE the noodles.)

(BLUE addresses the bag of noodles.)

BLUE   *(manic)* Hello there, little noodles. Look at you—so innocent, so above it all. "We had nothing to do with the water disappearing. We're just a pack of noodles." But you don't fool me. I see through your lies. It's a conspiracy, isn't it? OHHH YES, YOU'RE ALL IN THIS TOGETHER!

(BLUE throws the bag of noodles into the pot and turns up the heat.)

BLUE   I'm gonna teach these noodles a lesson. I'm gonna burn the shit out of these noodles!

GREEN   You're in one of your moods today, aren't you?

BLUE   You would be too if someone stole your water.

GREEN   No one stole the water, dumbass—

BLUE   I HAD WATER IN THE POT, OKAY? I FILLED THE POT UP WITH WATER AND NOW THERE'S NO WATER. SO DON'T TELL ME—

(He starts coughing violently.)

GREEN   Okay, okay. No need to get so worked up about it.

(Pause, as BLUE recovers his breath.)

BLUE   How're they doing?

GREEN   They who?

BLUE   The noodles.

(She lifts the cover.)

GREEN   They're doing . . . okay.

BLUE	Are they frying? Are they burning in hell?
GREEN	Of course not.
BLUE	Fuck it. I'm going out.
GREEN	Why?
BLUE	I'm hungry.

(He waits.)

You coming?

GREEN	I have to watch.
BLUE	Right.
GREEN	There could be a fire.
BLUE	I can turn the pot off.
GREEN	You can't do that to noodles. Reverse direction on them like that. Bad karma.
BLUE	You're saying that noodles have souls? *(Thinks for a moment.)* Damn, you're screwing with my head again. Staying or going?
GREEN	Staying.
BLUE	Suit yourself.

(BLUE exits. GREEN watches him go. She waits to make sure he's left, then sneakily removes a bottle of water from her pants. GREEN holds it up and regards it. GREEN opens the bottle with a flourish and starts to drink, as if she's been dying of thirst, when RED enters, picking up just where BLUE left off. GREEN plays along like RED is BLUE, although there's definitely something "off" about him. GREEN does a spit-take of the mouthful of water.)

RED	I forgot my . . . keys.
GREEN	Uhh . . . hey.
RED	What is that?

GREEN   This?

RED   That.

GREEN   Uhh . . . looks like water.

RED   I KNOW THAT'S WATER.

GREEN   You asked.

RED   So what are you doing with water?

GREEN   What do you mean?

RED   Didn't we just establish my need for water? My need to boil the noodles?

GREEN   Yes. I believe we did establish that. I forgot, I guess.

RED   You saw him, didn't you?

GREEN   Him? Him who?

RED   You know damn well who. Him. The Him who I told you not to see.

GREEN   Ohhhh. Him. No, I didn't see him.

RED   No?

GREEN   No.

(Pause. RED fumes. GREEN looks at RED, tentatively at first, then stares at him.)

RED   Look, maybe we need some . . . what're you looking at?

GREEN   You look different.

RED   What?

GREEN   You seem different. Did you get a haircut or something?

RED   No.

GREEN   Turn around. *(RED turns around slowly.)* I can't put my finger on it. But you definitely seem different.

RED	Hey, you wouldn't happen to have anything else to drink, would you?
GREEN	Like what?
RED	Oh, I don't know . . . like a Diet Coke?
GREEN	What's the matter, water ain't good enough for you?
RED	I'd prefer something that's sweeter. Something that's got fizz.

2.0 BLUE

(BLUE *addresses audience.*)

BLUE   My name is Yi Sang. That's the idea anyway. A simple idea, sure, but open to interpretation. Am I Yi Sang? Or am I playing a character that resembles Yi Sang? Or am I playing a character that could have been created by the writer known as Yi Sang? (You decide.)

Yi Sang isn't even my real name. It's actually a pen-name. From 1910 to 1945, Korea was colonized by Japan. I spent my entire life as a Korean living under Japanese rule—actually, I was born in 1910. A *strange* little coincidence. Anyway, my real family name is Yi. A Japanese superior at work called me over in Japanese. He said, "Yi-San, blah-blah-blah . . ." I misheard him and thought he said, "Yi-Sang," which means strange in Korean. I started to laugh because here I was writing strange poems, thinking strange thoughts, and living a strange colonial life, and here someone had just given me a strange name. It was too good to pass up. That Japanese guy had called me "Yi Sang," so Yi Sang I would be.

(*He searches for a cigarette.*)

Shit. I need a smoke. Anyone have one?

(*He looks out into the audience.*)

No? Alright. We'll just have to pretend then. By the way, right now

I'm speaking to you in Korean. So you gotta pretend that too. Also pretend that I'm still alive. Because I died in 1937 after all.

(Pause. BLUE *paces, trying to imagine that he's smoking. He inhales, exhales in frustration.)*

Okay, let's all pretend I'm smoking right now. Me with a cigarette in my hands, inhaling, the smoke filling my lungs, the nicotine and tar mixing with the oxygen and blood in my lungs.

Okay, this pretend thing isn't working for me. I mean, some things you can pretend and some things you can't.

Well, so what? It's not the same, not one bit. There are other things I'm not doing also. I'm not eating. I'm not taking a walk. I'm not sitting in a bar. I'm not staying up all night drinking with friends. I'm not writing a novel or a poem. I'm not talking to . . . her.

(Lights up on GREEN. *She gets up and walks over to* BLUE *and stares at him.)*

Hi, did you know that Yi Sang means strange in Korean?

*(*GREEN *takes a drag from her cigarette then blows smoke in his face.)*

I like her.

*(*GREEN *exits.)*

Are you into numbers? I am. I think there's more truth in numbers than people realize. Take thirteen, for example. A number most people think means trouble. I think I know why. Just look at it. The "1" standing next to the "3." There's a man and a woman there — there's passion and love and anger. Oh yeah, the trouble's built right into the number.

How about another one? 27. 27 is 3 cubed. That's 3 times 3 times 3. The significance of 3? I really only had 2 close friends in my life — sometimes it felt like the 3 of us were the only people on earth.

I died when I was 27.

I died of tuberculosis. Just in case you were wondering.

Against my doctor's orders, I kept right on smoking to the end. What the hell, sometimes you gotta do that. Keep right on smoking. No matter what.

I was a writer, among other things. What did I like to write about? Severed limbs. Mirrors. The number 13. Suicidal love triangles. You know, the usual Korean subjects.

One time, I wrote something about my right leg. It was like my right leg was a character. A woman who I was seeing at the time thought that was really weird. "Why do you write about things like that," she asked. "Why don't you write about love or flowers or . . . me?" So I thought about that and I took notes about her. The way she moved, the way she smoked a cigarette. The way she applied her lipstick. But somehow what I wrote didn't have any life for me. Then I noticed how when she walked into a room, my eyes always focused on her: elbow. Her elbow had this incredibly magnetic quality to it. So I started writing about her beautiful elbow. This made me think about my right leg. Naturally the two would have to meet. They would have a torrid love affair—her elbow and my leg. Their affair became more passionate than the actual relationship between us. And as I wrote the story, the distinction between HER and HER ELBOW became increasingly blurry. The same with ME and MY RIGHT LEG.

When I finally showed her what I had written—she hit me.

3.0 "THE CROOKED JOINT, EPISODE 1"

A shadow projection of a LEG *(played by* RED*) and an* ELBOW *(played by* GREEN*). The* LEG *is sitting in a chair, smoking a cigarette. Sound of sax music,* ELBOW *saunters in, sits down on the chair in front of* LEG*. It's like a scene from a detective noir movie.*

LEG [RED]　　If I had known what I knew now, I would have turned that lady away that day. But I didn't know then what I knew now. Because that's the way time works, and the past is the past and future is the future. Now is now. Or was just now. Then. Forget it.

Her name was Ms. Bow. But she went by—

ELBOW [GREEN]   You can call me El.

LEG   As in the train?

ELBOW   Yeah. That's right, smartass.

LEG   So what can I do for you?

ELBOW   I need you to find someone for me.

LEG   Yeah?

ELBOW   Yeah. A sophisticated character. Likes to wear leather. Is tough, though. Can withstand all sorts of weather.

LEG   Hmmm. You wouldn't happen to be talking about a glove, would you?

ELBOW   Maybe I am and maybe I ain't.

LEG   My fee is 250 a day, plus expenses.

ELBOW   What kind of expenses?

LEG   I like nice socks. Calvin Klein, preferably.

ELBOW   Look, you can have Armani, as long as you go find this guy.

LEG   Yeah. So what he'd do to you?

ELBOW   It's what he didn't do.

LEG   Don't tell me—he gave you a bad case of tennis elbow?

ELBOW   *(bursting into tears)* He only worried about his hands. Never went for the longer gloves, said they were out of fashion. Left me out in the cold. So now I have incredibly dry skin. It's horrible!

LEG   Is it?

ELBOW   I don't get invited to parties anymore. I'VE BECOME A SOCIAL OUTCAST!

LEG	Listen, you're a cute limb, kid. I'll find him for you. And I'm not pulling your leg. Heh-heh-heh. And remember—I like my socks in silk. Much easier on the skin.

4.0 MOEBIUS #1

RED and BLUE. RED is walking around BLUE, making a strange turning motion every revolution. It looks like bad modern dance. BLUE is writing.

BLUE	So I think I'm in love. Did you hear me?
	(Notices what RED's doing.)
	What the hell are you doing?
RED	I'm trying to feel what it's like to be a Moebius strip.
BLUE	A Moebius strip?
RED	You know when you take a strip of paper and you give it a half twist to form a loop, but it only has one side to it. I'm trying to figure out how that feels.
BLUE	You know, one day I'm going to kick your ass. Really.
	So I saw this woman. She's works at the teahouse. She must be about twenty years old. But she looks sixteen. I think to her I might seem like I'm forty. Though when I was around her I felt like a boy of ten or eleven. She had this magnetic quality about her. I felt drawn to her immediately.
RED	How'd you get in? You have no money.
BLUE	I took some of yours.
	(Beat.)
	You don't mind, do you?
RED	No, I love working a full-time job so that you can mooch off of me.
BLUE	I would think that you'd be honored.
RED	Honored?

BLUE   Yeah. I make you a generous individual. If it weren't for me, you'd be hopelessly selfish and materialistic.

RED   You have to try this. It's pretty amazing.

   (Reluctantly, BLUE gets up and "walks" with RED.)

   So did you ask her out?

BLUE   No. I recited a poem.

RED   What'd she say?

BLUE   She said that poets are pretentious assholes.

RED   So that pretty much ended it for you?

BLUE   No, it only made me want her more.

RED   You're strange, man.

BLUE   So I've been told.

   (They stop, winded.)

   What was the purpose of this again?

RED   To feel what it's like to have only one side.

BLUE   You mean to feel totally subjective.

RED   Exactly. How does it feel for you?

BLUE   I feel slightly nauseous. What about you?

RED   It makes me feel . . . like going to a bar.

BLUE   And what're we going to do there?

RED   Well, what're we doing here?

5.0 THIRTEEN

RED, BLUE, and GREEN in some situation that suggests war. As the scene progresses, the lights go out one by one, until the end of the scene is in near darkness.

RED	Thirteen kids dash madly down the street. The first kid says . . .
BLUE	"It's scary." The second kid says . . .
RED	"It's scary." The third kid says . . .
BLUE	"It's scary." The fourth kid says . . .
RED	"It's scary." The fifth kid says . . .
BLUE	"It's scary." The sixth kid says . . .
RED	"It's scary." The seventh kid says . . .
BLUE	"It's scary." The eighth kid says . . .
RED	"It's scary." The ninth kid says . . .
BLUE	"It's scary." The tenth kid says . . .
RED	"It's scary."
GREEN	*(interrupting)* WOULD YOU KIDS CUT THAT SHIT OUT! Dumb scared kids.
	(Pause.)
RED	*(whispering)* The eleventh kid says . . .
	(Pause. BLUE doesn't answer.)
	Hey, I'm talking to you . . .
BLUE	Not now.
RED	The eleventh kid says . . .
BLUE	Didn't you hear her? She said that we should stop.
RED	It's better if we keep playing. She thinks it's wrong to play at a time like this. But it's always better to keep playing. No matter how bad things get.
BLUE	You think?
RED	Yeah.
BLUE	Maybe you're right.

RED	The eleventh kid says...
BLUE	*(resuming)* "It's scary." The twelfth kid says...

(Suddenly the lights shift and RED *and* BLUE *are blinded by floodlights. They are led offstage as if by some unseen power. As they leave, the lights dim.)*

GREEN	*(continuing)* So the thirteenth kid says...

(Silence. GREEN *becomes uneasy.)*

AND THE THIRTEENTH KID SAYS...

Hey, you guys forgot thirteen. If you're going to play the game, then at least go all the way to... thirteen.

The thirteenth kid says...

6.0 WATCHING DIET COKE

RED *and* BLUE *look out at the audience as if they are watching a woman perform.*
They stare for a long while.
They both gasp. A look of pain, which turns to relief, then amazement.

RED	Shinto?
BLUE	Yin.
RED	Yang.
BLUE	Feng.
RED	Shui.
BLUE	Nutra—
RED	—Sweet.
RED	You drink that stuff?
BLUE	Shhhhh. Look at that, man. Isn't that just so, so—
RED	Sexy?

BLUE	No.
RED	Erotic?
BLUE	Sensual. Stop being such an ape.
RED	Sorry.
BLUE	She's so still, yet she's moving. It's Zen.
RED	Zen . . . or Shabu-Shabu.
BLUE	You see the whole range of influences in the subtlest gesture. It has African flavors even. And the obvious Buddhist undertones.
RED	I see traces of Catholicism. And Nintendo.
BLUE	How can you leave out Dreamcast?
RED	Or Kurosawa?
BLUE	Wong Kar Wai.
RED	Ang Lee.
BLUE	Bruce Lee.
RED	Geddy Lee.
BLUE	Lee Majors.
RED	Jamie Sommers.
BLUE	Suzanne Sommers.
RED	"Three's Company."
BLUE	"Three Amigos."
RED	"Three Tenors."
BLUE	"Three Stooges."
RED	Bugs Bunny.
BLUE	Elmer Fudd.
RED	Anime.

BLUE	Akira.	
RED	Kurosawa.	
	(Beat.)	
	Look at that.	
BLUE	Amazing.	
RED	I'm—	
BLUE	Astounded?	
RED	*(holding his breath)* No.	
BLUE	Electrified?	
RED	*(still holding)* No.	
BLUE	Mesmerized?	
RED	*(exhaling)* Thirsty.	
	(He starts choking from thirst.)	
BLUE	Did you see how she worked that straw?	
RED	*(hoarse)* Water . . . . I need water.	
BLUE	She made that straw come to life.	
RED	*(hoarse)* Water . . .	
BLUE	That straw was like—	
RED	like scoring—	
BLUE	the winning—	
RED	goal—	
BLUE	in the—	
RED *and* BLUE	WORLD CUP! *(Spontaneously, like the Spanish sportscaster.)* GOOOOOOOOOOOOAAAAAAAAAALLLLLLLLLLL!	
RED	*(cont'd)* GOOOOOOOOOOOOAAAAAAAAAALLLLLLLLLLL!	

(BLUE yells various "Sportscenter" phrases over RED.)

BLUE   *(Scarface voice)* SAY HELLO TO MY LIL' FRIEN'! *(As Chris Berman.)* SHE — WILL — GO — ALL — THE — WAY!

BOO-YAH! AND SHE BUSTS OUT THE WHIPPING STICK! AND THE YANKEES WIN, THE YANKEES WIN!

(They both stop, emotionally spent.)

RED   Whew.

BLUE   That was intense, man.

(Beat.)

I'm gonna go talk to her.

RED   But she's, she's . . .

BLUE   What?

RED   You know.

BLUE   I don't care.

RED   Alright. Do what you want.

BLUE   Well, thank you, father.

RED   What's that supposed to mean?

BLUE   I think you get it. Daddy.

RED   Stop it.

BLUE   Alright. Ahbuhji.

RED   I'm not your father.

BLUE   Then stop acting like it. Otosan.

RED   Shut up.

BLUE   Pappy.

RED   Not only am I not your father. I'm not your father's father. Or your

	father's father's father. Or your father's father's father's father's father's father's father.
BLUE	You left one out. And the most important one too.
RED	Come on, let's go.
BLUE	No. I have to see her.
RED	She looks like bad news, man. Women like that? They can screw around with your whole life.
BLUE	My life could use some screwing around with.
RED	You don't have the wings you used to. You should realize that.
BLUE	*(pissed)* What do you mean by that? My wings aren't clipped! I can still fly! Don't tell me I can't fly anymore! I'm still breathing clouds, I'm still inhaling the clear blue sky.
RED	Have fun.

7.0 DRINKING DIET COKE

We now see what RED and BLUE just watched. It is GREEN performing a strange version of a Japanese tea ceremony, but using a can of Diet Coke, a small cloth, and a straw.

Every movement is slow, stylized, like Noh movement. But there's a little MTV thrown in, too.

GREEN kneels in front of a small table. This is her START position. She "addresses" the table with a small bow. She wipes the surface clean in slow, deliberate strokes. She pauses.

GREEN places the cup on the surface far from her. She goes back to START. Then she places the Diet Coke can in front of her. She moves the cup a few inches closer to her. She moves the can a few inches away from her. Between each movement is a pause. She finally gets the can and cup so that they are in the center of the table and side by side. Now she takes out the cloth and wipes the table again, in circular strokes around the can and cup.

Now she picks up the can and brings it to her face. She hesitates and puts the can back down where it was. She pauses, concentrates. She picks up the can again, then puts it back down. She repeats this several times like a martial artist who is trying to concentrate on breaking a big block of cement. Finally she finds the right "groove" and brings the can to her face. She breaks into a huge grin, like an Asian woman in a Diet Coke commercial. She holds this grin for a few seconds, then brings the can back down to the table. She opens the can and pours it into the cup, filling about one-fourth of the cup. She dabs her own face as if what she just did took the most strenuous effort.

Now she brings out a straw. She places it on the table, parallel to her body. She tears off the end of the paper wrapper. She places the paper on the table in the upper right-hand corner. The rest of the wrapper she takes off the straw, but it takes like a million years, because she's doing this like it's a religious act. Finally the wrapper is off and she lays it perpendicular to the other piece, so that to the audience it looks like an exclamation point.

Now for the moment of truth. She places the straw into the cup and draws out a little bit of Diet Coke (by placing her finger over the open end of the straw) and brings the straw to her mouth. She leans her mouth back and lets the Coke from the straw drop into her mouth. She then places the straw on the table, parallel to the paper. She goes back to the START position and bows.

8.0 "THE CROOKED JOINT, EPISODE 2"

LEG and GLOVE. RED plays LEG, as in earlier scene. BLUE plays GLOVE.

LEG [RED]   You know your wife's been looking for you.

GLOVE [BLUE]   She's not my wife.

LEG   No?

GLOVE   No.

LEG   Come on, quit your stalling. Or else.

GLOVE   Or else what?

LEG   I ship you off to Isotoner. You hear what they do to gloves at Isotoner?

GLOVE   No, what?

LEG   They'll recycle you. Turn you into a pair of driving gloves. Some bus driver picks you up. He's a large, somewhat overweight man. Sweats a lot. Drives a screaming load of hyperactive third graders. He grips the wheel, out of frustration. The gloves get dirty, sweaty, grimy . . . *infected.*

GLOVE   I get the picture! She's been playing you, though.

LEG   You trying to step on my toes or something?

GLOVE   Hey, if the shoe fits.

LEG   I oughta stomp you right now. So you'll never play the piano again.

GLOVE   I don't play the piano.

LEG   Yeah, well you should.

GLOVE   Why?

LEG   Everyone should play a musical instrument.

GLOVE   You underestimate me. These gloves have killed. They've strangled. They've pulled triggers. They've choked. They've felt the last dying breath of some poor soul who just happened to be at the wrong place at the wrong time.

LEG   Oh yeah? I have toothmarks from all the faces I've kicked in. Like I got dental records in here that go back ten years. I'm thinking of selling them to an orthodontist.

GLOVE   I know you're just doing your job. But you gotta understand. She's a dangerous . . . limb. I bet she gave you that ole elbow in distress routine.

LEG   Well . . .

GLOVE   Yeah. Don't need to say a word. Can see it all in your shins. Written all over your hamstrings. I bet she offered you silk socks, didn't she?

LEG   Calvin Klein.

GLOVE   She's got you in a leg-lock, doesn't she?

LEG   What do you want me to tell her?

GLOVE   Tell her that my hands are tied. I ain't going back to her.

9.0 GLASS

　　GREEN alone.

GREEN   when i'm alone with people

　　　　when i'm in front of people

　　　　i become

　　　　i become those people

　　　　i scan their eyes

　　　　and feel thin

　　　　naked

　　　　their eyes take hold of me

　　　　their eyes inhale me

　　　　devour me

　　　　i don't mind

　　　　i feel like it's only my body

　　　　only

　　　　i become their mirror

　　　　i start becoming them

　　　　i lose my sense of i

　　　　i lose my sense

　　　　i lose my

　　　　i lose

　　　　　i

and so

so i proceed

i entertain

sing

dance

do the things i'm supposed to do

make it seem effortless

like it's an art form

all the while a flame

is bubbling under me

slowly burning my dreams

i don't like mirrors

i see

i see too

i see too much

them

me

me

one day, i'd like to turn it back on them

take all those stares

all those pupils

those gaping eyes

send the light back

blind them with the fire

fry them with the same glare

the same hot light

that melted

the wings

of icarus

sent him

crashing

to the sea

10.0 FLOWERING TREE

    BLUE *is writing. He's trying to get something "right."* GREEN *and* RED *speak as if they're inside his head.*

GREEN   *(sensual)* In the middle of the middle of the middle of a field . . . there is a tree that flowers, that towers above everything else. This tree thinks itself into being, such that to dream this tree is to bring its leaves into **green** swaying life. How ardently it blossoms, this tree. This tree cannot be anything else, yet it knows not what it is, nor what it wants to be. And so I ran through the wild, tall grass, the sky laughing in silver streaks. For this one tree, I have **lived** . . . I have **cried.**

RED   *(organic)* In the middle of the middle of the middle of a field . . . there is a tree that flowers, that towers above everything else. This tree thinks itself into being, such that to dream this tree is to bring its leaves into **red** swaying life. How ardently it blossoms, this tree. This tree cannot be anything else, yet it knows not what it is, nor what it wants to be. And so I ran through the wild, tall grass, the sky laughing in silver streaks. For this one tree, I have **loved** . . . I have **tried.**

BLUE   *(impassioned)* In the middle of the middle of the middle of a field . . . there is a tree that flowers, that towers above everything else. This tree thinks itself into being, such that to dream this tree is to bring its leaves into **blue** swaying life. How ardently it blossoms, this tree. This tree cannot be anything else, yet it knows not what it is, nor what it wants to be. And so I ran through the wild, tall grass, the sky laughing in silver streaks. For this one tree, I have **laughed** . . . I have **spied.**

11.0 COURTSHIP

A café. BLUE *and* GREEN *are meeting for the first time. There is a long awkward silence.*

BLUE   Well.

GREEN   Well.

BLUE   Thank you.

GREEN   For what?

BLUE   For agreeing to meet me. I'm honored.

(Pause.)

BLUE   I brought you a present.

(He brings out a two-liter bottle of Diet Coke that's wrapped in a gift box. She doesn't know what to say.)

GREEN   Gee. Thanks. Ummm. It's . . . huge.

BLUE   Yeah. I had it ordered special. Shall I open it?

GREEN   No.

BLUE   Really?

GREEN   Yeah. You see. That's what I do for work.

BLUE   Right. *(Embarrassed.)* Idiot!

GREEN   But I'm flattered. Thank you.

(Pause.)

BLUE   I think we should get married.

*(*GREEN *stares at* BLUE *and ponders this.)*

GREEN   Okay.

BLUE   Okay?

GREEN   Yes.

BLUE   But why?

GREEN   Because you asked me.

BLUE   But—

GREEN   You weren't serious?

BLUE   I was serious.

GREEN   Then what?

BLUE   You barely know me.

GREEN   Do you care?

BLUE   No.

GREEN   If you don't care, I don't care.

BLUE   Good. It's settled then. I think.

GREEN   There's only one thing I ask of you.

BLUE   What?

GREEN   You don't ask questions.

BLUE   *(confused)* Okay.

GREEN   You don't ask, you accept. I disappear for a week, you don't wonder where I am. Okay, maybe you wonder, but you don't go looking for me. I return, you accept me back. You don't pester me with accusations.

BLUE   And what about me? You won't ask anything of me?

GREEN   Of course not.

BLUE   I'd like to kiss you.

GREEN   Please don't. Not right now. Do you have a job?

BLUE		Does it matter?
GREEN		No.
BLUE		I'm in a transitional phase at the moment. But my friend has a job.
GREEN		Your friend?
BLUE		Yes. He usually pays for me. You should meet him. He's like a father to me.
GREEN		I see.
BLUE		Maybe the three of us can hang out together.
GREEN		Sure. Tomorrow.
BLUE		Great.

(Pause.)

GREEN   I have a personal question.

BLUE   Okay.

GREEN   *(secretively)* Do you have water?

BLUE   Water?

GREEN   Really cold, clean, pure spring water. The kind that comes from the mountains somewhere. The kind that when it hits the back of your throat with its icy sting, you can feel it in your toes. The kind of water that makes you feel like a new person, that you've turned a corner in your life, that makes you want to stand up and sing to the whole world: *(singing from "A Chorus Line")*

KISS TODAY GOODBYE,

THE SWEETNESS AND THE SORROW.

WISH ME LUCK, THE SAME TO YOU,

BUT I CAN'T REGRET

WHAT I DID FOR LOVE, WHAT I DID FOR LOVE.

LOOK, MY EYES ARE DRY.

>   THE GIFT WAS OURS TO BORROW.
>
>   IT'S AS IF WE ALWAYS KNEW,
>
>   AND I WON'T REGRET WHAT I DID FOR LOVE,
>
>   WHAT I DID FOR LOVE.
>
>   GONE,
>
>   LOVE IS NEVER GONE.
>
>   AS WE TRAVEL ON,
>
>   LOVE'S WHAT WE'LL REMEMBER.
>
>   KISS TODAY GOODBYE,
>
>   AND POINT ME T'WARD TOMORROW.
>
>   WE DID WHAT WE HAD TO DO.
>
>   WON'T FORGET, CAN'T REGRET
>
>   WHAT I DID FOR LOVE.
>
>   WHAT I DID FOR LOVE.
>
>   WHAT I DID FOR . . . LOVE.

BLUE   Yeah. I can get you that water. I *will* get you that water.

12.0 BUS STOP

A plaza in Seoul. GREEN *is waiting. She paces, looks at her watch.* RED *shows up. He looks around, stares at* GREEN. *She ignores him.*

RED   Excuse me, are you—

GREEN   Yes. You must be—

RED   Right. He and I are good friends.

GREEN   He seems to be late.

RED   He has a very poor sense of time.

(Pause.)

You look familiar.

GREEN You do too. I think it's the black hair.

RED No, I'm serious. Oh, wait a minute. You're the performer. You do that Diet Coke ceremony.

GREEN I thought he would have told you.

RED He actually has told me nothing about you. Except that you and he have reached a kind of agreement.

GREEN An agreement? That's how he described it?

RED He's very secretive about things like that. You should feel honored that he wanted to introduce us. I've never met any of his other female friends. And believe me, he's had . . . looks like rain.

GREEN He used to be an architect?

RED A very good one too.

GREEN What happened?

RED I think he developed problems with geometry. He stopped seeing right angles. Couldn't draw straight lines. That kind of thing.

GREEN So what does he do now?

RED We hang out in bars a lot. He and I drink and smoke together a lot. Sometimes we don't say anything for hours. Just smoke and drink. Smoke and drink.

GREEN Men like that kind of thing.

RED What kind of thing?

GREEN Boredom. They relish repetition. They don't mind doing one thing over and over.

RED I don't know about that. I like variety.

GREEN I can't imagine sitting in a room all day.

	I heard you have a job.
RED	I'm an architect too.
	(Pause.)
	I build things. I figure out how things work.
GREEN	Do you think you know how I work?
RED	I think I have an idea.
GREEN	Let's take a walk.
RED	But what if he shows up?
GREEN	What if? This was his idea anyway. He wanted your approval. He thinks of you as a father-figure.
RED	I think of *him* as a father-figure.
GREEN	You boys need to talk more, I guess.
RED	Where should we go?
GREEN	Surprise me.

13.0 LIMB REMOVAL SERVICE

Tableaux.

BLUE is sleeping. There is a knock on the door. He wakes up. RED barges in. He hands him a slip of paper, forces BLUE to sit down. He straps BLUE down, then removes a cutting instrument of some kind. There is a whirring noise. BLUE cries out in silent pain. RED removes his arm, places it in a plastic bag, packs it into a suitcase. He thanks BLUE and leaves. BLUE is left sitting without his arm. He stares at the business card that RED has left him.

Later. BLUE goes to a café. He sits at a table and tries to read. After a moment he notices that RED and GREEN are sitting at a nearby table. They are chatting and laughing. BLUE notices that RED's arm keeps waving to him, as if to taunt him. He gets up to talk to RED, but RED and GREEN pay their bill and leave.

Another evening. BLUE is sleeping. A knock at the door. BLUE wakes up. GREEN barges in this time. GREEN straps BLUE down and removes his other arm.

GREEN *wraps it up, leaves a business card and leaves.* BLUE *sadly goes back to sleep, now armless.*

BLUE *goes back to the café. He sits at a table and tries to read. He notices that* RED *and* GREEN *are sitting at the nearby table, and they are "all arms," wrapped around each other romantically. Periodically one of the arms will wave to* BLUE, *as if it were mocking him again. He goes up to confront them, but they leave as before.*

Another evening. BLUE *is sleeping. A knock at the door.* BLUE *wakes up.* RED *and* GREEN *barge in together this time. They hover over him, reattaching his arms, then leave, apologizing profusely.* BLUE *reads their business cards again. He tries out his new arms. They seem to suit him well. He beams happily and thinks of what to do. He decides to pour himself a glass of water. He sits down and tries to drink, but the arm doesn't obey him and the water "misses" his mouth. He does this a few times and realizes that these are not his arms. One of his arms slaps him. The arm slaps again and again. Soon he is cowering, in fear of his own arms.*

14.0 MOEBIUS #2

BLUE *alone, playing with a Moebius strip.*

BLUE   The Moebius strip. Has only one side to it.

    (He tries to "feel" what it's like to be a Moebius strip again. He stops in disgust. BLUE *breaks the strip—now it's just a strip of paper.)*

There. You are no longer Moebius. I have freed you from the bonds of Moebius . . . ness . . . ity. You are now a free strip of paper. Go forth, be merry, and prosper.

    *(*BLUE *goes back to his writing.* RED *walks in. He's got a can of Diet Coke in his pants pocket.)*

RED   Hey.

BLUE   Yo.

RED   We waited for you.

BLUE   You did not.

RED	We did!	
BLUE	What, for like three minutes?	
RED	Longer than that.	
BLUE	So what did you do?	
RED	We walked. And talked.	
BLUE	Where?	
RED	The park. Around the city.	
BLUE	And?	
RED	You're a lucky man.	
BLUE	Oh?	
RED	Yeah. I didn't know you were engaged.	
BLUE	She told you?	
RED	Yeah.	
BLUE	It was supposed to be a secret.	
RED	It's called conversation. It's what normal people do.	
BLUE	You're supposed to be my friend.	
RED	You're overreacting. She and I came to an agreement.	
BLUE	An agreement?	
RED	We decided she should marry you.	
BLUE	What if I don't want to marry her.	
RED	Well, that's another variable.	
BLUE	This isn't math class.	
RED	But it is. It's like you're one function, she's another function, and the two of you can be graphed. See, it's all very rational.	
BLUE	What about you? What's your "function"?	

RED		I'm more like a constant. Like the speed of light. I don't change, no matter what the frame of reference. I'm a rock.
BLUE		You are not the speed of light. You're one of those fucking irrational numbers. Like pi. I waited an hour, you know.
RED		She didn't want to wait. She's restless.
BLUE		I guess you are too.
RED		I'm impatient with life these days.
BLUE		Yeah, me too. I think I'm falling to earth.
RED		We've been through this—you don't got wings.
BLUE		Oh, I've been up there. I know what it feels like.
RED		Yeah?
BLUE		You're no longer you up there. You're it—us—we—me—them—you're the whole world . . . the sky, the air, the sun, the moon, the ocean. All of it inside of you and yet outside of you too.
RED		And now?
BLUE		Now, I'm screaming toward the earth. It's coming up fast. My wings have been clipped.
RED		You're getting married. You're just growing them.
BLUE		It all depends on what side you look at it from.
RED		If you're a Moebius strip, there's only one side to look at it from.
BLUE		I prefer having more than one side, thank you very much.

    (He shows him the strip of paper.)

    And another thing, are you really happy to see me or what?

    (They stare at his can.)

RED		Oh yeah. I forgot about this.

    (He pulls out a can of Diet Coke.)

	Uh, you want some?
BLUE	No, thanks.

15.0 "THE CROOKED JOINT, EPISODE 3"

Now it's GLOVE *and* ELBOW. BLUE *plays* GLOVE *and* GREEN *plays* ELBOW.

GLOVE [BLUE]	You done good, kid, you dug me up. You sent that Leg after me and you blew my cover. So now what? What you got in store for me now?
ELBOW [GREEN]	*(Far away.)* Good question.
GLOVE	I thought we had an understanding.
ELBOW	Sure.
GLOVE	Refresh my memory, because I'm not sure I understand anymore what our understanding was. Is.
ELBOW	Our understanding was—
GLOVE	Yes?
ELBOW	That we'd ask no questions.
GLOVE	Good. Now let's see: you hire a private investigator to come after me. Does that in any way follow the spirit of that understanding?
ELBOW	I was bored. What can I say?
GLOVE	You had this goon terrorize me with stories of bus drivers because you were bored?
ELBOW	Yeah, and I'm not terribly excited right now either. I'm going out. See ya.

*(*GLOVE *grabs her and shakes her.)*

GLOVE	Why do you always have to do this to me?
ELBOW	*(Screaming.)* HELLLPPPPPP! HELLPPPPPP!
GLOVE	Hey, shut your yap.

ELBOW   You're such a bully. Mister Leg is so much more of a gentleman. He has such nice . . . knees.

GLOVE   Well, excuse the shit out of me. You know what, the two of you deserve each other.

ELBOW   How dare you talk to me like that? I'm a high-class . . . joint! I used to model gloves and jewelry. The crook of my arm was on the covers of fashion magazines around the world. But then I fell in love—

(She breaks down in tears again.)

GLOVE   *(Aside.)* I knew right then that the smart thing to do would be to run and never look back. But I was never all that smart. Book-smart, maybe, but not street-smart. I was like a big dumb dog running to his big blue water dish on a hot hazy humid summer day. Women say that men are dogs. If that's true, then dogs might be men. *(Woof-woof.)* Look, I'm sorry I said all that. Let's turn the page and start fresh. Every page has two sides, after all.

ELBOW   *(sniffling)* Okay. I feel like you're mixing your metaphors, but I don't mind.

16.0 BOTTLES

BLUE and RED's room. BLUE is lying in bed with a sea of two-liter plastic Coca-Cola bottles around him.

RED   What the hell were you thinking? A man's got to know his limits. What are you, a child?

BLUE   I know, I know.

RED   Do you have a death wish or something?

BLUE   Or something.

RED   I'm worried about you.

BLUE   *I'm* worried about me.

(GREEN enters.)

BLUE *and* RED   Hey.

                 (Pause.)

GREEN   Are you okay?

BLUE   Yeah.

RED   He's so damn lucky. Look how much of this stuff he put into his body.

GREEN   What the hell were you thinking? A man's got to know his limits. What are you, a child?

RED   I already said all that.

GREEN   You can't mess with this stuff. Only a seasoned professional can consume that much. This stuff is not like *water*.

BLUE   Water! That sounds really good. What I would do for a nice, cold glass of pure, refreshing H_2O.

RED   I'll get you some.

BLUE   Not from the tap. From the source. From a fresh mountain stream. The water rushing over sharp rocks. A babbling brook. *(Making a sound like water.)* Shhhhhh-shhhhh-shhhhhh . . .

RED   Okaaaaay.

GREEN   Would you mind?

RED   Mind what?

GREEN   Getting him some water. You know, water is very important.

RED   Where am I going to get water like that?

GREEN   The mountains.

RED   And how am I going to get to the mountains?

GREEN   There's a bus.

RED   Are you going to come with me?

GREEN   I'll stay. I'll watch him.

RED		Yeah? *(to BLUE)* Is this what you want?
BLUE		Yes. Thanks.
RED		Okay. You need anything else?
BLUE		I'm good.
RED		*(to GREEN)* How about you?
GREEN		No, thanks.
RED		*(to BLUE)* How about a book? Whenever I'm sick I like to have a good book to read. A Russian novel is the perfect thing to read when you're sick. It just fits your mood. Remember that woman I used to see, the one with the great Dostoevsky collection?
BLUE		Ohhh, yeah. Whatever happened to her?
RED		I don't know. It's funny, though. I remember her books more than I remember her. She had great books.
BLUE		She had voluptuous books. Really hot titles.
RED		She was the best library system in the world.
GREEN		*(looking at bus schedule)* You'd better hurry. The last bus is leaving in twenty minutes.
RED		Right. Which bus is it again?
GREEN		The number 13.
RED		Uh-huh.
BLUE		Thanks, man, I really appreciate this.
RED		Sure, no problem.
GREEN		You need money?
RED		No, I'm fine.
		(Pause.)
		So. I guess I'll be going.

GREEN   See you.

RED   Hope you get better.

(He exits.)

(Pause.)

GREEN   I thought he'd never leave.

BLUE   He was just trying to help.

GREEN   That story he was telling was so obnoxious. *(Imitating.)* "She was the best library system in the world."

BLUE   It was just a joke.

GREEN   Is that what you guys do when you're together, make up little jokes about all the women in your life? *(Imitating.)* "Oh, she wasn't much to look at, but she's got a *great* record collection."

BLUE   I don't understand why you're so annoyed.

GREEN   You don't?

BLUE   No.

GREEN   What do you think I deal with every night? You think I'm having witty conversations about Tolstoy? No, I'm dealing with men. Men who look at me. Men who talk about me just like you guys do.

BLUE   We don't talk about you that way.

GREEN   No?

BLUE   No. You're different. You're not like all the others.

GREEN   How am I different?

BLUE   I don't know. You're . . . you know . . . you're . . . just different.

GREEN   You know, for someone who's supposed to be a poet, you sure are fucking inarticulate!

BLUE   From the moment I saw you, I felt like you were different. That's why I asked you to marry me.

GREEN	That's supposed to prove something?	
BLUE	I would think that proves something.	
GREEN	Do you know how many men have proposed to me? I've lost count.	
BLUE	Well, what do you want me to do? Kill myself?	

(GREEN stares at him. BLUE stares at her. Pause.)

GREEN	Let's take a drive.
BLUE	Where?
GREEN	To the ocean.
BLUE	Now?
GREEN	Yes.
BLUE	But—
GREEN	But what?
BLUE	Let's go.

17.0 "THE CROOKED JOINT, EPISODE 4"

ELBOW is sitting in LEG's office.

LEG	I never trusted those hands. They weren't honest hands. They were deceitful hands. Was there anything that he left? Some trace? A note?
ELBOW	Just this.

(She shows him a lone white glove. She bursts into tears.)

LEG	If it's one thing I can't stand, it's some female joint coming in here and turning on the faucets.
ELBOW	I'm sorry. I just miss him so.
LEG	Why'd he leave anyway? *(She bursts into tears again.)* Hey, would you stop that?

ELBOW   We had a fight.

LEG   What'd you fight about?

ELBOW   You.

LEG   Me? How'd I get dragged into this? I'm just a gimpy gumshoe, trying to earn an honest buck in this crummy little world.

ELBOW   I told him that I loved you.

LEG   You what?

ELBOW   I'm sorry.

LEG   Why'd you tell him that?

ELBOW   Because it's the truth. Ever since I walked into your crummy little office and seen how you walk around in the gimpy way you have.

LEG   Miss Bow. This is unprofessional.

ELBOW   Well, I had to be honest. But it passed.

LEG   Passed?

ELBOW   Yeah, I told you: I lov*ed* you. I use the past tense. After I saw you a few more times I realized that you were just a gimpy gumshoe trying to make an honest buck in this crummy little—

LEG   Hey, I get the picture.

ELBOW   But he wouldn't believe me. I tried to make him see that you were nothing to me, that you really meant nothing to me at all.

LEG   Uh, thanks.

ELBOW   But he never listened. He grew wings. He flew away.

        (*Long pause.* LEG *lights a cigarette.*)

LEG   I never thought he could fly. Now that's the stuff dreams are made of.

18.0 WET

BLUE and RED's apartment. RED is sitting on a chair. There is a large bottle of water in front of him. He is reading a book. He frequently looks at his watch from impatience and anger.

BLUE enters. He is sopping wet. They look at each other, but don't say anything. Pause.

RED   Well?

BLUE   Well what?

RED   Well, what the hell happened?

BLUE   I don't know.

RED   You don't know?

BLUE   It's complicated.

RED   You know how long it takes to go into the mountains? Two hours. I had to climb through the woods to find this little stream where I could find your precious water—Shhhhh-shhhh-shhhh. Then I gotta lug the bottle all the way back here, only to find that the two of you are gone.

RED   You're wet.

BLUE   Yup.

RED   How'd you get so wet?

BLUE   We went to the ocean.

RED   The ocean?

BLUE   She has a car.

RED   Okay.

BLUE   We drove out to the water. She thought it would be good for me.

RED   I thought you were deathly ill.

BLUE   I guess I got better.

(Pause.)

Hey, look . . . I'm sorry.

RED Sorry?

(Beat.)

Okay, so you're at the ocean. Did you decide to go swimming or something?

BLUE Or something, yes.

RED Could you be a little more specific, here?

BLUE I'm not in the mood at the moment. I'm wet. I'm tired. My mouth has a funny aftertaste from all that Diet Coke I drank.

RED *You're* tired? How about me? How did I spend my afternoon? I was walking in the woods, trying to find you some water. *(He slams the bottle of spring water on the table.)* Here's your damn water, by the way.

BLUE Thanks.

(Pause.)

RED Well?

BLUE What?

RED Aren't you going to drink it?

BLUE Not now. Later. I'll have some later.

RED Later?

BLUE I'm not in the mood right now.

RED I don't give a shit about your mood. I went to a lot of trouble to get this damned water, so I'd like to see you drink it right now, if you don't mind.

(Pause.)

BLUE *(lost in thought)* We were going to jump in together.

RED	Who?	
BLUE	She and I. We decided that life was too much for the both of us. She's tired of performing. I'm tired of . . . hell, I'm just tired. So we decided to run into the ocean together.	
RED	How romantic.	
BLUE	It was a spiritual moment.	
RED	So what happened?	
BLUE	We both ran in. The water was cold at first, but once I got in deeper, it felt great. So I kept running. I didn't notice that she had turned back.	
RED	She turned back?	
BLUE	Yeah.	
RED	So what were you doing? You can't even swim.	
BLUE	I was drowning. *(RED starts laughing.)* This isn't very funny, you know. I could have died.	
RED	So how'd you get out?	
BLUE	Luckily a fisherman was nearby. He pulled me out.	
RED	You were saved by a fisherman? What did I tell you about women like that? They're trouble, man, trouble.	

(RED opens the bottle of water and starts pouring it into a bucket.)

BLUE	Hey. That's wasteful.
RED	What were you expecting, some beautiful death at sea?
BLUE	I don't know what I was thinking. Don't throw that all away.

(BLUE tries to cup the water into his hands, but RED keeps pouring it into the bucket. They struggle for a moment, and then RED gets the bottle away from BLUE. There is just a little water left.)

I SAID, DON'T THROW IT ALL AWAY!

RED	What a day. What . . . a . . . day.

> *(Long pause. BLUE doesn't know what to do, but after a moment, he gets up and goes offstage. He returns with two wine glasses. He pours the remaining water into the glasses. He gives one to RED.)*

RED	*(making a toast)* To . . .
BLUE	To . . .

> *(Pause. They can't think of anything to say.)*

RED	Friendship.
BLUE	Right.

> *(They raise their glasses and are about to drink when GREEN enters. She stares at the two of them. After thinking about it for a moment, she wordlessly goes up to BLUE and puts her head on his shoulder. He gives his glass to RED, then holds GREEN. RED stares at the two of them while holding both glasses. He slowly drinks both glasses of water while BLUE continues to hold GREEN.)*

19.0 NOODLES #2

Same scene as the Noodles #1 scene, with BLUE and RED reversed. It is suggested that this scene start faster than Noodles #1. The scene should become increasingly fast-paced until the end.

Lights up on a pot simmering. We hear the sound of burning magnified.

RED stares at the pot. He stares for a really long time. He glares out into the audience, then resumes his staring. He looks at his watch. He takes his watch off, listens to it, winds it.

GREEN enters. They look at each other in surprise. Then they play it cool. With a flourish, she pulls out a package of instant ramen noodles.

She peers into the pot.

GREEN	You got no water in there.
RED	What do you mean, I got no water.
GREEN	Look.

(RED *does a double-take.*)

RED — Dammit!

GREEN — What?

RED — Someone stole my water!

GREEN — Stole?

RED — Yeah! Of all the low-down, dirty things someone could do.

GREEN — I think you forgot.

RED — Forgot? You think I forgot to put the water in? What kind of an idiot do you think I am? Don't answer that.

GREEN — Well, here're your noodles anyway.

(GREEN *gives* RED *the noodles.* RED *addresses the bag of noodles.*)

RED — *(manic)* Hello there, little noodles. Look at you—so innocent, so above it all. "We had nothing to do with the water disappearing. We're just a pack of noodles." But you don't fool me. I see through your lies. It's a conspiracy, isn't it? OHHH YES, YOU'RE ALL IN THIS TOGETHER!

(RED *throws the bag of noodles into the pot and turns up the heat.*)

RED — I'm gonna teach these noodles a lesson. I'm gonna burn the shit out of these noodles!

GREEN — You're in one of your moods today, aren't you?

RED — You would be too if someone stole your water.

GREEN — No one stole the water, dumbass—

RED — I HAD WATER IN THE POT, OKAY? I FILLED THE POT UP WITH WATER AND NOW THERE'S NO WATER. SO DON'T TELL ME— OWWWWW!

(*He grips his leg violently, as if he has cramps.*)

GREEN — Okay, okay. No need to get so worked up about it.

(Pause, as RED *recovers.)*

RED   How're they doing?

GREEN   They who?

RED   The noodles.

(She lifts the cover.)

GREEN   They're doing . . . okay.

RED   Are they frying? Are they burning in hell?

GREEN   Of course not.

RED   Fuck it. I'm going out.

GREEN   Why?

RED   I'm hungry.

(He waits.)

You coming?

GREEN   I have to watch.

RED   Right.

GREEN   There could be a fire.

RED   I can turn the pot off.

GREEN   You can't do that to noodles. Reverse direction on them like that. Bad karma.

RED   You're saying that noodles have souls?

(Thinks for a moment.)

Don't answer that. Damn, you're screwing with my head again. Staying or going?

GREEN   Staying.

RED   Suit yourself.

(RED exits. GREEN watches him go. She waits to make sure he's left, then sneakily removes a bottle of water from her pants. GREEN holds it up and regards it. GREEN opens the bottle with a flourish and starts to drink, as if she's been dying of thirst, when BLUE enters, picking up just where RED left off. GREEN plays along like BLUE is RED, although there's definitely something "off" about him. GREEN does a spit-take of the mouthful of water.)

BLUE   I forgot my . . . keys.

GREEN   Uhhh . . . hey.

BLUE   What is that?

GREEN   This?

BLUE   That.

GREEN   Uhhh . . . looks like water.

BLUE   I KNOW THAT'S WATER.

GREEN   You asked.

BLUE   So what are you doing with water?

GREEN   What do you mean?

BLUE   Didn't we just establish my need for water? My need to boil the noodles?

GREEN   Yes. I believe we did establish that. I forgot, I guess.

BLUE   You saw him, didn't you?

GREEN   Him? Him who?

BLUE   You know damn well him who. **Him.** The Him who I told you not to see.

GREEN   Ohhhh. Him. No, I didn't see him.

BLUE   No?

GREEN   No.

        (Pause. BLUE *fumes.* GREEN *looks at* BLUE, *tentatively at first, then stares at him.)*

BLUE   Look, maybe we need some . . . what're you looking at?

GREEN   You look different.

BLUE   What?

GREEN   You seem different. Did you get a haircut or something?

BLUE   No.

GREEN   Turn around.

        *(*RED *turns around slowly. She stops him and slowly traces out the outline of imaginary wings protruding from his back.)*

        Strange, but you seem to have wings.

BLUE   I used to have wings.

GREEN   You did?

BLUE   Years ago. They fell off. The harsh light of the world burned them off of me. But I still feel them. They're like phantom wings, you know?

GREEN   You still feel like you're flying?

BLUE   Sometimes. When I close my eyes real tight. When I can convince myself that all of this — everything we see — is just an illusion.

20.0 SMOKE

BLUE *alone. He is in "his" room. His wife's room is either up- or offstage.*

BLUE   We had a simple ceremony. Just the three of us. It was the best thing, trust me.

        Our honeymoon was walking along the river, then coming back to this apartment. I tried to carry her over the threshold like they do in those Hollywood movies, but I didn't have the strength.

That first night she and I shared the same room. But the next morning, she tells me that she needs her own room, and I'll have the other. She says she needs her privacy. And she has to continue with her entertaining.

Now, I'm not stupid. I have an idea about what goes on in her room. But I don't want to know. She expressly forbids me to go in there in the evening.

One night I decided to go out. I took some money out of her drawer and went out into the streets. But I found that I had nowhere to go. I felt stupid sitting in some restaurant all alone. So I walked around a little, and I came home, not thinking, or maybe I was halfway thinking, but I opened the door because I have to go through her room to get to my room and I saw—something that I definitely should not have.

> *(There is the sound of* RED *and* GREEN *laughing. Some empty Diet Coke cans get tossed into* BLUE*'s direction and clang noisily on the floor.)*

You know, when you see something like that, it affects you. It changes you. It makes you want to . . . drink. And smoke. Drink and smoke.

My room has started to feel like a prison. I try to write. I try to laugh. I try to taste. I try to remember. I try to feel all sides of the world—that feeling when I had wings. That indescribably delicious, joyous feeling.

> *(He spreads his arms. The lights shift and for a brief moment there is the sound of rushing air—it looks like he's flying.*
>
> *Then the lights shift back.*
>
> BLUE *lowers his arms.)*

But you see, I have no wings anymore. To fly—it's just a distant memory. Like a dream. Like those eyes you remember. Those lips. The poem you stayed up all night to write, in a fit of passion. It's all like water slipping through your fingers. Did you write that poem?

Did you know her eyes better than the sky? Did you really even touch her lips?

Look, I still need that cigarette. I really would like one. How about it? Come on. Whattya say?

(He holds out his hand.)

(Blackout.)

—— END OF PLAY ——

SATELLITES
Diana Son

Born in Dover, Delaware, in 1965, Diana Son grew up in what she recalls as a typical American suburban neighborhood. She decided to become a writer at a young age and saw her first major play in high school during a field trip to New York City's Public Theater. She attended New York University as a dramatic literature major. Her plays include *Wrecked on Brecht, Stealing Fire, Joyless Bad Luck Club, R.A.W. ('Cause I'm a Woman), 2000 Miles, BOY, Fishes, Stop Kiss, Happy Birthday Jack,* and *The Moon Please.* Her play *Stop Kiss* won the GLAAD Media Award for Best New York Production and was on the Top 10 Plays lists of *The New York Times, New Newsday, New York Daily News,* and others. Her plays have been presented at the Public Theater, Oregon Shakespeare Festival, Seattle Repertory Center, La Jolla Playhouse, Ohio Theatre in SoHo, Geva Theatre Center, Delaware Company, Woolly Mammoth Theatre Company, and People's Light and Theatre Company. Winner of the Berilla Kerr Award for Playwriting, she has received an NEA/TCG Residency grant at the Mark Taper Forum and a Brooks Atkinson Fellowship at the Royal National Theatre in London. She has also written for film and television and was co-executive producer of the TV series *Law & Order: Criminal Intent.* Son wrote *Satellites* (2006) after the birth of her first child, and while it is not an autobiographical play, it is, of all of her plays, Son's most direct commentary on Korean American identity and culture.

Diana Son. Photo courtesy of Diana Son. This photo was taken during the shooting of the KYOPO Project, www.kyopoproject.com.

Satellites was commissioned by the Public Theater (Oskar Eustis, artistic director; Mara Manus, executive director) and was presented in the series "New Work Now!" in 2004. The play premiered at the Public Theater in New York City on June 18, 2006, as part of the company's fiftieth anniversary season. It was directed by Diana Son's longtime collaborator Michael Greif; the set design was by Mark Wendland; the costume design was by Miranda Hoffman; the lighting design was by Kenneth Posner; the sound design was by Walter Trarbach and Tony Smolenski IV; the original music was composed by Michael Friedman; and the stage manager was Martha Donaldson. The cast was as follows:

Nina	Sandra Oh
Miles	Kevin Carroll
Eric	Clarke Thorell
Kit	Johanna Day
Mrs. Chae	Satya Lee
Reggie	Ron Cephas Jones
Walter	Ron Brice

The play has since been produced at the Aurora Theatre in Berkeley, California, in 2008 and at Swine Palace in Baton Rouge, Louisiana, in 2009.

CAST

NINA, mid-thirties, Korean American, an architect and new mother
MILES, mid-thirties, African American, an unemployed dot-com casualty and new father
ERIC, late thirties, Caucasian, MILES's brother, an entrepreneur
KIT, late thirties, Caucasian, NINA's business partner, an architect
MRS. CHAE, mid-fifties/early sixties, Korean from Korea, a nanny
REGGIE, early/mid-forties, African American, the king of the block
WALTER, any age, any race, a tenant in the brownstone

SETTING

Various rooms in MILES and NINA's unrenovated Brooklyn brownstone.

Kevin Carroll (right), Satya Lee (left), and Sandra Oh (center) in the Public Theater production of *Satellites*. Photo by Michal Daniel.

TIME

    Now.

    The symbol (.) denotes a barely perceptible (and yet perceptible) pause where a character chooses not to say something.

    Unitalicized text within parentheses, such as (this), indicates the word/s not spoken when a character is cut off.

    A forward slash (/) indicates overlapping text. The next character begins speaking at this point.

SCENE 1

Late night/early morning—they've bled into another. NINA, *still tender from a C-section, bounces her two-week-old newborn as best as she can and pats her back, trying to soothe the crying baby.*

NINA   OK, sweetie, I'm trying, I'm trying— *(Reacting to harder crying.)* I'm sorry it hurts so much, I never knew gas could be so painful and hard to get out— *(NINA pats harder.)* You know, if only it were this hard for adults to fart, riding the subway would be a much pleasanter (experience)—

(We hear the tiny pop of a baby passing a puff of gas. NINA reacts with the pride of a mother who's just watched her daughter win Olympic gold. The baby makes a happy, gurgling sound.)

You did it! Oh, I'm so happy for you! *(NINA holds the baby in front of her to look at her face. She gives her an encouraging little shake.)* My little champion!

(The baby starts to cry again. To herself, out loud.)

Holy shit, don't shake the baby. I'm such a fucking—

(She puts the baby back over her shoulder.)

Mommy didn't mean that, sweetheart, Mommy wasn't shaking you, Mommy was vibrating—

(MILES walks in, wearing pajamas.)

MILES   Sorry I didn't hear you guys, I was out cold. Did she want to nurse?

NINA   *(Not ironic.)* No, she wanted to watch *The Godfather*. Did you know that *The Godfather* is on every night? On different channels at the same time. If you turn on your TV after midnight, you have no choice but to watch *The Godfather*.

MILES   You want to watch it now?

NINA   Why don't you take her, so I can go back to bed.

(NINA carefully puts the baby in MILES's arms. The baby starts to cry harder.)

Look at her, Miles, chocolate skin, almond eyes . . . she's the best of both of us.

MILES   . . . I hope so.

NINA | What do you think about hiring a Korean woman to be her nanny? So she could speak Korean to her.

MILES | *(Distracted by crying baby.)* Is that important to you?

NINA | I just started thinking about it. I can't speak Korean so she's not going to hear it from me.

MILES | All right, sounds like a good idea. *(Re: baby)* You want to take her?

NINA | Why don't you try singing a song? Like a lullaby or something—

MILES | *(Sings.)* "The eensy weensy spider went up the water—"

NINA | That's not soothing.

(A bang from the apartment above.)

MILES | Aw, come on, man.

NINA | Fucking asshole. *(To upstairs neighbor.)* My baby has gas, man, I'll kill you, motherfucker.

MILES | Hopefully we'll close on the house next month, and finally be able to move in.

NINA | It's impossible to have a baby in this cramped little tenement. We've outgrown this apartment, this whole neighborhood.

MILES | Remember when we used to have wakes for our friends who moved to Brooklyn?

NINA | They're laughing at us now. Still, as much as we paid, it'll be worth it.

(The baby wails; the neighbor bangs on the ceiling again.)

MILES | You'd better take her.

(NINA opens her arms. The baby quiets down a little.)

NINA | What should I sing?

(MILES thinks a beat.)

MILES   "Hush little baby–"

    (NINA *joins in, a beat behind, singing what* MILES *sings.*)

MILES and NINA   "Don't say a word, Papa's gonna buy you a mockingbird . . ."

MILES   "If that—

NINA   "When that—"

MILES and NINA   ". . . mockingbird won't sing, Papa's gonna buy you a—"

    (*They look at each other, unsure what the rest of the words are. Finally—*)

NINA   I can look up the words. I found this website that has the lyrics to all the—

MILES   (*Sings, cues* NINA.) "Rock-a-bye—"

    (NINA *joins in.*)

MILES and NINA   (*Singing.*) "—baby, on the treetop. When the wind blows, the cradle will rock. When the bough breaks, the cradle will fall—"

    (NINA *stops, thinks about the words.*)

MILES   (*Still singing.*) "And down will come baby, cradle and all."

NINA   We are never singing that song to her again.

MILES   Why not?

NINA   The baby falls, Miles, the baby falls and the cradle falls on top of it. What kind of lullaby is that?

SCENE 2

  MILES *and* NINA*'s brownstone. It's dark, lit by a standing lamp near the kitchen. The living room blends into the kitchen, a stairwell leads to the bedrooms above, another connects to the garden level office below. Many moving boxes are piled on the floor, some opened, most not. There is very little furniture.* MILES *carries in a box as* NINA *comes down the stairs.*

NINA   I just got her down. Miles, that box belongs in the kitchen. It says "kitchen" on it.

MILES   It doesn't matter. I've been putting things wherever there's room.

NINA   Well, I've been putting everything exactly where it's/gonna go—

MILES   But I haven't. We'll deal with it later.

(NINA *grabs an end of the box, starts pulling toward the kitchen.* MILES *pulls it back.*)

NINA   You know we won't. Half of these boxes are going to be sitting in our living room for the next year and a half because we're not going to have the time or energy to/move them later.

MILES   We'll move them tomorrow. Or next week . . . or next month, it doesn't—

NINA   No, we're not. We'll get used to them being there. We'll start putting things on them, like our feet when we're sitting on the sofa. Or our drinks, they'll become end tables. We'll choose the paint color for the walls by whether or not it matches the boxes. You know we will.

MILES   No, we won't.

NINA   How many years did we use a plastic shopping bag hanging on the front doorknob as a garbage can?

(MILES *makes a dismissive sound.*)

Seven years. I bought us our first trash can on my thirtieth birthday because I couldn't stand it anymore. Miles, please, let's just move the goddamn box to the kitchen. I need to finish here and go downstairs to—

MILES   Stop bossing me around.

(NINA *starts to pull him toward the kitchen again.* MILES *resists. She stops in her tracks when she feels a cutting pain. She drops her half of the box.*)

NINA: Ow, motherfuck.

(MILES *sets the box down, walks over to her, helps her to sit onto a nearby box.*)

MILES: Honey . . . you shouldn't be doing all this. You need to stop pushing yourself so much.

NINA: I'm not pushing myself, Miles.

MILES: So, what—I am?

NINA: There's no one else to help us. We've burned through all the friends who offered to . . . let's just finish. After I'm done here, I have to go downstairs and help Kit work on the site plan.

MILES: You're gonna work tonight?

NINA: Kit's been carrying my weight for the past month.

(MILES *starts to massage* NINA'S *shoulders.*)

She's been working on the Tillman job and on the Barcelona competition. Not to mention she set up the whole office by herself.

MILES: Yeah, well, Kit can do that. She has the time. You should just . . . take it easy, you know? Relax a little.

(MILES *touches* NINA'S *breasts. She wriggles out of his reach.*)

Hey!

NINA: I'm sorry . . . honey, it's just . . . these aren't mine anymore.

MILES: Nina, I've been keeping it all to myself here for the past four months.

NINA: What're you—counting?

(MILES *tries to nuzzle her.*)

MILES: C'mon, the baby's asleep.

NINA: I can't believe I just told you everything I have to do tonight and you want to have sex?

MILES   Yes, I want to have sex! Remember sex? It's how we made the baby and got ourselves into this mess in the first place.

NINA   That's seductive.

(MILES *lets go of her hand, walks away angry and rejected.*)

MILES   I'll get the rest of the boxes myself. You just . . . relax.

NINA   I don't have time to—

MILES   You need to/relax—

NINA   I'm not relaxing!—

(ERIC *runs into the house, shuts the door behind him. His jacket pocket is torn.* MILES *and* NINA *look as surprised to see him as he is to see them.*)

ERIC   Two fucking guys just chased me for four blocks. They took my iPod and backpack, they had a gun!

NINA   Eric! Where did you—

MILES   Are you OK? You want me to call the cops?

ERIC   Yeah, no, it's OK, I just—

(*He walks over to the window, looks out.*)

MILES   Where was this?

ERIC   Like a block from the subway, by the projects. All of a sudden, these two (.) guys came up from behind me and ripped my iPod out of my pocket—

(NINA *examines at* ERIC's *pocket.*)

MILES   Did they get your wallet?

ERIC   No, I have a hole in my pocket so it drops down into the lining of my coat. They grabbed my backpack, and then I just . . . took off. I just kept running until I saw Rosa Parks Avenue.

NINA   How'd you know how to get here?

MILES: You want a glass of water or something? A beer?

ERIC: In a minute, I just— *(Changing gears.)* Hi, how are you?

(ERIC kisses NINA on the cheek.)

NINA: I'm fine.

(MILES and ERIC embrace, clap each other on the back.)

MILES: I thought you were in Malaysia.

ERIC: I just got off the plane. I'm fucking lagged.

NINA: Where are your bags?

ERIC: I put them in a mini-storage near the airport. *(Looks around.)* Get a load of this place. What's the deal?

MILES: . . . This is . . . our house.

ERIC: This is outrageous, man, your other apartment was like a dorm room. How many floors is this?

NINA: Four. We converted the garden level into an office for me and Kit, so we're only living on this floor and the one above.

ERIC: That where the bedrooms are?

NINA: Yes.

ERIC: So how many bedrooms are there?

NINA: Three. We use the third bedroom as a family office.

MILES: My office.

ERIC: Sweet, man. Mom and Dad said it was nice but I didn't expect it would be like this.

MILES: Why, what'd they say?

ERIC: Don't sweat it, Miles, they liked it. They were just more into the baby. Where'd you put the baby?

NINA: She's upstairs sleeping.

ERIC   Can I get a peek at her?

MILES   Sure.

NINA   I don't think it's a good idea.

ERIC   How old is she, a month?

MILES   Six weeks.

ERIC   Is she sleeping through the night?

NINA   *(On the verge of tears.)* No!

MILES   *(An apology.)* The baby gets up every couple hours to nurse. Nina's up all night.

ERIC   I noticed the moving van out front. You guys need a hand?

MILES   You don't have to, man, you must be exhausted.

ERIC   Getting mugged got me pumped. Let's do it.

(KIT walks upstairs, carrying a pizza box.)

KIT   Your pizza came. They rang the bell downstairs.

MILES   *(Turns to ERIC.)* Let's eat something first. *(To KIT.)* Kit, you've met my brother before, haven't you? This is Eric.

(KIT extends her hand.)

KIT   Not yet, but I've heard the stories.

ERIC   Uh-oh . . .

KIT   You've been bitten by a rattlesnake and lived to tell the tale, and you sold the Dalai Lama a laptop.

ERIC   His Holiness is addicted to Tetris.

KIT   *(To NINA.)* Nina, I've started regrading the site plan.

NINA   I told you I'd pitch in with that.

KIT   We've got to finish this by tonight. We should be cutting out shapes for the model by tomorrow.

NINA		We will. I'm going to work all day tomorrow.
ERIC		*(To KIT.)* Are you guys doing a charette?
MILES		Listen to you and your "charette."
ERIC		*(To MILES, a frequent joke.)* Just because I didn't go to Columbia, like some of us in the room—
MILES		*(Looking at KIT.)* All of us, actually.

(NINA's mobile phone rings. MILES and ERIC help themselves to pizza.)

NINA   *(To KIT.)* Audrey Tillman.

KIT   Why's she calling you?

NINA   *(Into phone.)* Hello? Yes, Mrs. Tillman . . . no, I wasn't at the jobsite today but Kit was—

(NINA looks at KIT who nods, yes, I was, everything was fine.)

No, the carpenters are going to fill that in . . . It's going to look exactly as we discussed. *(Brightens.)* Oh, yes, thank you. She's six weeks old, she's just— *(Mrs. Tillman could give a fuck.)* I'll make sure Kit takes a look tomorrow morning. Thank you, Mrs. Till—

(Mrs. Tillman has hung up.)

KIT   Why didn't she call me? I'm the one who's been holding her shriveled little liver-spotted hand for the past two (months.)—

(The baby starts crying upstairs. NINA reacts as if she's been electrically jolted.)

NINA   You guys, go ahead, eat. I'll bring her down when I'm done nursing her.

KIT   I guess I'll be working by myself after all.

(ERIC hands KIT a slice of pizza on a plate.)

ERIC   Here you go.

(He goes to the fridge to get her a beer. MILES touches KIT consolingly.)

So, do you live in Brooklyn too?

(ERIC hands her a beer.)

KIT — Ha! Thanks. Noooo. Look, Brooklyn's great, it's beautiful and cheaper, but . . . I want to be able to drop off my dry cleaning, go to a gallery opening, see an eight-hour Hungarian movie, then drink overpriced green apple martinis—all within a block of my house.

ERIC — That's what's great about New York, right?

(Suddenly, we hear a smash—the sound of glass being shattered and falling on the floor.)

MILES — What the—

(KIT grabs a flashlight. They see glass pieces on the floor and a jagged hole in the window.)

ERIC — Shit, man—

MILES — What just happened?

(KIT walks toward the window, surveying the debris. Finds a rock, picks it up.)

KIT — It's a rock. Someone just threw it at your window.

(MILES walks over. KIT shows him the rock.)

MILES — Why would someone do that?

ERIC — You've got a stereo, TV, all kinds of computer equipment . . . People in this neighborhood probably saw all that gear and thought Puffy was moving in.

KIT — Or, maybe they weren't trying to steal anything. Maybe they were just trying to send you a message. *(Goes for phone.)* Want me to call 911?

(NINA walks a few steps downstairs.)

NINA — Miles? What was that, what broke?

MILES — Stay upstairs, honey. There's broken glass down here.

(NINA, *holding the baby, walks down, sees the broken glass on the floor.*)

NINA — What the fuck! Who broke my fucking window?

MILES — I'm checking it out, don't worry. Go back upstairs where it's safe.

(NINA *ignores him, keeps walking.*)

NINA — It's going to take weeks to get a replacement glass . . . what are we supposed to do with a fucking hole in our house for three fucking weeks?

MILES — I don't know. Just take the baby upstairs, okay? *(To ERIC.)* Her first word's gonna be fuck if Nina keeps—

NINA — What?

MILES — Just please take the baby upstairs.

(*She goes upstairs.*)

KIT — You should call the cops, Miles.

(*Beat.*)

MILES — I don't want to do that. *(Beat.)* We're new here. I don't want people to get the wrong impression.

KIT — What would that be?

MILES — I don't want to dwell on this. The most important thing to do is cover up that hole.

KIT — Home Depot's open twenty-four hours. You can buy a four-by-eight piece of plywood and some hardware to anchor it to the wall.

ERIC — I'll go. Will you come with me so you can show me?

KIT — I'll get my jacket.

(MILES *shakes his brother's hand.*)

MILES Thanks, man. Can you believe this happened?

(ERIC *looks out the window, at the sky.*)

ERIC It's a full moon. Maybe it's a sign of good luck. Getting all the bad things over with first.

MILES Or it's a sign that moving my family here is the biggest mistake of my life.

(KIT *comes back with her jacket, she and* ERIC *walk out, leaving* MILES *alone and feeling it.*)

SCENE 3

Early morning. MILES *tries to set the plywood into the wall, manual labor is not his forte. A man walks by on the street,* REGGIE, *his clothes not quite clean, his hair in need of a comb. He stops in front of the broken window. The hole still uncovered.*)

REGGIE Oh, shit! What happened, man?

(MILES *looks at* REGGIE.)

MILES What happened? Somebody smashed the window.

REGGIE And you ain't hardly even moved in yet—that ain't a way to welcome a brother to the neighborhood.

(MILES—*a small reaction to "brother."*)

MILES It's not exactly a pie on the stoop, is it?

REGGIE That's what I'm saying! You done a lot of work on this house, man.

MILES Not really. I mean, we bought a door and . . . we put glass in the—

REGGIE We got all kinds of people up in here now, building new condos and renovatin' these old brownstones . . . You see that house over there? Two homosexuals bought that, fixed it up to historical accuracy, and all that. I'm glad you came to the neighborhood, man. What you do, you a lawyer or something?

MILES I'm . . . an interactive producer.

REGGIE A producer! You know Biggie grew up two blocks from here, right? I used to send that punk to the store to buy me Milk Duds.

MILES Actually, I produce websites for corporate clients. But, I like Biggie.

REGGIE I'm glad you came to the neighborhood, man. This glass was custom-made, wasn't it?

MILES *(A little surprised.)* Yeah, it was.

REGGIE 'Cause 'round here all the brownstones have one seventy-two-inch window or two thirty-six-inch ones. That was the style in the 1870s when most of these buildings was built. But this one here is eighty inches, only one like it. I know they charged you a lot of money for that piece of glass.

(MILES waits to see where REGGIE's going with this.)

Mm hm, a lot of money.

(REGGIE nods gravely.)

MILES You seem to know a lot about my house—

REGGIE I got a guy I can go to—he'll cut that glass for you cheaper than you paid for.

MILES Thanks, but my wife's got her sources. She's an architect so she has reliable (vendors.)—

REGGIE *(Insistent.)* Listen, man, you don't know me. But, I'm telling you— *(Extends his hand.)* I'm Reggie, I live across the street from you, I lived on this block for—matter of fact, I was born on this block. I'm forty-two years old—I got three grown kids, they live with they moms, but everybody 'round here know Reggie. If you need something, I'm your boy.

(NINA walks downstairs carrying the baby.)

NINA Miles, you take the baby. Kit's going to be here any— *(To REGGIE.)* Hi, I'm Nina.

(She can't offer her hand because she's holding the baby.)

REGGIE Alright.

MILES This is Reggie, he lives across the street.

REGGIE *(To MILES.)* Like I said, you make up your mind, you come to me.

(MILES, feeling awkward, turns to NINA.)

MILES Oh, I should tell you, Reggie mentioned that he, uh, he has a glazier that he recommends.

NINA He's done work for you?

REGGIE *(A nod.)* Mm-hm.

NINA Do you have his card or can you give me his phone number?

MILES *(To NINA.)* I thought you would want to use Frankie again.

NINA I'll call Frankie, but if this guy's in the neighborhood—

(REGGIE sees someone offstage.)

REGGIE I gotta talk to this—Hey, Mo! You need to settle up with me, son. *(To MILES.)* Look, I'm a go get my boy's card and you talk to him. Whatever you want, he'll do it.

NINA Thanks, Reggie. *(To MILES.)* I don't know what kind of work this guy does, I'm just saying let's get a price from him.

MILES Doesn't it seem weird to you, this guy who's always hanging out on the corner, coming up first thing in the morning, telling us "I got a guy who can fix that for you . . ."

NINA So?

MILES And where were those guys last night? They're always out

	there, doing whatever they're doing, selling whatever they're selling, but last night—they're not there. Where were they?
NINA	What—you think Reggie or one of those guys broke the glass?
	(MILES *gestures—I'm just saying.*)
	. . . I don't think Reggie did it. Why would he do it?
MILES	Maybe he gets a fee. Whenever Reggie finds some sucker to give this guy business—
NINA	And what's the deal with your brother? He tell you how long he's gonna stay?
MILES	No. But he usually stays a week or two—you have a problem with that?
	(NINA *turns to the baby for unconditional love.*)
NINA	Look, she's dreaming. Look at how her expression changes every couple seconds. *(Narrating the baby's thoughts as she goes from a smile, to a frown, to tears, to a smile again.)* Flowers . . . car alarms . . . mmm, Mommy's nipples . . .
	(ERIC *comes downstairs.*)
ERIC	Alright, let me see her. *(Looks at baby.)* She's beautiful.
NINA	She's the perfect mix of the both of us, don't you think?
ERIC	She's herself. You, on the other hand, seem to have turned into a completely different person. Didn't I just hear you talking baby talk?
NINA	I was giving voice to her thoughts.
ERIC	Can I hold her?
	(NINA *hesitates.*)
MILES	Of course, man.
NINA	Just—make sure you support her neck.
	(NINA *gingerly hands the baby to* ERIC.)

ERIC Ohmigod, it's so much responsibility. If I don't hold her right, her neck will break off.

(MILES *goes to get a camera.*)

MILES Hang on a second, let me take a picture of you two.

NINA Miles—don't put him on the spot.

ERIC I don't mind.

(ERIC *smiles for the camera.* MILES *clicks the shutter.* NINA *responds to the sound of the downstairs door being opened.*)

NINA Shit, Kit's here. I'd wanted to get a head start before she showed up. Miles, take the baby.

MILES Eric's got her.

NINA (*To* MILES.) You said you'd watch the baby today—

MILES I will. But, just today. Remember I have an interview at Poseidon tomorrow—

(NINA *heads downstairs.*)

ERIC You guys don't have a nanny?

MILES Not yet. But we'd better soon, because I can't go on interviews if I'm stuck here taking care of the baby.

ERIC Look at you, man, you've got a wife, a kid, a house . . . Not just any house, a Brooklyn brownstone.

MILES Yeah, but it needs a lot of work, man. I mean, this kitchen is like, from *Sanford and Son*. This linoleum floor . . . I was gonna fix it but then we ran out of money.

ERIC What do you mean you ran out of money—look at this place, you're swimming in bucks.

MILES Look at this place, exactly. I don't even want to tell you how much we paid for it. I had to cash in the last of my stock options for the down payment. If it weren't for the income we get renting the top floor apartment, we couldn't afford to live here.

ERIC   There's another apartment?

MILES   On the fourth floor. Eventually, we hope to take it over but right now we need the money.

ERIC   You've got something set aside, I know you, Miles. You've probably got ten thousand dollars in quarters all rolled up and stuffed inside a pair of tube socks upstairs.

MILES   Dude, InTech laid me off six weeks before the baby was born. Nina's the only one making a steady check now—

(ERIC *holds the baby with one hand, undoes his pants with the other.*)

ERIC   Check this out. This is what I got for spending three months in a tropical Asian paradise.

(ERIC's *pants crumple around his ankles, revealing small piles of blue currency rubber-banded around each leg.*)

MILES   What the hell are those?

ERIC   Ringgits. I sold hot dog carts to street vendors in Kuala Lumpur. This is my take home. Thirty thousand ringgits. Which is about ten thousand U.S. dollars.

MILES   What're you, waiting to deposit them in Chicago?

ERIC   Oh. Did I say I was going back to Chicago? My building went co-op so they kicked me out. How are the rents in this neighborhood? Think I could find a one-bedroom in the six-hundred-to-seven-hundred-dollar range?

MILES   Aw, no, man, maybe three years ago but now—

ERIC   Fucking yuppies coming in, jacking up the rents so that even a guy like me can't afford to live in the ghetto.

(*A smile, he pats* MILES *on the back.*)

MILES   It isn't exactly the (ghetto.)—

ERIC   I'm just kidding, man.

MILES	I know it's still rough around the edges, but, it's got a good history. A lot of families have been in these brownstones for six or seven generations. You've got teachers, artists, musicians—Biggie grew up a couple blocks from here.
ERIC	OK, I get it.
MILES	It'll be good for Hannah to grow up around (.) . . . all kinds of kids.
ERIC	It's a great place to start a business. What does this neighborhood need?
MILES	We have to drive two neighborhoods over to get organic milk.
ERIC	What else?
MILES	You know—pasta sauce, good cheese, bread . . .
ERIC	So, a place where you can buy upscale groceries, sit down and get a good cup of coffee, and—meet other people like you in the neighborhood.
MILES	Sounds good, man. I hope someone opens one.
ERIC	Why not you?
MILES	The thing I need to do right now is get a job. Bring some money into this house. Starting a business costs money.
ERIC	That's what investors are for.
MILES	Plus, it's risky.
ERIC	Man, don't you know you're taking a bigger risk waiting around for the right position to open up in the right company. Starting a business gives you control. Look, I've got these ringgits. We can use them to get us off the ground.
MILES	OK, I'll . . . think about it, man.

(WALTER, the tenant, walks down the steps and out the door. He tries not to notice MILES and ERIC, standing there in his underwear with the ringgits. He heads up the stairs.)

ERIC   Who the hell is that?

MILES   That's the tenant, Walter.

ERIC   He walks through your house to get to his apartment? That is weird, man. Come on, let's take a walk around the neighborhood. Scope out some old storefronts. I'll carry the baby.

MILES   We can't leave with the window like that.

ERIC   It'll be fine. We'll be back in ten minutes.

(MILES *picks up the BabyBjörn.*)

MILES   You want to wear the Björn?

ERIC   No, man. I don't want that thing. Think about it—two dudes walking down the street with a mixed-race baby in a BabyBjörn? It's not like people are gonna guess we're brothers. I'll just carry her like this, okay?

(ERIC *holds* HANNAH *in the football hold.*)

MILES   She hasn't made a peep this whole time, she likes you.

ERIC   Of course she likes me, man. I'm crazy Uncle Eric. She needs me.

MILES   For what?

ERIC   To be everything you're not.

(*They exit.*)

SCENE 4

NINA, *holding* HANNAH, *sits across from* MRS. CHAE, *who is dressed neatly and paying a little more attention to* HANNAH *than* NINA.

NINA   I didn't expect to have to go back to work so soon. The good thing is I get to work at home—unlike other working mothers who have to go to their midtown (offices.)—

MRS. CHAE *(Korean accent.)* Yes, I know. My daughter is lawyer and she (works.)—

NINA But most working mothers get three months' maternity leave and I have to start working after only six weeks. My partner and I have made it to the finals in a major design—

MRS. CHAE These days, woman has to work. My daughter says—

NINA —A major design competition for a new arts center in Barcelona.

(She looks to MRS. CHAE for approval, signs she's impressed. She gets none. Clearing throat.)

Arts Center in Barcelona. It's an international competition and only four groups made it to the final. It's an honor and a huge—

(MRS. CHAE makes clicking noises at the baby.)

Anyway, the deadline is in six weeks so that's why I need a nanny to start right away—

MRS. CHAE Can I hold her?

(NINA unconsciously hesitates.)

NINA Yes, of course, just—be careful of her (neck.)—

MRS. CHAE *(Soothing to NINA.)* I know . . . I know . . .

(MRS. CHAE takes the baby, while saying in Korean, "Oh, look at you, you're such a pretty girl." This unexpectedly touches NINA.)

Your mommy and daddy must be very happy.

NINA I think my dad liked her, it's hard to tell.

MRS. CHAE But your mommy, she was so proud.

NINA No, Mommy's dead.

MRS. CHAE Tsk tsk tsk. You take care of baby, your mommy suppose take care of you.

(This moves NINA again. The baby makes a sound. MRS. CHAE immediately soothes her by patting her on the back and saying a few words in Korean.)

NINA She's smiling at you.

MRS. CHAE Babies love me. And I love the babies too. The family I worked for before? Husband got the new job in Ohio. They ask me to move with them, "Please, nanny, come with us." But I cannot go. I have my family here. I have a grandson, did you know?

NINA Oh, how old is he?

MRS. CHAE My daughter, she work at big law firm, they have daycare center in building. I told my daughter, "I quit my job to take care of him, he's my grandson." But she say, "Mommy, don't be selfish, I want him near me."

NINA Her name is Hannah, did I tell you?

MRS. CHAE I think maybe you name her Hannah *(Pronouncing it huh-NAH.)* because she's first one born.

NINA Actually, we just liked the name. And it's HA-nah, not huh-NAH. That would be weird, wouldn't it? Naming her "number one"?

MRS. CHAE You know Huh-nah?

NINA *(Counts in Korean, pronunciation shaky.)* Hana, tul, set . . .

MRS. CHAE Oh. Because when you tell me you don't speak one word of Korean, I think you don't speak one word.

NINA I do know one word. I know "hana." Actually, I can count to ten. My parents did teach me that. I just don't know how to say . . . eleven or twelve. I don't know any Korean lullabies, or how to say "koochie koo—"

MRS. CHAE	*(Starts to sing; insert first couple lines from a Korean lullaby.)* Your mommy sang this to you.
NINA	*(Moved, wishing she weren't.)* Yes, I think she did.
MRS. CHAE	*(Looking at* HANNAH.*)* She has the curly hair.
NINA	Yes, from my husband. I'm thrilled.

(MRS. CHAE looks at the baby again.)

MRS. CHAE	She looks like . . . your husband?
NINA	I don't know. My family thinks she looks like my husband and my husband's family thinks she looks like me.
MRS. CHAE	Your husband . . . he is . . . architect too?
NINA	No, he's uh . . . he's a computer guy.

(MILES hurries in.)

MILES	I'm sorry I'm late, the interview went long—
NINA	So, it must've gone really well. What did they—
MILES	I'll . . . tell you later. *(To* MRS. CHAE.*)* Hi, I'm Miles.

(He goes to shake MRS. CHAE's *hand, she bows.)*

NINA	Oh, uh, Miles, this is Mrs. Chae. Mrs. Chae, this is my husband Miles.
MRS. CHAE	*(Not skipping a beat.)* Congratulations. She is beautiful baby.
MILES	Thank you, thank you.
MRS. CHAE	So, you don't mind? Nina says she want the Korean nanny to speak Korean to Hannah. You don't worry?
MILES	No, I—I think it'd be great. I think it'd be wonderful for Hannah to understand Korean. You thought I might be worried?
MRS. CHAE	Maybe some American parent don't want the child to get confused or handicapped.

MILES No, no, I think it's totally a good thing.

(MRS. CHAE *looks at* HANNAH, *then* NINA *and* MILES.)

MRS. CHAE She is lucky baby.

(MILES *smiles, puts his arm around* NINA.)

MILES Hey, why don't I take a picture of you three together?

(MILES *gets his camera.*)

NINA Um . . . Miles? It's a little premature—

MILES It'll be nice.

(NINA *stands next to* MRS. CHAE, *not quite committed.* MRS. CHAE *holds* HANNAH *closer and smiles into the camera.*)

That's great.

(*Flash. The doorbell rings.* NINA *turns to* MRS. CHAE.)

NINA Thank you for your time. Let me walk you to the door.

MRS. CHAE Should I call you tomorrow?

NINA I'll call you, thank you.

MILES You guys look great together!

(*She opens the door to let* MRS. CHAE *out, sees* REGGIE.)

NINA Oh, hi Reggie. Um, come on in.

(MRS. CHAE *leaves as* REGGIE *comes in carrying a large, ornate chandelier.*)

REGGIE (*To* MILES.) Check this out, man. I just bought it for fifty bucks, I sell it to you for seventy-five.

MILES Where did you get that?

REGGIE I told you, I bought it. (*Looks at their ceiling.*) I see you got a hook where one used to be. All you got to do is slip it on. You got a ladder?

MILES   Listen, Reggie, thanks, but we don't want to buy that.

REGGIE   It ain't gone be that hard, here—

(He hands it to MILES, *who reluctantly takes it.* REGGIE *moves some boxes underneath the hook.)*

I could probably reach it like this.

MILES   Can you get down, please? You're stepping on some fragile electronic equipment.

REGGIE   You got some computer stuff in here?

MILES   Can you just come down?

*(*REGGIE *steps down.)*

REGGIE   *(To* MILES.*)* So, I talked to my boy over at the glassworks, I told him it was a eighty-inch window, and he says he can do it for fifteen hundred dollars.

NINA   *(To* REGGIE.*)* Oh. Did you get his card? 'Cause I should talk to him about some details.

*(*REGGIE *digs through his pockets.)*

REGGIE   I got his card, I got his card, here—

(He hands her a folded piece of paper, then turns back to MILES.*)*

But if you want to pull the trigger on this, tell me. I'll set it up for you. Even with my fee, you ain't paying what you'd pay if you walked in there yourself.

*(*MILES *looks at* NINA.*)*

MILES   Your fee. That's part of the fifteen hundred.

REGGIE   *(Goes to fridge.)* Oh, shit. You still got that fridge? That ugly-ass fridge been here since the seventies.

*(*REGGIE *opens the fridge.)*

MILES   Do you mind?

	REGGIE	You know, I been in your house before. Yeah, I been in here before. Had some good times up in here, man. The night of the blackout, 1977, city was coal-black. People were running around crazy, smashing store windows, grabbing up anything they could get—bananas, turntables, diapers . . . Me and my friends climbed through that window, lay down on our backs, and looked straight up, man, saw stars we never get to see—the constellations. Aquila the eagle; Cygnus the swan; Hercules the warrior—he took on the labors, man. He brought down the lion, the hydra, Cerberus, himself. After the riots is when the monsters took over this neighborhood—drug dealers, gangs, robbers. Hercules should've stuck around, we coulda used him. But when the power came back on, all the stars faded away.

(MILES hands REGGIE the chandelier.)

SCENE 5

The office. There are two drafting tables and stools, a desk with a computer and printer. KIT and NINA are building the landscape their model will sit on. KIT finishes gluing on a layer of gator board and is waiting for NINA to cut out more shapes. Meanwhile, NINA is looking for something.

	KIT	Nina, I'm ready for more shapes. What're you doing, what're you looking for?
	NINA	A green and yellow receiving blanket. It was mine when I was a baby. I have this picture of my mom holding me in it . . .

(Their office phone rings. KIT checks the caller ID.)

	KIT	Don't get it, it's Mrs. Tillman. She's called three times already.
	NINA	Not about the wall again.
	KIT	The first two calls were about the wall. The third call was about the bathroom. She said the light made the wall tiles look "too shiny." I am so sick of these overly entitled, ignorant, tantrum-throwing rich people.

NINA	Me, too. I just want to be one.	
KIT	I want to be in a whole new league. Get the hell out of residential work, be rid of these idiots forever.	
NINA	I wonder what Mrs. Chae is doing to try to soothe her.	

(KIT *listens, hears nothing.*)

KIT Hannah's not crying.

NINA She is, they're upstairs in the bedroom.

KIT You're saying you can hear them two floors above? I can't hear anything.

NINA *(Standing up.)* I'm gonna go up there and offer to nurse her —

KIT *(Also standing.)* Nina, don't. Just . . . leave her, it's disrespectful. If the baby really needed you . . . or your breasts . . . the nanny would bring her down here. I don't even think she's crying.

NINA I hear her. Being a mother has given me superhero powers. And Hannah — Hannah can smell me from twenty feet away.

KIT You measured?

NINA I read it and I tested it. And her crying — it triggers my milk. I was in the bathroom yesterday and she started crying, and milk shot out of my nipples. Smacked right into the back of the door. Sometimes my milk attacks her.

(*We hear* HANNAH *crying.* MRS. CHAE *has brought her downstairs to the living room.* NINA *looks at* KIT.)

KIT No, Nina, concentrate. We blew the first two months of our deadline already. We have six weeks to do what all our competitors have had four months to do. I didn't mean blow.

NINA I couldn't stand up —

KIT *(To* NINA.*)* I know, honey.

NINA Any woman who has a planned C-section is a fucking moron.

KIT · I like the image of the doctor grabbing your intestines by the handful and piling them on your stomach, then shoving them back in after she gets the baby out. You know, I think you've broken some kind of sacred code of silence by telling me the details of your horrible birth experience.

NINA · Are you afraid to have a baby now?

KIT · Hell yeah! Not that it's an option right—

(ERIC *comes downstairs, puts a set of keys on* KIT's *desk.*)

ERIC · Thanks for letting me borrow these, Miles made a spare set for me.

KIT · No problem.

ERIC · Hey, you know that radio station you told me about? I tuned into it this morning. They play some great music.

KIT · I figured since you lost your iPod . . .

ERIC · I appreciate it. Well, I'll leave you gals to your work.

(ERIC *heads upstairs.*)

NINA · What the hell was that about? You loaned him your keys?

KIT · Yeah. What's wrong with that?

NINA · I don't want him getting too comfortable. I don't want him to be here at all. Eric is not the kind of person Miles should get into business with.

KIT · Why not?

NINA · He's never done anything legit, he's never had a proper job . . . and he's never been able to commit to a relationship.

KIT · That was unsolicited.

NINA · Stream of consciousness. The thing is, I think Miles is using Eric and this business as a way of avoiding having to spend time with the baby.

KIT   If you think that there's some guy out there who's going to do more than what Miles is doing . . . you're nuts.

NINA   Fucking Joe.

KIT   You think Joe's a shit because he wouldn't marry me after six years, but I think Joe's normal. Every guy in the world is like Joe. You've had it lucky, Nina, you don't know—

NINA   How hard it is out there? It's hard in here. This is hard.

    (Beat.)

KIT   Last night, I went to a Salvadoran restaurant with this guy. I kept telling him in a nice way, "It's not El Salvadorean food. It's Salvadoran." But all night he kept saying "I've never had El Salvadorean food before," "I have to tell my friends I went to an El Salvadorean restaurant."

NINA   Sounds like another online loser. Where was the restaurant?

KIT   Deepest Queens. To get there we had to take the Z train. The Z train to Jamaica Center. Then we had to walk twelve blocks to get to this little piece-of-shit restaurant that served the most heavenly pupusas made on the planet.

NINA   You bring some back for me?

KIT   No. Hot off the griddle—the crust was crisp and toothsome and when you bit into them the cheese and pork oozed out—

NINA   *(Putting out her hand.)* Stop—

    (KIT reaches into her desk, pulls out a bag of pupusas, tosses them to NINA.)

KIT   They're not going to be as good cold, but—

NINA   Love.

    (MILES comes downstairs.)

MILES   Nina, have you seen my camcorder?

NINA   What? No.

MILES: I know I put it on the bookshelf yesterday but now I can't find it. I wanted to shoot some video of Hannah on her first day with Mrs. Chae.

NINA: You know what, Miles, I want you to spread the word that this office is off-limits to anyone who doesn't work here.

MILES: What—?

NINA: We're on a serious deadline here.

KIT: Yes, and it's ticking away every minute that you stand there arguing with your (husband.)—

MILES: This office is part of my house, Nina—

NINA: Our house. But Kit and I pay rent here.

MILES: You have to throw that in my face?

NINA: This is our space, Miles, and I don't want anyone else down here.

MILES: That is so— *(He storms off.)*

NINA: *(Calling after him.)* Except Hannah and Mrs. Chae! They're still allowed to (come.)—

(The office phone rings.)

KIT: *(Into phone.)* Hello? What?! Javier, I told you twice before I left last night those pipes had to be flush with the I-beams— alright, look, just tell Mrs. Tillman to put her ass on ice, I'll be there in an hour. *(Off his reaction.)* I'll take a cab, but I'm in fucking Brooklyn.

(She hangs up the phone, dials another number.)

NINA: Want me to call a car service?

KIT: I'm already doing it. *(Into phone.)* Yeah, can I get a car at 127 Rosa Parks Avenue? Thanks.

NINA: I'll finish the shapes for the foundation by the time you—

(MRS. CHAE *walks downstairs carrying the crying* HANNAH.)

MRS. CHAE   I'm sorry, Nina, I try give her pacifier, I try my finger, I play nice music—

NINA   *(Looks to* KIT.*)* Can you try taking her for a walk outside? Could you try that?

MRS. CHAE   Okay, yes, okay. I'm sorry I interrupt—

NINA   It's okay.

(NINA *looks at* HANNAH, *feeling she might lose her resolve, she turns away. Sound of a car horn outside.* MRS. CHAE *starts to leave,* HANNAH *cries harder.* KIT *grabs her bag.*)

KIT   That's my car. If you finish the layers by the time I get back, we might be able to stay on schedule.

(One quick look at NINA, *who continues working, then* KIT'S *out the door. When* NINA *hears the door close, she stands up. She starts for the stairs—then stops, starts—stops . . . then runs upstairs.)*

SCENE 6

Afternoon. Living room. There are fewer moving boxes—the place looks more settled. The window is still broken, a piece of plywood has been anchored to the wall to cover it. REGGIE *walks in carrying two boxes of ceramic tiles and sets them down on the kitchen floor, near another open box of a different shape. He can't resist looking into the other box.* MILES *walks in carrying another two boxes, sees* REGGIE.

MILES   Can I help you, man?

REGGIE   I see you got a Xbox. I can get you some games that go with it real cheap. They still in the plastic, let me show you what I got—

(He starts for the door.)

MILES   It's alright. I don't have time to play games these days.

REGGIE   They factory sealed. They ain't no cheap-ass Chinese—

(Oops. REGGIE *does a quick scan for* NINA.)

MILES   She's not Chinese. And if they're meant to be sold in a store, how'd you get them?

REGGIE   I got a guy, he works in a Circuit City. He say sometimes they order twenty-five copies of a game, they get twenty-six.

MILES   So, they're stolen.

REGGIE   How's it stolen, the store ain't paid for it!

MILES   If you take something from a store without paying for it, you stole it!

REGGIE   Man, who lives like that?

MILES   *(Trying to get rid of him.)* Yeah, right, thanks for your help, Reggie. I can get this from here.

REGGIE   You got ten more boxes out there.

MILES   I can handle it.

REGGIE   Where you gone lay them tiles down any way, the kitchen?

(MILES *hesitates, he knows where this is going.*)

MILES   I've got it all taken care of.

REGGIE   That will look nice, man. But you gotta take up all that linoleum, then you gotta patch up the holes and put something smooth down to glue the tiles to—you can't do all that by yourself.

MILES   Well, I have the time right now so I think I'll be alright.

REGGIE   We done did this in my mom's house in the eighties, man, I'm telling you—you gone need some help. Pulling that old stuff off piece by piece—ain't nothing for that but a pry bar. I don't mind an honest day's work. You hire some guy in the phonebook, he gone charge you two bills a day. I'll do it for half.

(NINA, *wearing the baby in a sling, walks in carrying plastic bags loaded with groceries in both hands.*)

NINA What's this—you bought tiles? How much did they cost?

(MILES *glances at* REGGIE, *wants to get rid of him.* MILES *reaches into his pocket and hands* REGGIE *a five-dollar bill.*)

MILES Here you go, man, thanks.

(REGGIE *looks at the money, doesn't take it.*)

REGGIE That's alright. We do it another way.

(REGGIE *heads out the door.* MILES, *embarrassed, puts the money back in his pocket.*)

MILES Eric paid for the tiles, says it's his housewarming gift to us.

NINA Miles, take the baby. You haven't held her since yesterday.

MILES No, I don't want to wake her.

NINA What about your interview this morning?

MILES I went. *(Opens a box of tiles.)* Look, I got those tiles that you circled in the catalog—

NINA Miles, how'd it go?

MILES I don't want to take a job that I'm going to resent going to every day. You know what I really want to do.

NINA Open a store with your brother? Miles, we make fun of your brother and his ridiculous schemes.

MILES This isn't a scheme; it's a good idea.

NINA I don't trust your brother, Miles. I'm sorry, but I don't. He doesn't have the experience—

MILES He has tons of experience!

NINA He's never opened a business here. He just goes to these Western-worshipping little Asian countries with his all-

	American good looks and he bamboozles them. He sells them shit.
MILES	How can you talk like that about my brother?
NINA	You don't need your brother. If you really want to start a business, then why don't you start something yourself?
MILES	Start a business—what business, with what? I don't have any ideas—
NINA	Look what Reggie does, Reggie doesn't have anything but he's out on that street corner, paying attention to what's going on, looking for opportunities—
MILES	I'm not one of the guys on the corner, Nina. Are you telling me to stand on the corner with the rest of the unemployed black guys?
NINA	No.
MILES	This store is my idea. It's how I want to present myself to the community. A lot of these families living in these brownstones, they stayed committed to the community during the rough times. And now people like us are moving in and I want to be connected to their history. I don't want to be the intruder. I want to bring something.

(MRS. CHAE *walks in.* MILES *and* NINA *brighten like schoolchildren.*)

NINA *and* MILES   Good morning, Mrs. Chae.

(MRS. CHAE *makes a beeline for the baby.*)

| MRS. CHAE | She's asleep? You give me whole sling. This way you can work and I can keep Hannah while I do her laundry. And I do your laundry too. |

(MRS. CHAE *picks up a few stray pieces of dirty clothing lying around.*)

| NINA | Oh, you don't have to do that. |

MRS. CHAE   I do this for my daughter too.

(MRS. CHAE *starts picking up stray laundry from around the living room.*)

NINA   . . . Huh. Do you . . . cook for her too?

MILES   Nina—

MRS. CHAE   Yes, of course. She and husband spend every weekend at my house. I cook a lots of food—chapchae, bulgogi, kimchee chigae—then Sunday, pack it up and they take home.

NINA   Man, I haven't had home-cooked Korean food in a long, long—

MRS. CHAE   You like the Korean food? Even the stinky kimchee?

NINA   I love kimchee. But I used to have to sneak it because my mom wouldn't let me eat it. She'd say, "You'll never have an American boyfriend."

MILES   Unless he also eats kimchee. *(Re: laundry)* Let me get you something for that.

(He heads upstairs.)

MRS. CHAE   Your mommy want you to have American boyfriend?

NINA   That's all we had where I grew up. Except for this one Filipino boy.

MRS. CHAE   I see. That's why she don't teach you the Korean language.

NINA   I don't think she knew I'd live in a place where I could speak Korean every day. Where every time my local Korean deli got a new cashier, I'd have to explain no, I'm not Japanese, I'm Korean, I just can't talk to you.

MRS. CHAE   If you want, I teach you the Korean words I speak to Hannah.

NINA   That would be amazing.

MRS. CHAE   That way you both learn together. And maybe someday I make kimchee for you. You work hard all day. You spend evening with Hannah instead of cook, clean and do laundry, eh? Hannah misses the mommy.

NINA: Do you think?

MRS. CHAE: She love the mommy and daddy. She talk about you all the time.

(MILES *comes downstairs with a laundry bag.*)

MILES: Here you go, you can put things in here.

MRS. CHAE: Oh, thank you, Miles. Such a good husband, hm? My husband, he never touch the laundry, never change the diaper, but Miles . . . he does so much.

(MRS. CHAE *touches* MILES's *cheek then goes upstairs.* ERIC *opens the front door. Pushes in half a dozen large pieces of luggage.*)

MILES: You need a hand with that, man?

(*He goes over to help.*)

NINA: What's going on, Eric?

ERIC: Miles was running out of clothes that fit me. Plus it was costing me twenty-one bucks a day to have this stuff in storage.

NINA: You took all of this to Malaysia?

ERIC: I was there for three months. I wanted to have my options.

MILES: I don't know if all that's gonna fit in the upstairs office.

ERIC: What about the basement? I don't need to put my hands on all this stuff every day. A bunch of these bags can go downstairs.

NINA: How long do you plan on staying here, if you don't mind my asking.

ERIC: To get a store off the ground could take a year. But, I don't have to stay here the whole time —

MILES: Where else are you going to stay?

ERIC   I can get a sublet—

NINA   It's just that we're still trying to get settled here—

MILES   I don't want you to do that, man. You're family.

NINA   Miles—

MILES   I asked him to stay here and help me launch the business. The least we can do is offer him a place to stay. We have the room—

NINA   No, we don't. That's supposed to be our office—

MILES   You have your office downstairs. The upstairs is my office and I say Eric is welcome to stay.

ERIC   I'm sorry, Nina, if I'd've known you were against me staying here, I wouldn'ta brought all my shit—

NINA   This isn't personal, Eric, you just happen to have shown up at a time when we're . . . we're still trying to figure things out ourselves and . . . I just need to put my family first.

MILES   *(To NINA.)* Eric is family. *(To ERIC.)* Come on, man, let's get these things upstairs.

SCENE 7

Night. ERIC sits at NINA's desk, KIT stands with her coat on; she's just come into the office.

KIT   Does Nina know you're down here?

ERIC   No, she's asleep. Why?

KIT   Well, she said she didn't want anyone else down here anymore.

ERIC   Oh—

KIT   Anyone except for me, her, Mrs. Chae, and Hannah, of course . . . which only leaves you and Miles.

(ERIC *turns to the computer.*)

ERIC   I didn't know, I'll close my document right now.

KIT   (*Stopping him.*) So—what were you working on? Something to do with the store?

ERIC   I was drafting a proposal. Miles scoped out a great location. So, what do you think of our idea?

KIT   S'pretty good. Neighborhood's changing . . . yuppies love their pesto and their lattes, I know I do.

ERIC   You know, I don't know why Miles never had the idea to run his own business before.

KIT   It's a lot of extra work. And it doesn't always pay off. You know this.

ERIC   I just wonder if Miles leans on Nina too much. If she ends up holding him back. Because Miles—

(*They hear a sound from the floor above.*)

I should get out of here—

KIT   Go on.

ERIC   Miles can do anything, man.

KIT   He's smart and hard-working, he's creative—

ERIC   What? He's way more than that, man. Miles came into the world a four-pound, undernourished, heroin-addicted, premature little bird you could hold in the palm of your hand.

KIT   Miles was a heroin baby?

ERIC   His birth mother was some junkie, shot ten bags of dope to induce her labor. Then after she gave birth, she snuck out of the hospital. My parents adopted him when he was still in the pediatric ICU.

KIT   I've known Nina and Miles for fifteen years, I've never heard that story.

ERIC Ask Nina. When Miles was a kid, he had to go to physical therapy, occupational, speech . . . he rode the little special ed bus to school with the retards. And then in the fifth grade, pow! He just shot up and shot out. Next thing we knew he was doing karate, playing piano . . . writing code on the Commodore computer I got for Christmas.

KIT Wow, a Commodore. Your parents were cutting edge.

ERIC All I did was play Pong on it so they ended up giving it to him. That's why I say Miles can do anything. And it's just . . . weird to come here and see him so . . .

KIT Well, getting laid off right before you have a baby isn't exactly an ego booster.

ERIC Guess not.

KIT I've watched Nina and Miles's relationship for a long time. They try to pass the power back and forth between them, but one person always ends up holding the ball. That's true with most relationships, it's true with two women.

  (Beat.)

ERIC This is so embarrassing.

KIT What?

ERIC I'm such an idiot.

KIT Why?

ERIC Are you gay?

KIT No!

ERIC I thought . . . because you said two women—

KIT I'm talking about my friends Stephanie and Laura.

ERIC OK, good.

KIT Why would it have been embarrassing?

ERIC   I don't know. Listen, I should go. I'm in your way.

KIT   I can still do my work with you here.

ERIC   I know. But, I'm not sure I can.

SCENE 8

Office. The sound of scraping and prying from above—MILES and REGGIE working on the floor. KIT and NINA work on the model—they are gluing on a cantilevered roof onto its beam. KIT applies the glue as NINA balances the top-heavy roof piece.

NINA   Your birthday is already? What's today's date?

KIT   The third.

NINA   I completely lost track of time—okay, Thursday, your birthday. Is it— . . . are you gonna turn (forty?)—

KIT   Let's not touch on that.

NINA   Okay, okay, what do you want to do? Do you want me to throw you a party?

KIT   *(Re: roof)* Press down harder on this side.

NINA   Dinner with a bunch of our friends?

KIT   No.

NINA   Kit, you gotta ring it in. Your fortieth—

KIT   Do not speak the number.

NINA   You can't do nothing.

KIT   I don't want to do nothing. I want to go out to a nice, quiet dinner, just you and me. We can go to that new French place on Smith Street. You can be home in time to nurse Hannah.

NINA   You sure you don't want to go somewhere fabulous in Manhattan?

KIT   With you constantly checking your watch, worried that your breasts are going to explode?

NINA   I guess you're right.

             (KIT *finishes, leaves* NINA *holding the newly glued-on piece.*)

KIT   So, Hannah being such a big baby and all, I was wondering — were you a big baby?

NINA   Normal. My body was skinny but my cheeks clocked in at about a pound each.

KIT   Miles must've been a big baby, then, huh?

NINA   Mm . . . no.

             (KIT, *having hoped for a longer answer, fishes for more.*)

KIT   Have you ever seen pictures of him as a baby?

NINA   I have a picture of him when he was about a year old in my desk.

KIT   Can I see it?

NINA   Uh . . . sure. It's in my top drawer.

             (KIT *opens* NINA's *top drawer, sifts around to find it. Looks at it.*)

KIT   Well. Looks like a perfectly healthy one-year old to me. Perfectly healthy.

             (*She puts the photo back, goes to her desk, silently kicking herself for believing.* NINA *watches her, unsure what this is about.*)

NINA   Actually, a normal one-year-old should weigh about twenty pounds and Miles only weighed seventeen.

             (KIT *turns to* NINA — *enthused.*)

KIT   Tell me more.

NINA   His mom said he was a fussy eater —

(KIT's disappointment is visible.)

KIT ...Right.

NINA He wouldn't drink milk or eat cheese which are good sources of fat.

(NINA looks at KIT, trying to read her reaction.)

KIT That makes sense.

(Beat.)

NINA Plus he was addicted to heroin for the first two months of his—

KIT Yes!

NINA You're in love with Eric! He told you about Miles. That's Miles's big secret.

KIT It came up in conversation.

NINA Pillow talk.

KIT Eric and I haven't even gone out yet, let alone slept together.

(Half beat.)

NINA Don't trust him, Kit.

KIT What do you resent so much about Eric? Has he ever hurt you or Miles?

(Beat.)

NINA He's never there when it counts, you know, he didn't even come to our wedding. Then out of nowhere, he just swoops in and inserts himself into our lives.

(MRS. CHAE carries downstairs a tray with two bowls of soup.)

MRS. CHAE It's lunch time for the hard-working woman. *(She means "women.")*

NINA *(Smelling, just saying it fills her.)* What is that? Seaweed soup?

(MRS. CHAE places a bowl on NINA's desk.)

MRS. CHAE   Mi yuk guk. I write it down for you. Very good for the mommy after delivering the baby, because it has iron and protein. Good for you now because of the breastfeeding. You need the strength.

NINA   Thank you! I'll have it as soon as—

(MRS. CHAE places another bowl in front of KIT.)

MRS. CHAE   Good for you too, because it also helps to make the baby.

(KIT gently pushes the soup bowl away from her.)

KIT   Hmmmm . . . Thanks . . .

(MRS. CHAE notices. So does NINA, she's embarrassed.)

MRS. CHAE   Your husband don't want the children?

KIT   My husband . . . right. He says he's not ready.

(NINA flashes her a look.)

MRS. CHAE   You cannot wait for him. The man is never ready for the children, he is still his mommy's baby. But, having the child will make him a man.

NINA   You can still eat it, Kit, the soup won't impregnate you.

MRS. CHAE   *(To NINA.)* If you like, I teach you how to make it.

NINA   God, I would love that. *(NINA looks at the soup, she still can't move her hands. To MRS. CHAE.)* Would you mind moving that a little closer to me?

MRS. CHAE   Of course.

(MRS. CHAE does so. NINA leans her head down, without moving her hands, trying to get her mouth close enough to the bowl. She manages a sip.)

NINA   Mm, smells fantastic.

(She blows on it. MRS. CHAE watches NINA struggle to drink the soup.)

I'm dying to eat it but I can't move my hands until the glue—

(MRS. CHAE *picks up the bowl, scoops up a spoonful of soup and blows on it before offering it to* NINA.)

MRS. CHAE *(In Korean.)* Eat well.

NINA Oh, gosh, um— (NINA *takes a sip of soup.)* Mm, that's delicious.

(MRS. CHAE *continues to feed* NINA.)

MRS. CHAE Soon it will be Hannah's paek il. We must have a big party.

NINA Paek il? What's that?

MRS. CHAE Paek il is for one hundredth day because back in old times, when a baby did not die by one hundred days, we have a big party. We say now she will live long life.

(MRS. CHAE *feeds* NINA *another spoonful.)*

KIT Where's Miles's camera when you need it?

NINA Gosh, I really appreciate this but . . . you don't have to feed me.

(We hear MILES's *and* REGGIE's *voices in disagreement.)*

MRS. CHAE It's okay. Hannah is sleeping and I am in the way upstairs. Miles and his brother are working so hard.

NINA Eric's helping?

MRS. CHAE Yes.

(NINA *looks at* KIT.)

NINA I thought he was going to the realtors—wait a second. Who do you mean by Miles's brother?

MRS. CHAE The man, his brother. The one who's helping him.

NINA Is he black?

MRS. CHAE Yes.

NINA That's not Miles's brother.

MRS. CHAE   Oh—

NINA   You met his brother. Eric. Eric's his brother. Reggie's . . . just some guy who lives on our street.

(KIT notices NINA's tone of voice.)

MRS. CHAE   Oh, I see . . .

(A beat. NINA's uncomfortable.)

Miles is adopted?

NINA   Yes.

MRS. CHAE   *(A Korean sound.)* Oh . . . *(Tsk tsk tsk.)* Such nice parents.

NINA   . . . They're nice because they're white people who adopted a little black baby?

(KIT tastes the soup.)

KIT   Mmmm, Mrs. Chae, this is good. What kind of seaweed is this?

MRS. CHAE   We call it mi yuk.

NINA   Because actually, I think Miles's parents were—they did things that were kind of . . . like raising him in an all-white neighborhood, sending him to schools where he was the only black kid—

KIT   I thought you liked your in-laws—

NINA   Miles was teased a lot. The reason he'll be emotionally enslaved to Eric the rest of his life is because Eric would beat the shit out of kids who picked on him.

MRS. CHAE   But Miles grew up so nice. Clean and smart, handsome.

NINA   Did you just say (clean.)—

KIT   Mrs. Chae, you mentioned your daughter has a child Hannah's age. Maybe he and Hannah can have a playdate! *(To NINA.)* It'd be good for Hannah to have another kid she can speak Korean to because . . . you don't really have Korean friends.

MRS. CHAE *(Hesitates.)* I don't think—

NINA What—you're afraid your daughter won't let him come because Hannah's black?

KIT Nina—

MRS. CHAE Hannah is not black. If you look at her, maybe you cannot tell. People cannot tell the daddy is black. She is just beautiful baby.

(MILES walks in through the outside door.)

MILES Nina, I've got to use your computer for a minute.

(He sits at her desk, launches a web browser.)

NINA Why can't you use your computer upstairs?

MILES I told Reggie I was going to the hardware store to get something. I hid a little webcam so I can watch him. Mrs. Chae, do you mind staying down here for a few minutes?

KIT Watch him do what?

MILES Steal from me.

MRS. CHAE *(A Korean expression of shock.)* Aigu.

NINA Miles, you have no reason to think that Reggie stole your—

MILES The man openly offered to sell me stolen goods, Nina. This is what he does. He insinuates himself into people's homes, and then he takes things he can sell. The gentrification of this neighborhood is the best thing to happen to him in years.

(MILES checks the web browser.)

See that—look, he's looking in one of our boxes. I put my portable DVD player in there on purpose.

(NINA looks.)

NINA This is wrong. I'm going upstairs to tell him—

KIT Nina, don't let go of that—

(NINA *starts for the stairs.* KIT *rushes to the model to grab the roof.* MILES *goes after* NINA.)

MILES Nina, stay. I want to catch him.

NINA You've set up a trap.

KIT Look at it this way. If he doesn't take anything, you'll have won.

NINA You approve of this?

KIT No, but I admit I'm on the edge of my seat.

(MILES *looks at the browser.*)

MILES He's looking around . . . he's walking toward my iPod . . . he's picking up a pry bar—

(*We hear the corresponding sound on the ceiling.*)

And . . . he's pulling up the linoleum off the kitchen floor.

NINA I am so embarrassed, Miles.

MILES Well, someone took my camcorder.

NINA You should go up there and apologize.

MILES I'm not going to apologize. But I will let him keep working for us. And keep my eye on him.

(MILES *goes out the front door.*)

MRS. CHAE Can I . . . go upstairs now?

NINA Yes.

(MRS. CHAE *goes upstairs.* NINA *takes over the job of holding down the roof from* KIT. KIT *goes to her desk.*)

KIT Do you want . . . me to feed you the soup?

NINA No, I don't want it anymore. Do me a favor and throw it away.

SCENE 9

Living room. The next day. REGGIE *holds one end of a tape measure while* MILES *pulls the rest across the length of the floor.*

MILES   One hundred and thirty-five inches. Divided by two, that's sixty-seven and a half inches.

(He walks to that number on the measuring tape, then makes a mark on the floor.)

So this is the center of the room.

REGGIE   Why you doing this the hard way? All you have to do is start at this wall— *(Walks to the border between kitchen and living room.)* —get your tiles going across, then whenever you run into your fridge or your stove, you just cut the tile to fit. That's it.

MILES   No, if you do it that way then that's the only line that will look like full tiles. It's better to start in the center. That way I can distribute the error factor around the periphery of the room. *(After a beat.)* I'm going downstairs to ask Nina to take a look at—

REGGIE   Man, why do you have to—

(MILES turns to him.)

Alright, alright, I get you, man. Now, I get you. I ain't never been married yet so I wasn't feeling you before, but now I am.

MILES   What?

REGGIE   'Cuz I notice how you talk to your female, see what I'm saying. 'Cuz you always saying, "I gotta ax Nina this," or "I can't 'til I ax Nina—" and I've been thinking, "What is this brother, henpecked or some shit?" But now I know that's how you do her to do you right. I'm'a try that shit myself.

MILES   Man, Nina's done this before.

REGGIE   I done this before! I keep telling you!

MILES	Nina's done this hundreds of times before. Not just once in her mother's house. Anyway, why are you still living in your mother's house?
REGGIE	She getting old, she need somebody.
MILES	Yeah, but, you never moved out, right? So, who's taking care of who?
REGGIE	I got four brothers and three sisters, seven nephews and eight nieces, we all there.
MILES	All living in that house?
REGGIE	We family, man. We got seventy-seven years history in that house. Ain't no yuppie gone come up in here and buy us out.

(ERIC *walks in.*)

ERIC	I tracked down the owner of the diner, he's this Hasidic guy who hangs out with his buddies in this bakery in Williamsburg. I made an appointment for Friday so you can meet him.

(REGGIE *starts arranging the tiles the way he wants them. Not gluing them, just placing them down to make a point.*)

MILES	Awesome.
REGGIE	"Awesome, dude."
ERIC	The landlord said another party approached him about the space last week. They want to open a tea lounge.
MILES	A tea lounge? Who around here is going to go to a tea lounge?
REGGIE	I would. I drink tea.
ERIC	To get an edge on these guys, I think we should put down a deposit. Are you ready to do that?
REGGIE	He gone ax his wife.
MILES	It's your money. If you want to be that aggressive—
ERIC	That's how you compete, little brother. You have to be fierce,

you have to use that big brain of yours to think—how do I get the advantage? What idea can I come up with that no one else could?

MILES
I can do that.

ERIC
I'm gonna go to the bank tomorrow, convert my ringgits.

(ERIC *heads for the stairs just as* WALTER *comes down. Once again, he goes straight out the door, without acknowledging anyone.* ERIC *gives* MILES *a look—weird. As* ERIC *goes upstairs,* NINA *comes up from the office.* REGGIE, *having placed a few rows of tiles on the floor, seizes the opportunity.*)

REGGIE
(*To* NINA.) Mommy, look at this here. How this looks? You walk into the room, you see one solid line. That's the way to do it.

NINA
You're . . . right, Reggie. That is . . . a way to do it. But—

REGGIE
You hear that? She said I'm right. She said I'm right and she know more about this than you. But you ain't never said nothing like that.

MILES
Oh, Nina's your hero now?

NINA
Miles—

MILES
I've been telling you since the minute I met you that she's an architect. But you keep treating her like she doesn't know anything.

REGGIE
(*To* NINA.) Is that true? That ain't true. You the one who act like I don't know anything. I done did this before and you ain't. But you gotta be like one of them new niggas who always think—

(*The baby starts crying upstairs.* NINA *can't decide whether to get the baby or stay with* MILES.)

MILES
No, man. No. I'm not any kind of nigger. You hear me?

REGGIE
Man, I ain't mean it like that. Over here when somebody say

	new nigga we mean somebody who turn they nose up at something 'cause it ain't new or good enough —
MILES	I don't care what you say it means, man. I don't want to hear it in my house.
	(The baby's cries become jagged and intense. NINA can't take it anymore and goes upstairs to soothe the baby.)
REGGIE	Man, you all new niggas to me, buying up these here brownstones for a million dollars when they done sat here for decades all boarded up — shit, city couldn't give these buildings away.
MILES	Don't try to give me that back in the day bull(shit.) —
REGGIE	This house that you living in now been abandoned so long it had a tree growing out of it — right through the roof. When we was little kids, we called it the tree house — *(Walks to window.)* We used to climb through that window and sit under the tree — *(Points to a spot on the floor.)* Right here — and smoke cigarettes, kiss, party, you name it. This was our house.
MILES	Man, don't try to make it sound like it was better back in the old days 'cause I know this house went on to be a shooting gallery and a crack house before the city took it over.
REGGIE	I ain't saying it was better. Shit, I got shot walking down my street just going to buy some chicken wings at the Chinese restaurant. So I ain't saying nothing 'bout no back in the day. All I'm saying is — this is the way you do your tiles, son. You get them going across, ain't nothing else to worry about.
MILES	Reggie, man, if you want to help, I'll pay you. But we're gonna do it the way I want it. Okay? It's my house now.
	(Beat.)
REGGIE	Alright. *(Checks watch.)* I gotta go check on my girl, wake her ass up otherwise she ain't gone get to work —

(He goes out the door. NINA *comes downstairs carrying* HANNAH.*)*

NINA   Miles, is everything okay?

MILES   Where's Mrs. Chae? Why isn't she here taking care of the baby?

NINA   I told her to come in a little later this morning. I wanted to talk to you about her. I think we have a problem.

MILES   What're you talking about? She seems to be working out great.

*(*ERIC *hurries downstairs carrying a pair of boxer shorts.)*

ERIC   This is fucked up, man. This is out of line, this is fucked up.

MILES   What's going on, man?

ERIC   My ringgits are gone.

MILES *and* NINA   What?

(He holds out his boxer shorts.)

ERIC   I hid the money in here—I folded these up and put them underneath the mattress in the sofa bed—not the most inventive hiding place, I admit, but I figured we were all family here.

MILES   Man, what is going on around here?

ERIC   You got a lot of new people coming in and out of this house. The tenant passes by all our bedrooms to get to his floor. He's got a lock on the door to his apartment, but all our rooms are wide open. Maybe he took your camcorder. What do you know about that guy?

MILES   Not much.

ERIC   If you ask me—you guys need to close ranks. Clean house. How much is he paying in rent?

NINA   Twelve hundred a month.

ERIC   I could pay that. Or close to that. I've got some money in the bank, plus I've built in salaries for me and you in the business proposal.

(NINA *looks at* MILES—*you're not going for this, are you?*)

MILES   We can't just kick him out, we gave him a two-year lease.

ERIC   I should be part of this community, too. It'll be good for the profile of the business.

MILES   We'll see what we can do to make that happen, man.

NINA   We will?

ERIC   Let me go upstairs and have another look.

(He goes upstairs.)

NINA   *(To* MILES.*)* We need twelve hundred for the upstairs apartment. I cannot meet our mortgage payments without—I can't take it on, Miles. I can't have one more thing on my back.

MILES   It's not going to be on your back. Eric said he's going to pay rent.

NINA   No, he's not. Eric came here with the intention of getting us to give him a free place to live.

MILES   He just got off a plane! He came here to meet the baby.

NINA   We haven't seen or heard from him in months—

MILES   That's usual for him.

NINA   Then on the day we move in, he shows up at our doorstep with no place to live. He comes up with this business idea, says he's got the money to get it started, gets you all riled up about it, then all of a sudden—the money's gone. He never had the money, Miles.

MILES   You never saw it, but I saw it.

NINA   He probably bought it at a party store with a pack of tropical drink umbrellas. What bothers me the most, Miles, is that we've always laughed at your brother . . . together, we've indulged him, we'd listen to his stories and wink-wink at each other knowing that it was all a big show . . . but now I look over at you, and you're rapt. You're like a kid listening to his con-man uncle and hanging on every word.

(HANNAH *starts to cry.*)

MILES   You really think that I'm that gullible?

NINA   I think you're . . . vulnerable, I think you think you're cast out in some way . . . and that your brother's going to bring you in. But you're not cast out. Hannah and I are your family, now. Why don't you hold her? She'll stop crying if you do.

(NINA *tries to hand* MILES *the baby. He doesn't take her.*)

MILES   No, she won't. She only cries harder.

NINA   Only when she senses your fear. Just focus on how much you love her, and she'll calm down.

MILES   You know she's going to reject me.

NINA   No, she won't.

MILES   She only wants you. I don't have anything she needs.

NINA   Miles, take her—

MILES   No, you want me to fail. You want me to.

(*He storms off.* NINA *turns to* HANNAH.)

NINA   It's OK, sweetie, daddy loves you. Daddy loves you.

SCENE 10

Office. KIT *is working.* NINA *is nursing* HANNAH.

KIT   Nina, you can't take time away from work to look for a new nanny. I won't let you.

NINA   It won't take that long this time. I'm not going to hold out for

	a Korean woman. I'll take anyone who isn't going to poison my baby with racist thoughts.
KIT	I think you're blowing this whole thing out of proportion.
NINA	I'm not. I know that as sure as someday Hannah's going to fall off her bike and scrape her knee, that someone is going to call her a chink, and a nigger—
KIT	Cover her ears!
NINA	I can't stop it. I can't protect her from it—I can't stop it from happening to me as a grown woman. Last month, I was standing in the front lawn of my childhood home, where I used to play cowboys and Indians, and ride my banana seat Schwinn, and eat Creamsicles from the ice cream man, and some teenager shouted from a car, "Go back to Vietnam—"
KIT	It's horrible, it's embarrassing, but I still think that's completely different from what Mrs. Chae—
NINA	My whole bright idea about hiring a Korean nanny was to give Hannah a reason to be proud to be Korean. I thought if she could, I don't know, speak the language, have some sense of belonging—it would help those names bounce off of her. We had the same reasons for wanting to raise Hannah in a mostly black neighborhood.
KIT	Look, you guys are making great choices for her—
NINA	No, we're not, we're failing in every way. The Korean nanny's denying her blackness, the black neighbors are throwing rocks through our window . . . Miles won't hold our baby and . . . I see how hard you're working and I'm trying my best—I know I'm not pulling my weight—but I swear I am giving this everything I have left. And all I ask from Miles, all I want him to do . . .

(*A beat for* NINA.)

. . . is to be in it with me. |

	(NINA *covers her mouth to hide that she's crying—something she saw her mother do.*)
KIT	Hey—
	(KIT *walks over, kneels in front of* NINA.)
NINA	But instead, he wants to know when we're going to start having sex again. And I can't—I swear, Kit, I don't have anything left to give.
	(NINA *hides her face by nuzzling* HANNAH.)
KIT	When we're in Barcelona, I'm gonna take you to this fantastic little tapas place I read about. We'll eat little plates of fried octopus eyes and beef snout on toast while we watch them build our building.
	(NINA *nods but aims all her need at* HANNAH, *kissing her, holding her close.* KIT *goes to touch* NINA *supportively, but* NINA *has closed the circle—there's only room for her and her baby.* KIT *stands up, walks back to her drawing table. She draws for a minute.*)
NINA	Eric tell you about the missing money?
KIT	I heard about it.
NINA	What do you think? Do you think someone really stole it?
KIT	I think a ghost took it. I think that first night when your window got smashed, the ghost of all the neglected communities past—who couldn't get the city to fix their sidewalks, or keep their electricity going on hot days, let alone provide them with a local source of organic half-and-half—wafted in here and is trying to spook you into leaving.
	(KIT *puts something down on the table,* NINA *picks it up—a matchbook from a restaurant.*)
NINA	What's this?

KIT	It has the restaurant's name and address on Smith Street. The food was good. You and Miles should go there some time.
NINA	What? Ohmigod. Oh please God, please please please let it not be—
KIT	It's new, so it's not that crowded yet. They let me sit for a while.
NINA	You waited for me? Why didn't you call?
KIT	I have some dignity, you know.
NINA	Why didn't you remind me during the day!
KIT	Just, let it pass, Nina.
NINA	No, it's totally my fault. I can't believe I forgot to show up for your fortieth birth(day.)—
KIT	Just stop talking about it, OK? I don't care that you didn't show up, I don't care. I ate dinner, went to a bar, I fucked a guy in the bathroom—it was perfect. The best birthday ever. All I want from you, Nina, is for you to do your work. Fucking do your work. I can't finish this model by myself, not with less than six weeks left. I waited for you, Nina, I could've started two months ago without you, but you told me to wait.
NINA	I shouldn't have done that. It's just—I never . . . it's like this feral—this animal drive to take care of my daughter. I can't even apologize for it, it fucking feels right.
KIT	So you shouldn't be trying to work.
NINA	I want to work. I don't want to be a stay-at-home mom. I know it doesn't add up, okay? But I still love my work.
KIT	Look, Nina, you're a good mom—my mom, she took Dexatrim when she was pregnant with me because she didn't want to get fat. And I—I don't think women should have children if they're not going to be like you. But this work is all I have and I fucking want to win this competition.
NINA	I do too.

KIT   Don't say that.

NINA   I know it doesn't make sense to you—

KIT   Nina, I'm forty years old, I already don't have what I thought I would have by now but I know I can make beautiful buildings. It's not fucking fair for you to hold me back. Between Mrs. Tillman's unreasonable demands and your constant distractions, we're way behind already.

NINA   I'll take care of Mrs. Tillman.

KIT   No, you won't.

NINA   When she calls today, tell her I'll meet her at the house.

KIT   That's nice of you to finally offer, but Mrs. Tillman isn't going to call today because I told her we quit.

NINA   What—?

KIT   This morning, she insisted I go all the way to the Upper East Side just to show me some dust from the living room had "penetrated" her bedroom. And I just—I fucking had it.

NINA   You quit—you . . . you quit before she finished paying us?

KIT   Now we can focus on the model.

NINA   Kit—how could you do that to me?

KIT   We need to concentrate on the model.

NINA   Mrs. Tillman is my livelihood. That money is what my family lives on.

KIT   We split the money but I do all the work.

NINA   I designed the plans with you. I did my share until the baby was born.

> (NINA *thinks a beat, looks at the baby, then picks up her bag. Calling upstairs.*)

Mrs. Chae? *(To KIT.)* I'm going to apologize to Mrs. Tillman.

KIT	Go ahead.
NINA	*(Yells.)* Mrs. Chae! *(To KIT.)* I'm getting this job back, Kit.
KIT	Fine, you can run up there every time a nail gets hammered in crooked.
NINA	Mrs. Chae!

(MRS. CHAE *rushes downstairs.*)

MRS. CHAE	Sorry, Nina, I could not hear you.
NINA	I need you to take Hannah right now.
MRS. CHAE	Yes, yes, I will take.

(MRS. CHAE *reaches for the baby, says in Korean, "It's okay, baby, Mommy is very busy so Grandma will take care of you."*)

NINA	What did you just say?
MRS. CHAE	Mh?
NINA	What did you say to her?
MRS. CHAE	I say you are very busy, so I will take her upstairs—
NINA	Did you call yourself "halmoni?"
MRS. CHAE	. . . Yes?
NINA	Grandma?
MRS. CHAE	In Korean language, a child will call any woman my age—
NINA	When I come back, we need to talk.

(NINA *flies out the door.*)

KIT	I'm sorry—
MRS. CHAE	*(Consoling herself, but aiming it at HANNAH.)* It's okay, it's okay, I know everything will be okay.

(MRS. CHAE *heads upstairs as* ERIC *walks in through the front door. He walks up to* KIT, *stands close to her.*)

ERIC   Hey.

KIT   Hi.

ERIC   Now I know why you take a car service. It's a bitch to get here from your house by train. Do you feel hungover?

KIT   Eric, I don't have the money.

ERIC   You didn't get to stop by the bank on your way in?

KIT   No.

ERIC   Well, you still have a couple hours—

KIT   I'm not going to loan you any money. I'm sure both of us said things last night that we don't intend to follow through on. We were drunk, we were having a good time—

ERIC   You called me up, lured me to that restaurant with your sob story—

KIT   I invited you to join me, you ordered the most expensive thing on the menu, I picked up the tab . . . everything that happened after that was fun, but it wasn't worth five thousand dollars. You're just going to have to tell your brother you never had the money.

ERIC   I had the money. I had it until last night.

KIT   Well, I'm sure you'll find a way around it, Eric, you're fast on your feet.

SCENE 11

Living room. MILES *comes downstairs in a suit and jacket—he's missing a tie. He starts looking through some boxes, pulling out kitchen utensils from one box, winter clothes from another . . .* ERIC *comes downstairs wearing a dress shirt and tie.*

ERIC   You look sharp, man.

MILES   I'm looking for my ties—

ERIC   You don't need a tie, you look crisp without one.

>   (MILES *lifts a box off the top of a stack and looks in the box underneath it.*)

MILES   I want to make a strong appearance, those tea lounge people probably wear thrift store T-shirts and flip-flops.

ERIC   Don't bring up the tea lounge unless he brings it up first. As far as I know, they haven't put down any money so we'll be on even ground.

>   (MILES *pulls his camcorder out of a box.*)

MILES   My camcorder . . . that's what I did with it. I put it in here after Reggie came in with his chandelier and was roaming all over the place.

ERIC   Well, alright. That's great.

>   (*A beat.*)

MILES   So, if my camcorder was never stolen . . . what happened to your ringgits?

ERIC   I don't know, man.

MILES   Eric . . . tell me straight up. Were those ringgits real?

ERIC   Of course they were real.

MILES   Where are they, man, I don't believe Walter took them.

ERIC   Oh, I think he has them.

MILES   Eric—

ERIC   What you want to do is watch his checking account. You have all his information from his credit report, right? Watch his account for the next couple weeks and you just might see a big deposit show up.

(Beat.)

MILES: Then, what, he's going to tell me he's moving out?

ERIC: Could be.

MILES: Is that what you did with the money, Eric? You wanted me and Nina to think Walter stole it, but really you paid him so he would move out?

(Beat.)

ERIC: I offered it to him, yeah.

MILES: Man—that money was supposed to be for our business.

ERIC: You want me to commit to this business but what're you doing for me? You own this whole brownstone, but you'd rather price gouge a stranger than give your brother a home.

MILES: We're not making decisions right now based on preference— we need to make ends meet.

ERIC: You always make ends meet, Miles. Why're you acting like you don't know that everything's gonna turn out your way— it always does.

MILES: You think things just snap into place—?

ERIC: Nina's gonna win her competition, the store's going to be an instant success, Hannah's gonna be the poster baby for the new Benetton campaign . . . you're going to have it all, like you always do—why do you have to deny me a piece of it?

MILES: Man, I've earned what I have. This is what I've always worked for. But you've been flitting around the world, cobbling together this little job with that one, never building anything, never digging roots, and now you're looking at me and saying, "I want some of that"?

ERIC: You don't think I want a house, a steady career and a family? What do you think I am, a circus performer? A pirate? Of course I want those things but I've never been able to work for them because I'm not allowed to have what Miles has. Miles is the super baby, the poor little black boy left on our doorstep who goes on to save the town and my job in life is to make sure I never overshadow him.

MILES   Mom and Dad gave you every chance they gave me. They cut everything straight down the line.

ERIC   I can see why you'd want to remember things that way, but they weren't. You were always the golden boy, the miracle . . . I could never live up to it, Miles.

MILES   Did you try? All you had to do was try.

ERIC   What, you think because I'm white, because I know who my biological parents are, because I can walk down the street of our hometown without some old lady calling the cops—that every door in the world is open to me? They're not, Miles. The doors are for you.

MILES   You want what I have? Do you know what it is like for me to look at my baby, and see her brown skin, and curly hair, and long eyelashes and know she got them from me—but I don't know who I come from? What am I giving her? What have I passed on? I don't know. Maybe there's some disease that skips a generation, and I've given it to her. Or maybe my great-great-grandfather was a Civil War hero, but I'll never be able to tell Hannah about it. All I can do is take her to Mom and Dad's house in Indiana, where Mom can explain every little tchochke and how it was handed down to her . . . and Dad can break out the family albums going back seven generations—but when she looks at those people in the photographs, she won't see herself, she won't see me.

ERIC   You think I see myself in those old pictures? All I see are a bunch of old people in stiff suits who had sixteen children and were half-dead from lung cancer by the time they were our age.

MILES   That's how you make it hard for yourself, Eric. Trying to invent yourself from scratch.

ERIC	You did. But I can't, no matter how hard I've tried.
	(NINA *walks upstairs, notices the camcorder.*)
NINA	You found the camcorder.
MILES	…Yeah.
NINA	Where was it?
MILES	…Where I put it.
ERIC	I'm gonna go to this meeting, man.
NINA	Miles, I want to fire Mrs. Chae this afternoon.
ERIC	If you want to catch up with me…
	(ERIC *leaves.*)
MILES	Why?
NINA	I just need you to trust me on this.

SCENE 12

Living room. MRS. CHAE *crosses the living room to get to the door.* MILES *sees her.*

MILES	Mrs. Chae, are you leaving?
MRS. CHAE	Yes.
MILES	You left your lunch—
MRS. CHAE	Not my lunch. It's jap chae for you and Nina. You have it for dinner.
	(*She heads for the door.*)
MILES	You'll still be with us for two more weeks, right?
MRS. CHAE	I am old woman with nothing to do. Husband is dead, no job, what I'm going to do?

MILES	I — I don't know what to say, you've been wonderful to Hannah . . . but —
MRS. CHAE	I try so hard, I want to make you and Nina happy. What have I done so wrong?

(NINA *walks upstairs from the office, having overheard the last part.* MRS. CHAE *takes a step toward her.*)

	Nina —

(*Without thinking,* MRS. CHAE *speaks to* NINA *in Korean.*)

	Nina, You're such a good girl, hm? Give me another chance. I'll do everything right.
NINA	I don't understand you.
MRS. CHAE	You are good girl, such a good mommy, hm? Best mommy. My daughter, she hire the British nanny to take care of my grandson. She tell me she don't want Mommy to take care of grandson. She don't want grandson to speak the bad English like Mommy. Kyung Soon say when she was little girl, she speak the English like Mommy, go to school and say "preejing," it's "preejing" outside. And children laugh, laugh.
NINA	. . . pleasing?
MRS. CHAE	So cold, it's preejing and Kyung Soon come home and say, "Mommy, you are dummy. You are such dummy!"
MILES	. . . Kids can be rough.
MRS. CHAE	So, she hire another nanny, not me. British nanny take care of my grandson.
NINA	You said your daughter has her son in daycare at her firm?
MRS. CHAE	Now I am telling you. British nanny comes at seven o'clock in morning, stay until eight o'clock at night. Then, Tibetan nanny comes on weekend, so Kyung Soon and husband can play golf.
MILES	She has two nannies?

MRS. CHAE Yes.

MILES That's a lot of nannies.

NINA So . . . you've been lying about all of that?

MRS. CHAE I tell you the truth now. Before, I wanted you to hire me, I see nice family, two good parents—happy baby . . . I wanted to be in this house, I wanted to be in this (family.) . . .

(MILES *turns to* NINA.)

MILES Nina, maybe firing her isn't the right thing to do.

NINA (*To* MRS. CHAE.) I know people like you. Some of my mom's friends, they came to this country in the sixties, people taunted them, told them their food stank, their faces were flat, called them gook, chink, chingaling—

MILES (*To* NINA.) Whoa—

NINA Made them feel like shit for what, for walking down the street, for sending their kids to school, for starting a business. For that they got beaten up, their stores got vandalized, right?

MRS. CHAE . . . Yes. My husband and I had a gift store in Yonkers. Somebody paint all over the windows.

NINA So what did you do?

MRS. CHAE We cleaned the windows. My husband and I scrubbed the paint off with our hands—

NINA You went looking for someone you could feel superior to. And you picked black people.

MILES Nina, I think you need—you need to take a step back.

NINA It makes me mad, it makes me ashamed of being Korean, fucking racists.

MILES Mrs. Chae is new to this country, she's from another generation . . . I don't like what she said to Hannah but I don't think she's a racist—

NINA	Bullshit. My mom was all those things and she never said anything like that. Even in that shitty little town we lived in. Mrs. Chae is from Queens, she has no excuse.
MILES	Well, she'll learn—
NINA	Who taught my mom—nobody. It was in her heart.

(Half beat.)

MILES	Oh, I get it. I get it now, Nina. It's like you hired Mrs. Chae to be your mom. And you fired her because she's not.
NINA	Geezus, Miles, is it too much to ask you to take my side?
MILES	Side—!? What do you want this to be, Nina?
NINA	I want you to . . . I want you to defend me.

(MILES looks at MRS. CHAE, who has kept her head down. He turns back to NINA.)

MILES	Nobody's attacking you!
NINA	That's not the point.
MILES	*(To MRS. CHAE.)* Excuse her, Mrs. Chae, Nina's under a tremendous amount of press(ure.)—
MRS. CHAE	She is working very hard.

(Moves towards NINA, who turns to MILES.)

NINA	Don't fucking apologize for me.
MILES	You just said you wanted me—
NINA	Not to apologize, I want you to—Christ, if you think I'm being unreasonable—
MILES	Yes!
NINA	Then, fucking . . . hold me or something.
MILES	You're not making me want to hold you.
NINA	I have to do something—?

MILES: Well, you're not making me feel like it—

NINA: So, making all the money for the family doesn't qualify me for a hug?

MILES: Why d'you— *(Looks at MRS. CHAE.)* Why d'you have to say that?

NINA: Because I'm tired of having to tiptoe around your ego. My work is totally stressful, I'm not giving the baby the time I want—but at the end of the day, I don't get to vent to you. If I say anything about the pressure that is fucking crushing me— you think I'm trying to make you feel bad.

MILES: So, what, you're discounting the fact that most of the down payment for this house came from cashing in my stock options?

NINA: I'm not counting money, I could give a shit about the money, Miles.

MILES: This is obviously about money, you resent me for not being able to provide for my daughter. Look at this house—it's crumbling down around us. We can't afford to fix it, we can't afford to live in it. This is no way to raise a baby. We never should have . . . we were not ready to have a baby.

(KIT walks upstairs.)

KIT: *(To NINA.)* Is everything OK?

NINA: You're blaming me because we have a healthy, beautiful baby?

MILES: No, I'm blaming you because we have a baby that I don't deserve.

NINA: All she needs is for you to love her, Miles.

MILES: It's not enough.

(The doorbell rings. REGGIE appears on the other side of the broken window.)

REGGIE: Hey yo, son, I got the guys with the glass, they gonna install it.

NINA   (Looks at MILES.) Now? They were supposed to have come at two, here they are at six-thirty.

MRS. CHAE   That's Korean time.

MILES   You deal with this, Nina, I'm—

                (He heads upstairs.)

NINA   (Calling after him.) You're what?

                (MILES continues upstairs. NINA looks at MRS. CHAE.)

                Fuck him, man, fuck all of you. I had this perfect, precious baby and all anyone wants to do is blame me for how she's changed our lives. Of course she's changed our lives. What was so fucking good about them before?

                (REGGIE knocks on the front door, then opens it.)

REGGIE   (To NINA.) Yo, mommy, they gone have to take the rest of that old glass out first. So I'm'a have to put some drop cloth down there so you don't get no glass shards on the floor.

NINA   Okay, Reggie.

                (A beat.)

REGGIE   I'm'a go to the hardware store, so, you gone have to hit me so I can get the drop cloth.

NINA   (Hands him a twenty.) Here.

REGGIE   I'm'a need sixty.

NINA   Sixty dollars for a drop cloth?

REGGIE   Okay, forty.

NINA   I don't have forty dollars, Reggie.

KIT   I have forty dollars. (Reaches into wallet.) Oh, no, I don't.

NINA   (To MRS. CHAE.) Do you have any money?

MRS. CHAE   Sorry.

NINA: Just—fuck it, Reggie.

REGGIE: All right, thirty dollars, I'll get the cheap stuff.

NINA: Forget it—forget the whole thing. Tell the guys they have to come back another—

(*Smash. The sound of the workmen smashing the glass to make way for the new window.*)

Goddamnit—!

REGGIE: What the fuck! Stupid motherfucker!

(*He heads for the door. Another smash. NINA releases a sound—something between a growl and a war cry. She picks up a pry bar and walks to the window and starts smashing the glass as KIT and MRS. CHAE watch. REGGIE, on the other side, backs up. NINA takes several whacks at it until there's little window left. The sound of HANNAH crying. NINA takes a breath, her demeanor changes. MRS. CHAE also responds to the sound. They both head for the stairs—*)

NINA: (*To MRS. CHAE.*) I'll get her.

(*She just gets to the stairs when MILES appears at the top of the stairs holding the baby.*)

MILES: I got her.

(*He walks downstairs toward NINA. Knows the words.*)

"Hush little baby, don't say a word. Papa's gonna buy you a mockingbird. If that mockingbird won't sing, Papa's gonna buy you a diamond ring."

(*He meets up with NINA.*)

You want me to teach you the rest of the words?

NINA: Yes.

MILES: (*Sings.*) "If that diamond ring turns brass."

(*NINA repeats after him as they walk toward the window.*)

NINA	*(Sings.)* "Turns brass."	
MILES	*(Sings.)* "Papa's gonna buy you a looking-glass."	
NINA	*(Sings.)* "—looking glass."	
MILES	*(Sings.)* "If that looking glass gets broke—"	

(They stop at the window. They look out into the street for a while. We start to hear the sounds of the neighborhood. Indeterminate voices in conversation. A basketball being bounced, music from a car stereo.)

NINA   You know what I think that rock coming through our window was?

MILES   What?

NINA   A meteorite. A chip off of some billion-year-old comet that came crashing through here to let out all the ghosts, all the stories, all the history . . . To let us know . . . we can make up the words ourselves.

(The sounds from the street swell as NINA and MILES look out.)

—— END OF PLAY ——

MINA
Kyoung H. Park

Kyoung H. Park was born in Santiago, Chile, in 1982, and received his BFA in Dramatic Writing from New York University's Tisch School of the Arts and an MA in Peace and Global Governance from Kyung Hee University's Graduate Institute of Peace Studies in South Korea. He is currently a Dean's Fellow at Columbia University's MFA program in playwriting and a member of Ma-Yi Writers Lab, Ensemble Studio Theater's Youngblood, and the Soho Theater's Hub. He is the author of *Sex and Hunger*, *disOriented*, *Heartbreak/India*, and *The Diamond Trade*. Park has worked in Chile, Brazil, the United States, the United Kingdom, South Korea, and India, and his plays have been developed or produced at Second Generation, Access Theater, Diverse City Theater, Ensemble Studio Theatre, La Mama, Ma-Yi Theater Company, Theater C, Vital Theatre, the Royal Court Theatre (London), and Lark Play Development Center. He is a UNESCO-Aschberg Laureate and recipient of an Edward Albee Playwriting Fellowship, Global Arts Village Fellowship, and Theater of the Oppressed Exchange Fellowship, as well as grants from the Arvon Foundation and GK Foundation.

Having grown up in Chile, Park initially felt closer to Latin American rather than Asian American communities in New York. It was in New York that he began to read Korean American literature and watch Asian American plays, which opened his eyes to new theatrical possibilities. *Mina* (2007) was written during his residency at Ma-Yi Writers Lab, and it was influenced by *Jaz*, a monologue written by the Ivory Coast playwright Koffi Kwahule, Pablo Neruda's *Canto General*, and Korean *pansori* storytelling. Park sees the play as an exploratory work on his multiple—and often clashing—cultural perspectives.

Mina was produced by Vital Theatre Company (Stephen Sunderlin, producing artistic director) in December 2004 as part of the Vital Signs: New Works Festival (Linda Ames Key, producer) at the McGinn Cazale Theatre in New York City. It was directed by C. S. Lee and featured Deborah S. Craig in the title role.

CHARACTERS

MINA, late twenties. A Korean woman, raised in Peru, living in New York City.

TIME AND PLACE

New York City. Now.

At rise: MINA *stands alone on stage. The stage is empty.*

MINA

Soy una mina,
coqueta y feliz.
Toda mi vida
fue un trampolín.

From Lima to New York,
I've been there.
Cosmopolitan metrosexuals,
Inca men—beware.

Soy una bestia—
una furia! —
mujer asiática
con raíces latinas.

Esa soy yo.

This is me.

On a yellow island
named Jejudo,
solitary, solid, singular,
I was born.

But I grew up in Lima,
where people called me a mina—

a *gal*.
Funny enough—that's my *name*.

During the nineties, my parents
followed the Japanese,
to live under the rule of Fujimori—
the president of Perú back then.
Ironically, my father would never say
anything nice about the Japanese:

"No trust them!
They took advantage
of our people—
we fermented cabbage,
because we were poor.
We made kimchi
with onions, garlic and chili.
We let the ingredients fester
for months
before we ate it.
But the Japanese invaded our shores
stole our fish, and
they had raw, expensive sushi!"

Don't think I'm judging.
I'm just relaying my father's words.
"Cooking facts," he said.

In New York,
my therapist calls facts a
trauma.
So I asked her:
His trauma or mine?

There was a silence.

They always want you to
answer your own questions.
They're tricky, aren't they?

I guess, looking back, Dr. Lee,
the trauma,
whether it was his,
or mine,
because history books said *this*,
but people said *that*,
were only facts.

Just facts.

Then again, little did I know that
I would fall in love with
a Japanese man.
A *Peruvian* Japanese man!

The shock just
made my father die.

"Mina-ya, no puede!
No puede!
You Korean woman,
you can't Japanese marry."

But dad, él es Peruano.

"Japanese blood is
in his body."

Pero papá, he was born in Perú.
He doesn't even speak Japanese.
He speaks Spanish.

"Mina-ya, you marry
Peruvian,
you're children will be
mutants."

Yes, Dr. Lee.
That's what he said:
"Mutants."

"Mina-ya, Japanese men
invaded Korea
and raped our woman!
Not your mother,
but woman like your
great-grandmother."

My omma,
she didn't say anything.
But she nodded.
And with that nod,
that silly domesticated
head-bobbing,
she said more than enough.

So Mina, whose trauma do you think it is?
His or yours?

I don't know Dr. Lee,
why don't you tell me
what you *think?*

Well, I grew up differently.
I grew up in America.
I don't know what it's like
to be Peruvian.

Well, Dr. Lee, you're
Korean too, aren't you?

Korean-American.

"Mina-ya, you
not love him.
You young!
You don't know!"

Lo único que sé
es que te quiero.
Hombre peruano,
a tí te quiero.

Te quiero desde que naciste,
te quiero porque eres de esta tierra,
from this earth,
you have been born!

Me? I don't know.
I wished I knew
where I belong.

"Mina-ya, tell me,
truthfully,
are you in love?"

I didn't answer.

My omma started crying:
"Oh-mo! Sae-sang he!
Ai-gu,
ai-guuuu!"

"Mina-ya,
truthfully,
you pregnant?"

Me? Pregnant?
Yes,
I was pregnant.

My Asian blood
was multiplying with
the golden blood
of the Inca empire.
My child was conceived
on the lands
robbed from their splendor
by the Spanish conquistadores
that held the Inca king's brother
imprisoned.
And they told the king:

"You must fill this room with
gold,
this high up,
and when you give us that much,
we will release your brother."

The Inca King complied—
his gold was shipped
to the Spanish kingdom
of Isabel la Católica
and the destitute people of Perú,
who valued plumes from exotic birds
as currency worth more than gold,
were robbed of its treasures
but persisted against
the imperialists—
imperialists like the Japanese
that raped
my great-grandmothers,
made my forefathers
ferment their food
and now,
between one victim
of history
to another,
we made love.

Love so strong,
sex so mighty,
our wet passion
made life
through fusion.

*"Ai-guuuu, Mina-ya,
Ai-guuuuuu!"*

As my omma howled,
in greater pain than
I have ever heard,

my father collapsed.
He had a heart-attack,
dropped the bul-gogi
on the floor,
tipped over the table,
the table-stove
fell on the kitchen mantle
and the bul
lit
'till there was bul
all over the house—
and our house burned down,
and my mom cried
"ai-guuuu"
as my childhood home
collapsed.

The ashes were swept up
by the Pacific breeze,
crossed the Iguazu falls and
reached the Amazonic canopy.

My parents' labor,
sweat,
and tears
silently found sleep
between the puma
and the iguana.

*"Ai-guuu,
ai-guuuu!"*

My fathers last words
were that he wanted his
body buried in Jejudo.

So there we went.
My mother stayed with him.
She didn't want to be alone.

I did.

I left.

I came back to Lima
where the father of my child
said:

We were different.
That our love couldn't be.

All of sudden,
there was this pain in my stomach.
As I vomited for hours
and saw from my mouth,
everything that I had eaten in Korea,
regurgitated
on the grass of my beloved's garden,
I felt ill.

Everything I had eaten since
my father's death
had been miscooked.

I bled.
I bled our child away
and with the little *soles* left,
I bought a plane ticket
for one,
for just me
and my empty womb
and alone,
I am here.

Because I'm a mina,
a gal,
just a gal,
with no roots.

In Spanish, a mina
is also a mine.

And in my dreams,
I picture myself a
Korean mine,
which I dig deeper
into,
into myself I look,
within,
to find nothing but
rocks.

But sometimes, I dream that
if I go inside myself,
with a jackhammer
and a flashlight,
with dynamite
to burst my
insides
I find—
among the:
rubble, dust, and dirt—
happiness, for I mine
the Inca gold which once was robbed.

(Lights fade.)

—— END OF PLAY ——

Esther Kim Lee is Associate Professor of Theatre
and Asian American Studies at the University of Illinois
at Urbana-Champaign.

Library of Congress Cataloging-in-Publication Data
Seven contemporary plays from the Korean diaspora
in the Americas / [edited by] Esther Kim Lee.
p. cm.
Includes bibliographical references.
ISBN 978-0-8223-5253-2 (cloth : alk. paper)
ISBN 978-0-8223-5274-7 (pbk. : alk. paper)
1. Koreans—America—Drama. 2. American drama—
21st century. 3. American drama—Korean American
authors. I. Lee, Esther Kim.
PS634.2S479 2012
812'.60808957073—dc23
2011041907